Java Generics and Collections

A comprehensive guide to type-safe data
structures and efficient coding

Meenu Jaiswal

Sunil Gupta

bpb

www.bpbonline.com

First Edition 2026

Copyright © BPB Publications, India

ISBN: 978-93-65893-663

LIMITS OF LIABILITY AND DISCLAIMER OF WARRANTY

To View Complete
BPB Publications Catalogue
Scan the QR Code:

www.bpbonline.com

Dedicated to

My beloved parents
Late Nand Kishore and Smt Kamlesh Kiran
and
my husband Pradeep and my kids Suryansh and Purvashi
-Meenu Jaiswal

My parents, on whose guidance and support I have built my path
Late Ramesh Gupta and Smt Kiran Gupta
and
my wife and son, my greatest source of strength and joy
-Sunil Gupta

About the Authors

- **Meenu Jaiswal** is a Java developer with over 13 years of experience in the software industry, contributing to numerous projects across various sectors. Her passion lies in both developing and educating. She is an Oracle Certified Associate Java programmer and holds a full stack engineer certification from IIT Roorkee. She offers advanced Java training sessions focused on practical, real-world applications, and she shares insights on Java, backend programming, and new technologies on LinkedIn. Her expertise spans advanced Java, Spring, Spring Boot, and microservices, which she uses to empower developers in building scalable and efficient solutions.

- **Sunil Gupta** is an architect and software developer with over 30 years of experience in application design and development. He specializes in **service-oriented architecture (SOA)** and design patterns. With 25 years of expertise in Java programming, he has developed innovative solutions across diverse domains, including Fintech, analytics, marketing, robotics, and CAD/CAM. His experience spans both startups and large enterprises, where he combines deep technical knowledge with a strategic approach to create impactful, high-performance products.

About the Reviewers

❖ **Roopa Sunder Raj** is a skilled enterprise software engineer and system architect with a strong foundation in designing scalable, cloud-ready, and secure technology solutions, focusing on real-world performance and business impact. Her technical expertise spans system architecture, including microservices, event-driven systems (Kafka), and legacy modernization; cloud and DevOps, with proficiency in AWS, CI/CD pipelines, Kubernetes orchestration, and various deployment strategies; integration and APIs, covering REST, SOAP, service orchestration, and asynchronous messaging; and core technologies such as Java/J2EE, Oracle SQL, and WebLogic. She is also adept in security and compliance, with knowledge of secure coding and OAuth-based authentication/authorization, and in the practical application of AI/ML in enterprise and SMB telecom domains. Her experience further includes OSS/BSS, encompassing end-to-end telecom systems, service lifecycle automation, and TM Forum standards. She has led major transformation initiatives at Charter Communications and Oracle Corporation, including international advisory roles such as optimizing telecom infrastructure for high-volume mobile orders in Australia. Her leadership has encompassed architectural reviews, data backup and storage strategies, and cross-functional solution validation across globally distributed engineering teams. An advocate for diversity in tech, she is also an active member of the National Association for Multi-ethnicity in Communications (Platinum Member), Women in Cable Telecommunications, and the Society of Cable Telecommunications Engineers.

❖ **Kavita Bora** is a highly skilled software engineer with 8.5 years of experience specializing in Java development, Spring Boot, Spring Cloud, Microservices, and web technologies. Demonstrated expertise in delivering innovative solutions for diverse projects, including automation of mail tracking, prevention of product brand delicacy, and open API banking. Strong proficiency in database management using MySQL and PostgreSQL. She is committed to delivering high-quality code and exceeding client expectations.

Acknowledgements

We would like to express our heartfelt gratitude to everyone who has supported us throughout the journey of writing this book.

Special thanks to the training programs and organizations where we worked, which enhanced our understanding of the subject matter and helped us strengthen our technical expertise.

Our sincere appreciation goes to the team at BPB Publications for their patience, guidance, and flexibility in allowing us the time and creative space to complete this work. Their support in structuring the content and making the publishing process seamless has been invaluable.

Meenu Jaiswal: I would like to thank my parents, my late father, whose wisdom and values continue to inspire me, and my mother, whose unwavering encouragement gave me the strength to see this project through.

Sunil Gupta: I extend my deepest gratitude to my parents, whose unwavering support, blessings, and guidance have shaped the person I am today.

To my beloved family, you are my world. My wife's boundless love and care, and my son's remarkable achievements and radiant smiles, inspire me to strive beyond my own expectations.

My deepest gratitude goes to my husband and children for their love, patience, and understanding during the many hours I spent researching and writing. Without their support, this book would not have been possible.

Preface

This book serves as a comprehensive guide to two fundamental pillars of the Java programming language: Generics and the Collections Framework. Mastering these concepts is essential for developers seeking to produce robust, type-safe, and highly reusable code. The text is structured to provide a logical and progressive learning experience, moving from foundational principles to advanced applications and best practices.

This book is crafted with a practical approach, aiming not only to educate on the theoretical aspects of generics and collections but also to empower readers to apply these principles effectively in their own projects. The clear structure and detailed content are intended to guide the learner from a basic understanding to confident, expert-level application.

The book is divided into twelve chapters, each dedicated to a specific aspect of generics or collections. The book emphasizes the synergy between these two concepts, illustrating how they work together to create more efficient and powerful applications. By understanding their combined functionality, readers will not only grasp the syntax but also the underlying design philosophy that underpins Java's most robust data structures.

Chapter 1: Introduction to Generics- This chapter introduces the core concepts of generics, explaining their role in enhancing type safety and code reusability. You will learn the basic syntax for type parameters and how to create your own generic classes and methods. This is the perfect starting point to understand why generics are such a powerful tool in modern Java.

Chapter 2: Bounded Types- This section explores how to restrict the types used with your generics. We will cover upper bounds, lower bounds, and wildcards, showing you how to build more flexible and secure code that prevents unexpected errors at compile time.

Chapter 3: Generics in Collections- This chapter bridges the gap between generics and the Collections Framework, detailing how to apply generics to everyday data structures like List<String>, Set<Integer>, and Map<String, User>. We will explore how this makes your collection management much safer and easier to read.

Chapter 4: Introduction to Collections Framework- This chapter provides a foundational overview of the Collections Framework's architecture. We will look at the main interfaces (Collection, List, Set, Map) and discuss how they all fit together in a logical hierarchy.

Chapter 5: List Interface and Implementations- This chapter explores the List interface and its primary implementations, including ArrayList, LinkedList, Vector, and Stack. You will learn the key differences between them.

Chapter 6: Map Interface and Implementations- This chapter explores the Map interface and its main implementations, including HashMap, LinkedHashMap, TreeMap, and Hashtable.

Chapter 7: Set Interface and Implementations- This section covers the Set interface, which is all about unique elements. You will explore the various implementations, including the fast-but-unordered HashSet, the ordered LinkedHashSet, and the sorted TreeSet, so you know exactly which one to choose for your specific needs.

Chapter 8: Queue and Deque Interfaces- This section discusses the specialized Queue and Deque interfaces and their implementations, like PriorityQueue and ArrayDeque.

Chapter 9: Utility Classes- This chapter covers essential utility classes, such as Collections and Arrays, which provide methods for sorting, searching, and manipulating data. You will discover powerful static methods for sorting, searching, and manipulating your data with ease.

Chapter 10: Best Practices with Generics and Collections- This section synthesizes the knowledge by outlining best practices for writing efficient, maintainable, and synchronized code. We will help you avoid common mistakes and write professional-level Java.

Chapter 11: Real-world Applications- This chapter demonstrates how generics and collections are used in practical, real-world scenarios through case studies and tangible examples, showing you how to solve common problems.

Chapter 12: Future Trends and Next Steps- The book concludes with a summary of key concepts and an exploration of what is next for Java. We will look at recent advancements and future trends, helping you stay ahead.

Code Bundle and Coloured Images

Please follow the link to download the
Code Bundle and the *Coloured Images* of the book:

https://rebrand.ly/091a3a

The code bundle for the book is also hosted on GitHub at
https://github.com/bpbpublications/Java-Generics-and-Collections.
In case there's an update to the code, it will be updated on the existing GitHub repository.

We have code bundles from our rich catalogue of books and videos available at
https://github.com/bpbpublications. Check them out!

Errata

We take immense pride in our work at BPB Publications and follow best practices to ensure the accuracy of our content to provide an indulging reading experience to our subscribers. Our readers are our mirrors, and we use their inputs to reflect and improve upon human errors, if any, that may have occurred during the publishing processes involved. To let us maintain the quality and help us reach out to any readers who might be having difficulties due to any unforeseen errors, please write to us at: errata@bpbonline.com

Your support, suggestions and feedback are highly appreciated by the BPB Publications' Family.

At www.bpbonline.com, you can also read a collection of free technical articles, sign up for a range of free newsletters, and receive exclusive discounts and offers on BPB books and eBooks. You can check our social media handles below:

Instagram   *Facebook*   *Linkedin*   *YouTube*

Get in touch with us at: business@bpbonline.com for more details.

Piracy

If you come across any illegal copies of our works in any form on the internet, we would be grateful if you would provide us with the location address or website name. Please contact us at business@bpbonline.com with a link to the material.

If you are interested in becoming an author

If there is a topic that you have expertise in, and you are interested in either writing or contributing to a book, please visit www.bpbonline.com. We have worked with thousands of developers and tech professionals, just like you, to help them share their insights with the global tech community. You can make a general application, apply for a specific hot topic that we are recruiting an author for, or submit your own idea.

Reviews

Please leave a review. Once you have read and used this book, why not leave a review on the site that you purchased it from? Potential readers can then see and use your unbiased opinion to make purchase decisions. We at BPB can understand what you think about our products, and our authors can see your feedback on their book. Thank you!

For more information about BPB, please visit www.bpbonline.com.

Join our Discord space

Join our Discord workspace for latest updates, offers, tech happenings around the world, new releases, and sessions with the authors:

https://discord.bpbonline.com

Table of Contents

1. Introduction to Generics..1

   Introduction..1

   Structure...1

   Objectives 2

   Generics 2

     Background..2

   Benefits of generics...3

   Basic syntax of generics 6

     Defining parameterized types...6

     Syntax overview 6

       Generic classes 6

       Generic methods..8

       Bounded type parameters 9

       Wildcard types 10

   Defining generic classes..11

   Using generic methods 12

   Generics with constructors 13

     No explicit type parameter on the constructor..14

   Conclusion...14

   Exercise 14

     Answers..16

2. Bounded Types 19

   Introduction..19

   Structure...19

   Objectives 20

   Upper bounds 20

   Lower bounds 21

     Key differences between upper and lower bounds 24

   Wildcards...24

     Best practice 26

Bounded type parameters 27

Examples of bounded types in practice 27

Conclusion 33

Exercise 34

    Answers 35

3. **Generics in Collections** 37

Introduction 37

Structure 37

Objectives 38

Overview of Java Collections Framework 38

Applying generics to List<T> 39

    Wildcards in generic lists 41

Applying generics to Set<T> 44

    Wildcards in generic sets 44

Applying generics to Map<K,V> 46

    Wildcards in generic maps 47

Common pitfalls and best practices 50

Type erasure in generics 53

    Impact of type erasure 54

Conclusion 55

Exercise 55

    Answers 57

4. **Introduction to Collections Framework** 59

Introduction 59

Structure 59

Objectives 60

Overview of Java Collections Framework 60

Collections hierarchy 60

Collection interface 61

    Key methods in the collection interface 62

Key methods in collections 65

Iterable interface and iterators 70

    Iterator interface 70

Understanding the enhanced for loop in Java 71

Using Lambdas for iteration 72

Nested classes in collections 72

Empty collections 72

Singleton collections 73

Synchronized collections 74

Checked collections 75

Immutable collections 75

Wrapper class 77

Conclusion 80

Exercise 80

Answers 82

5. List Interface and Implementations 83

Introduction 83

Structure 83

Objectives 84

List interface 84

ArrayList implementation 86

Use cases for ArrayList 88

Performance considerations 89

Custom implementation of ArrayList 91

LinkedList implementation 92

Internal structure of LinkedList 93

Performance considerations for LinkedList 96

Custom LinkedList implementation 97

Vector implementation 100

Synchronization in lists 103

Collections.synchronizedList() 103

CopyOnWriteArrayList 104

Unmodifiable collections 105

Checked collections 106

Advantages of using checked collections 106

Conclusion 107

Exercise 107

    Answers *109*

6. Map Interface and Implementations 111

Introduction 111

Structure 111

Objectives 112

Map interface 112

HashMap implementation 114

    Internal structure of HashMap *114*

    Constructors in HashMap *118*

LinkedHashMap implementation 118

    Internal structure of LinkedHashMap *119*

    Constructors in LinkedHashMap *120*

TreeMap implementation 120

    Internal structure of TreeMap *121*

    Constructors in TreeMap *124*

    Common methods in TreeMap *124*

Hashtable implementation 125

    Internal working of Hashtable *125*

    Constructors in Hashtable *125*

        Comparing Map implementations *127*

Performance considerations 128

Common use cases for Maps 129

Synchronization in Maps 129

Generic algorithms for Maps 130

Conclusion 131

Exercise 131

    Answers *133*

7. Set Interface and Implementations 135

Introduction 135

Structure 135

Objectives 136

Set interface 136

HashSet implementation 137

    Internal structure of HashSet.. 137

    Constructors in HashSet... 138

    LinkedHashSet implementation 138

    Internal structure of LinkedHashSet.. 139

    Constructors in LinkedHashSet 140

TreeSet implementation... 141

    Internal structure of TreeSet 141

        Eligibility requirements for elements in TreeSet............................. 142

    Constructors in TreeSet.. 143

    Common methods in TreeSet 143

    Comparison of HashSet, LinkedHashSet and TreeSet............................ 144

        Java 8 enhancements for the Set interface 145

Performance considerations.. 146

Synchronization in Sets 146

Generic algorithms for Sets 147

Conclusion... 148

Exercise 148

    Answers.. 150

8. Queue and Deque Interfaces 153

Introduction.. 153

Structure.. 153

Objectives 154

Queue interface... 154

    Characteristics of Queue interface 154

PriorityQueue implementation 156

    Internal structure of PriorityQueue.. 156

Deque interface... 160

    Common use cases... 160

    Key methods in Deque interface 160

    Using Deque as both Queue and Stack 161

ArrayDeque implementation.. 162

    Internal structure 162

Constructors...165

Common use cases of ArrayDeque...165

Implementing a Stack...166

Implementing Queue...166

Sliding window or fixed buffer...167

LinkedList as a Queue 167

Using LinkedList as a Queue 168

Using LinkedList as a Deque 168

Synchronization in Queues and Deques 169

Using concurrent collections..169

Wrapping with Synchronized Collections 170

BlockingQueue and BlockingDeque..170

ArrayDeque vs. LinkedList vs. PriorityQueue 171

Conclusion...171

Exercise 172

Answers...173

9. Utility Classes 175

Introduction..175

Structure..175

Objectives 176

Collections utility class 176

Sorting and reversing a List...177

Sorting and searching with collections 178

Sorting a List..178

Sorting with natural order...178

Sorting with custom comparator 179

Searching a List...179

Binary search with custom comparator 180

Modifying collections with Collections 180

Reversing a List..180

Shuffling elements..181

Filling a List with a value 181

Replacing all occurrences of a value..181

Copying one List into another..182

Arrays utility class..182

Sorting an Array 183

Searching in an Array...183

Filling an Array 183

Comparing Arrays 184

Copying Arrays...184

Working with Arrays and Collections...184

Converting an Array to a List..185

Using collection methods on Arrays 185

Wrapper class..185

Synchronization utilities...187

Making a List synchronized 187

Synchronized Set and Map 188

Unmodifiable collections...189

Predefined empty collections 190

Checked collections..192

Conclusion...194

Exercise 194

Answers...196

10. Best Practices with Generics and Collections............................197

Introduction..197

Structure..197

Objectives 198

Writing type-safe code with generics 198

Avoiding common pitfalls with generics.......................................200

Efficient use of collections..203

Designing collections-based APIs..204

Performance considerations..206

Synchronization best practices 208

Using generic algorithms 209

Conclusion..210

Exercise 211

       Answers..212

11. Real-world Applications..215

    Introduction..215

    Structure..215

    Objectives 216

    Case studies..216

    Practical examples..227

    Common usage patterns 231

    Solving typical problems...232

    Best practices in real-world scenarios 232

    Conclusion...233

    Exercise 234

       Answers..236

12. Future Trends and Next Steps..237

    Introduction..237

    Structure..237

    Objectives 238

    Recent advancements in Java generics...238

    Future updates in collections..241

    Trends in Java development 243

    Staying updated with Java innovations..246

    Future of generics and collections..248

    Conclusion...251

    Exercise 251

       Answers..253

Index 255-259

CHAPTER 1
Introduction to Generics

Introduction

This chapter introduces the concept of generics in Java, a feature that enhances type safety by enforcing strict checks at compile time, reduces runtime errors, and enhances code readability and reusability. We begin by understanding the need for generics in building type-safe collections and **application programming interfaces** (**APIs**). We will also explore the syntax of generics, demonstrating how to define generic classes, methods, and constructors. Through practical examples, we will illustrate the advantages of using generics and provide a foundation for applying them effectively in Java development.

Structure

The chapter covers the following topics:

- Generics
- Benefits of generics
- Basic syntax of generics
- Defining generic classes
- Using generic methods
- Generics with constructors

Objectives

By the end of this chapter, you will have a clear understanding of the purpose and benefits of using generics in Java. You will learn the foundational syntax and key concepts of generics, enabling you to define and implement generic classes, methods, and constructors. This knowledge will prepare you to confidently apply generics in practical scenarios as explored in subsequent chapters. Additionally, the chapter concludes with a set of exercises designed to test your understanding and reinforce the concepts covered.

Generics

Generics in Java were introduced as part of **Java Development Kit 5 (JDK 5)** in 2004, to make code safer and easier to reuse. They provide a mechanism to create classes, methods, and interfaces that work with different data types without having to rewrite the code each time.

For example, before generics, if you wanted a list of strings and a list of integers, you would often use the same list class but have to manually check the type of each item you added or retrieved. With generics, you can create a **List<String>** and a **List<Integer>**, and the compiler will automatically enforce the correct types, preventing errors.

Generics aim to address limitations in older Java code that need a lot of manual type checking (casting), particularly with collections.

Background

Before generics, Java developers had to use raw types, which allowed collections to store any object type. This approach often led to runtime errors when a developer unintentionally added incompatible types to a collection. For example, adding a string to a collection of integers would only cause an error when accessing the value at runtime, leading to a **ClassCastException** and potential program failures.

The following is an example without generics:

```
List listWithoutGenerics = new ArrayList();
listWithoutGenerics .add("A String");
Integer number = (Integer) listWithoutGenerics.get(0); // Runtime error
```

The following is an example with generics:

```
List<String> stringList  = new ArrayList<>();
stringList .add("A String");
// Integer number = (Integer) stringList .get(0); // Compile-time error
String text = stringList.get(0); // Compile-
time safety ensures no casting erro
```

Benefits of generics

The following are the main benefits of using generics in Java:

- **Type safety**: Generics guarantee that only compatible data types are used by enforcing compile-time checks. This eliminates runtime errors such as **ClassCastException** and makes the code more predictable and reliable.

- **Code reusability**: Before generics, developers often had to create separate versions of the same class or interface for different data types, leading to what is known as interface or class explosion. For instance, to handle different types in a type-safe manner, one might create:

```
class ListOfStrings implements List { ... }
class ListOfIntegers implements List { ... }
class MapOfStringToInteger implements Map { ... }
```

This repetition made the code harder to maintain and scale.

Generics eliminate this problem by allowing a single implementation to work with different data types. Developers can write a generic class or method once and reuse it across various types, reducing duplication and promoting cleaner, more maintainable code.

The following is an example:

```
public class CommonBox<T> {
    private T commonItem;
    public void setCommonItem(T item) {
        this.commonItem = item;
    }
    public T getCommonItem() {
        return commonItem;
    }
}
```

The **CommonBox** class can be used to create a class with different data types.

For example, to create a **CommonBox** of type **Integer**:

```
CommonBox<Integer> intBox = new CommonBox<>();
intBox.setItem(123);
```

To create a **CommonBox** of type **String**:

```
CommonBox<String> strBox = new CommonBox<>();
strBox.setItem("Hello");
```

- **Elimination of explicit casting**: Generics eliminate the need for manual type casting, which can cause errors during program execution. By specifying the type upfront, generics enforce type safety at compile time, preventing these runtime errors.

The following is an example without generics:

```
List commonList = new ArrayList();
commonList.add("Hello");
String text = (String) commonList.get(0); // Explicit casting is
required
```

The following is an example with generics:

```
List<String> stringList = new ArrayList<>();
stringList.add("Hello");
String text = stringList.get(0); // No casting required
```

- **Improved readability**: By specifying the type of data a collection can hold, generics make code easier to read and understand, improving maintainability and reducing the likelihood of errors.

The following is an example without generics:

```
List commonList = new ArrayList();
commonList.add("Hello");
commonList.add(123); // Adds an integer, which might not be intentional
for (Object obj : commonList) {
    String str = (String) obj; // Requires casting, prone to
runtime errors
    System.out.println(str);
}
```

The following is an example with generics:

```
List<String> stringList = new ArrayList<>();
stringList.add("Hello");
// stringList.add(123); // Compile-time error, prevents adding
 incompatible data
for (String str : stringList) {
    System.out.println(str); // No casting needed, easier to read
}
```

It is clear that the list can only contain string objects, improving readability and reducing confusion.

- **Performance optimization**: Generics can lead to performance improvements by avoiding unnecessary casts and type checks at runtime. This results in faster execution, especially in scenarios with frequent type operations.

  Note: **This is not officially confirmed or explicitly declared in the official Java documentation, and there could still be debates around the extent of these performance benefits.**

  The following is an example without generics:

  ```
  List commonList = new ArrayList();
  commonList.add("Hello");
  String str = (String) commonList.get(0); // Casting happens at runtime
  ```

  The following is an example with generics:

  ```
  List<String> stringList = new ArrayList<>();
  stringList.add("Hello");
  String str = stringList.
  get(0); // No casting required, type is known at compile time
  ```

  In the generic version, type safety is enforced at compile time, avoiding runtime type-checking overhead, which is especially beneficial in large-scale or performance-critical applications.

- **Backward compatibility**: Generics were designed with backward compatibility in mind, ensuring that existing non-generic code and libraries remain functional while allowing developers to adopt generics incrementally.

  The following is an example of pre-generics (Java 1.4 or earlier):

  ```
  List commonList = new ArrayList(); // Non-generic collection
  commonList.add("Hello");
  commonList.add(123);
  for (Object obj : commonList) {
      System.out.println(obj); // Outputs: Hello, 123
  }
  ```

  The following is the post-generics (Java 5+):

  ```
  List<String> stringList = new ArrayList<>(); // Generic collection
  stringList.add("Hello");
  // string_ist.add(123); // Compile-time error
  for (String str : stringList) {
      System.out.println(str); // Outputs: Hello
  ```

```
}
```

The following is non-generic, and generic collections can coexist:

```
List oldList = new ArrayList(); // Non-generic
oldList.add("Hello");
List<String> newList = oldList; // Allowed but with warnings
 (raw type usage)
System.out.println(newList.get(0)); // Still works
```

Basic syntax of generics

Generics let you define classes, methods, and interfaces that work with different data types. This happens when the code is compiled, providing flexibility and type safety. The syntax of generics revolves around the concept of parameterized types, allowing developers to create more abstract and adaptable code structures. This section explains how to use the correct syntax for generics.

Defining parameterized types

Generics are implemented using angle brackets (<>) to specify type parameters.

The most common types of parameters include:

- **Type (T)**: Represents a generic type.
- **Element (E)**: Typically used in collections, like `List<E>`.
- **Key (K) and value (V)**: Used in map structures, such as `Map<K, V>`.

These type parameters act as placeholders that get replaced with actual types during code execution or compilation.

Syntax overview

Generics have a rich syntax designed to cover a wide range of use cases, from defining generic classes to creating generic interfaces and methods. The following section is a detailed breakdown of the syntax, along with additional examples and explanations.

Generic classes

Generic classes define type parameters that can be specified when creating an instance of the class. We will learn more about generic classes in the next section.

The following is an example:

```
public class TemplateClass<T> {
    private T templateValue;
```

```
    public void setTemplateValue(T value) {
        this.templateValue = value;
    }
    public T getTemplateValue() {
        return templateValue;
    }
}
```

Let us break down the syntax in this example:

- **TemplateClass<T>**: This declares a generic class named **TemplateClass** with a type parameter **T**. **T** is a common convention, but you can use any valid identifier (for example, **E**, **K**, **V**, **Item**). T represents the type of the value field.

- **private T templateValue**: This declares a private instance variable **templateValue** of type **T**. The type of **templateValue** will be determined when an instance of **TemplateClass** is created.

- **public void setTemplateValue(T value) and public T getTemplateValue()**: These are the setter and getter methods for the **templateValue** field.

Note: Both the parameter type of setTemplateValue and the return type of getTemplateValue are T. This ensures type consistency.

Let us discuss the uses. To use a generic class, you must specify the actual type within the angle brackets when creating an instance of the class:

```
TemplateClass<String> stringInstance = new TemplateClass<>();
stringInstance.setValue("Hello, Generics!");
System.out.println(stringInstance.getTemplateValue());
```

The following is the explanation:

- **TemplateClass<String> stringInstance = new TemplateClass<>();**: This creates an instance of **TemplateClass** where the type parameter **T** is replaced with **String**. Now, **stringInstance** can only hold **String** values. The diamond operator **<>** on the right-hand side is shorthand for **GenericClass<String>**, inferring the type from the left side.

- **stringInstance.setTemplateValue("Hello, Generics!");**: This sets the value of **stringInstance** to a **String**. This is because **stringInstance** is of type **TemplateClass<String>**, the compiler ensures that only **String** values can be passed to **setTemplateValue**.

- **System.out.println(stringInstance.getTemplateValue());**: This retrieves the value of **stringInstance**, which is guaranteed to be a **String**. No explicit casting is needed.

Similarly, we can also do:

```
TemplateClass<Integer> intInstance = new TemplateClass<>();
```

Here, **T** is replaced with **Integer**, so **intInstance** can only hold **Integer** values.

Generic methods

Generic methods allow you to use type parameters within a method's scope, making the method work with different data types without requiring individual implementations for each type. This is particularly useful for utility methods that operate on collections or perform generic operations.

A generic method is declared with type parameters within angle brackets (<>) before the method's return type.

The following is an example:

```
public static <T> void printArrayObjects(T[] array) {
    for (T arrayObj : array) {
        System.out.println(arrayObj);
    }
}
```

The following is an explanation of how the code above works:

- **public static <T>**: This declares a **public static** method with a type parameter **T**. The **<T>** comes before the return type (**void**). This signifies that the method is generic.
- **void printArrayObjects(T[] array)**: This defines the method signature. The method takes an array of type **T** as a parameter.
- **for (T arrayObj : array)**: This enhanced for loop iterates through the array. Because the array is of type **T[ ]**, each element is also of type **T**.

Let us discuss the usage. When calling a generic method, the compiler often infers the type argument based on the arguments passed to the method. You can also explicitly specify the type argument, but it is usually not necessary.

The following are a few different examples:

```
Integer[] numbers = {1, 2, 3};
printArrayObjects(numbers);// Type inference: T is inferred as Integer
String[] words = {"Hello", "World"};
printArrayObjects(words); // Type inference: T is inferred as String
Character[] chars = {'a', 'b', 'c'};
printArrayObjects(chars); // Type inference: T is inferred as Character
//Explicitly specifying the type argument (less common):
printArrayObjects<Double>(new Double[]{1.0, 2.0, 3.0});
```

Bounded type parameters

As the name implies, bounded type parameters limit the types that can be specified as type arguments. This is done using the **extends** keyword (and the **&** symbol for multiple bounds). This provides greater type safety and allows you to use methods specific to the bounded type.

The general syntax for a bounded type parameter is:

```
<T extends BoundType>
```

For multiple bounds:

```
<T extends BoundType1 & BoundType2 & ...>
```

Note: **<T> is the type parameter, as usual.**

The keywords used above are explained in the following:

- **extends**: This keyword indicates that **T** must be a subtype of **BoundType**. This means **T** can be **BoundType** itself or any class that inherits from **BoundType** or any interface that is implemented by **T**.

- **BoundType**: This is the upper bound. It can be a class or an interface.

- **&**: Used to specify multiple bounds. If you use multiple bounds, at most one of them can be a class. The rest must be interfaces.

The following is an example:

```
public <T extends Number> void processNumber(T number) {
    System.out.println(number.doubleValue());
}
```

The keywords used above are explained in the following:

- **<T extends Number>**: This is the bounded type parameter declaration. It specifies that **T** must be a subtype of the number class. This means **T** can be a number, integer, double, float, long, short, byte, or any other class that extends number.

- **void processNumber(T number)**: This is the method signature. The method takes an argument of type **T**.

- **System.out.println(number.doubleValue());**: This is the method body. This is because **T** is bounded by a number; we know that number has the **doubleValue()** method (which is defined in the number class). This is the key benefit of bounded type parameters: you can safely call methods of the bound type.

The following is the usage:

```
processNumber(5);        // Integer is a Number
processNumber(3.14);     // Double is a Number
//processNumber("hello"); // Compile-time error: String is not a Number
```

The following is an explanation of how the above code works:

- **processNumber(5)**: This is valid because **Integer** extends **Number**.

- **processNumber(3.14)**: This is valid because **Double** extends **Number**.

- **processNumber("hello")**: This would cause a compile-time error because **String** does not extend **Number**. This demonstrates the type safety provided by bounded type parameters.

Wildcard types

Wildcards (**?**) in Java generics provide a way to handle situations where you do not know the exact type parameter or where you want to accept a range of types. They offer flexibility but also come with certain restrictions.

The following is an example:

```
public void printList(List<?> anyList) {
    for (Object listObj : anyList) {
        System.out.println(listObj);
    }
}
```

Let us break it down:

- **public void printList(List<?> anyList)**: This declares a method named **printList** that takes a **List** as a parameter. The crucial part is **List<?>**. The **?** (question mark) is the unbounded wildcard. This means that this method can accept a list of any type. It does not matter if it is a **List<String>**, **List<Integer>**, **List<MyCustomObject>**, or any other type of list.

- **for (Object listObj : anyList)**: Inside the method, the code iterates through the list using an enhanced for loop. This is because the type of the list is unknown (represented by **?**), and the elements are treated as **Object**. This is safe because every object in Java is ultimately an instance of the **Object** class. So, you can safely access each element as an object.

- **System.out.println(listObj);**: This line simply prints the current element (**listObj**) to the console. This is because **listObj** is treated as an object; the **toString()** method of the object will be called implicitly to get its string representation for printing.

In essence, this method is designed to print the contents of any list, regardless of the type of elements it contains.

The following is a usage:

```
List<String> listOfStrings = Arrays.asList("String", "List");
printList(listOfStrings); // Output: String \n List
```

```
List<Integer> listOfIntegers = Arrays.asList(101, 201, 301);
printList(listOfIntegers); // Output: 101 \n 201 \n 301
List<Double> listOfDoubles = Arrays.asList(3.14, 2.71);
printList(listOfDoubles); // Output: 3.14 \n 2.71
```

As you can see, the **printList** method works correctly with lists of different types because of the unbounded wildcard **?**. It provides a generic way to print the contents of any list without needing separate methods for each type.

Defining generic classes

A generic class is a class that can operate on different data types without the need for separate implementations for each type. You achieve this using type parameters.

Let us discuss the syntax. You define a generic class by adding type parameters, typically represented by single uppercase letters such as **T**, **E**, **K**, or **V**, within angle brackets **< >** following the class name:

```
public class Container<T> { // T is the type parameter
    private T product;
    public Container(T product) {
        this.product = product;
    }
    public T getProduct() {
        return product;
    }
    public void setProduct(T product){
        this.product = product;
    }
}
```

The following are the explanations:

- **Container<T>**: This declares a class named **Container** that is generic. **T** is a placeholder for the actual type that will be used when you create an instance of the **Container**.

- **private T product;**: This declares an instance variable product of type **T**. The type of product will be determined when an object of **Container** is created.

- **Type consistency**: The constructor **public Container(T product)**, getter **public T getProduct()**, and setter **public void setProduct(T product)** methods also use **T**, ensuring type consistency.

Let us discuss the usage. When you create an object of a generic class, you provide the actual type within the angle brackets:

```
Container<Integer> integerContainer = new Container<>(123);
// T is replaced with Integer
int intValue = integerContainer.getProduct(); // No casting needed
Container<String> stringContainer = new Container<>("Hello");
// T is replaced with String
String textValue = stringContainer.getProduct(); // No casting needed
Container<Double> doubleContainer = new Container<>(3.14);
double piValue = doubleContainer.getProduct();
```

Using generic methods

Generic methods are methods that have their own type parameters, independent of any generic class they might be in.

Let us discuss the syntax. You declare a generic method by placing the type parameters within angle brackets <> before the method's return type.

The following is an example:

```
public class Utility {
    public static <E> void displayArray(E[] dataArray) { // E is the type
parameter
        for (E displayItem : dataArray) {
            System.out.print(displayItem + " ");
        }
        System.out.println();
    }
    public static <K, V> void displayMap(Map<K, V> dataMap){
        for (Map.Entry<K, V> displayEntry : dataMap.entrySet()){
            System.out.println("Key: " + displayEntry.getKey() + ", Value: " +
displayEntry.getValue());
        }
    }
}
```

The following are the explanations:

- **<E>**: This declares a type parameter **E** for the **displayArray** method. This **E** is only in scope for this method.

- **E[] dataArray**: The method takes an array of type **E** as a parameter.

- **<K, V>**: This declares two type parameters **K** and **V** for the **displayMap** method.

- **Map<K, V> dataMap**: The method takes a **Map** with key type **K** and value type **V**.

Let us discuss the usage. The compiler usually infers the type argument based on the method's arguments. You can also specify it explicitly, but it is less common:

```
Integer[] numbers = {1, 2, 3};
Utility.displayArray(numbers); // E is inferred as Integer
String[] words = {"a", "b", "c"};
Utility.displayArray(words); // E is inferred as String
Map<String, Integer> ages = new HashMap<>();
ages.put("Alice", 30);
ages.put("Bob", 25);
Utility.displayMap(ages);
```

Generics with constructors

While classes themselves can be generic, constructors are not directly generic in the same way methods are. However, if you are in a generic class, the constructor implicitly works with the class's type parameter.

The following is an example:

```
public class Container<T> { // T is the type parameter
    private T product;
    public Container(T product) {// Constructor uses the class's type
parameter T
        this.product = product;
    }
    public T getProduct() {
        return product;
    }
    public void setProduct(T product){
        this.product = product;
    }
}
```

The explanation of the above code is that the constructor **Container(T product)** uses the type parameter **T** that was declared for the class. This means that when you create a **Container<Integer>**, the constructor will expect an Integer argument.

No explicit type parameter on the constructor

You cannot declare a separate type parameter for the constructor itself. The constructor automatically uses the class's type parameters; this is an important distinction. The following is incorrect syntax:

```
// Incorrect: You cannot do this
//public <X> Container(X product) { ... }
```

The above code is incorrect because the constructor cannot have its own type parameter `<X>`. It must use the class's type parameter `<T>`.

Conclusion

This chapter introduced Java generics, a versatile feature that improves type safety, promotes code reusability, and enhances readability. Generics allow for the creation of classes, methods, and interfaces that work with various data types without requiring repetitive code or manual casting, thus preventing runtime errors.

In the next chapter, we will learn about bounded types, which allow us to restrict the types that can be used with generics.

Exercise

1. **What is the primary purpose of generics in Java?**
    a. To improve runtime performance
    b. To provide type safety and code reusability
    c. To simplify syntax for collections
    d. To allow the use of primitive types in collections

2. **Which of the following correctly declares a generic class?**
    a. public class MySampleClass<T> { }
    b. public class MySampleClass<Generic> { }
    c. public <T> class MySampleClass { }
    d. Both A and B

3. **What will happen if you use a raw type instead of a parameterized type?**
    a. Compile-time error
    b. Runtime error
    c. Warning at compile time
    d. No effect

4. **What does <T> represent in the following method signature?**

    public <T> void print(T item);

    a. It declares a generic method with a type parameter T.
    b. It specifies the return type of the method.
    c. It indicates that T is a class in the Java API.
    d. It restricts the method to primitive types only.

5. **Which of these statements about bounded type parameters is correct?**

    a. Bounded type parameters must always use the extends keyword.
    b. T extends Number means T can only be a subclass of Number.
    c. T super Number allows T to be a superclass of Number.
    d. Both A and B.

6. **Which of the following correctly defines a generic method?**

    a. public void display(T item) { System.out.println(item); }
    b. public static <T> void display(T item) { System.out.println(item); }
    c. public static void display(<T> item) · System.out.println(item); }
    d. public <T> static void display(item) ¦ System.out.println(item); }

7. **What does the wildcard? Extends T represent in generics?**

    a. A type that is a superclass of T.
    b. A type that is a subclass of T.
    c. Any type that is unrelated to T.
    d. Any type that matches T exactly.

8. **What is the key difference between a raw type and a wildcard in generics?**

    a. Raw types allow primitive types, while wildcards do not.
    b. Wildcards provide type safety, while raw types do not.
    c. Wildcards enforce compile-time type checking, while raw types allow unchecked operations.
    d. Both B and C.

9. **Which generic type declaration is commonly used for elements in a collection?**

    a. T
    b. E
    c. K and V
    d. R

10. **What does the following method signature imply?**

    public static <T extends Comparable<T>> T findMax(T[] array);

    a. The method can only be used with numeric arrays.

    b. The method can accept arrays of any type that implements Comparable.

    c. The method requires explicit casting of the return type.

    d. The method can accept arrays of any type without restrictions.

Answers

1. b

   Explanation: Generics enhance Java by enforcing type safety at compile time and enabling code reusability. They prevent runtime errors caused by type mismatches and make the code more reliable.

2. d

   Explanation: Both options A and B correctly declare a generic class. A generic class requires a type parameter inside angle brackets (<>) immediately after the class name. The name of the parameter can be any valid identifier (commonly T, but not restricted to it).

3. c

   Explanation: Using a raw type generates a compile-time warning because it bypasses type safety checks. Although the code might still run, it risks runtime ClassCastException errors.

4. a

   Explanation: The <T> in the method signature declares T as a type parameter, making the method generic. This allows the method to accept arguments of any type, determined when the method is invoked.

5. d

   Explanation: Bounded type parameters use the extends keyword to restrict the type to a class or its subclasses. For example, T extends Number ensures that T must be a subclass of Number. The super keyword is not used in this context.

6. b

   Explanation: A generic method must declare the type parameter (<T>) before the return type (void). Option B is correct as it adheres to this syntax. Option A lacks a type parameter declaration, and options C and D have incorrect syntax

7. b

   Explanation: The wildcard? extends T represents a type that is either T or a subclass of T. It is used when the method or class can work with types derived from T.

8. d

   Explanation: Wildcards (?) ensure type safety and allow flexibility in type parameters. Raw types, on the other hand, disable type checking, leading to potential runtime errors. Wildcards enforce compile-time type constraints, which raw types lack.

9. b

   Explanation: E stands for "Element" and is commonly used in collections like List<E> or Set<E>. T is a general type placeholder, while K and V are typically used for key-value pairs in maps.

10. b

    Explanation: The type parameter T extends Comparable<T> means that T must implement the Comparable interface, enabling comparison operations. This ensures type safety and that the method can determine the maximum value in the array.

Join our Discord space

Join our Discord workspace for latest updates, offers, tech happenings around the world, new releases, and sessions with the authors:

https://discord.bpbonline.com

CHAPTER 2
Bounded Types

Introduction

This chapter explains the concept of bounded types within the context of generic programming. We will explore how to use bounds to restrict the types that can be used with generic classes and methods. We will learn about different types of bounds, including upper bounds, lower bounds, and wildcard bounds. Through practical examples, we will demonstrate how to effectively apply these bounds to create more robust and maintainable generic code.

Structure

The chapter covers the following topics:

- Upper bounds
- Lower bounds
- Wildcards
- Bounded type parameters
- Examples of bounded types in practice

Objectives

By the end of this chapter, you will have a solid understanding of bounded types in generics and how they help enforce type safety while maintaining flexibility in your code. You will learn how to apply upper and lower bounds to restrict the types that can be used with generics, explore the use of wildcard characters to handle unknown types, and implement bounded type parameters effectively. Additionally, you will see practical examples that demonstrate how bounded types improve code reusability and maintainability. At the end of the chapter, exercises will help reinforce your understanding and test your ability to apply bounded types in real-world scenarios.

Upper bounds

Upper bounds in generics restrict a type parameter to a specific class or its subclasses. This is achieved using the **extends** keyword. By using upper bounds, you can ensure that your generic code works only with types that meet specific constraints, ensuring type safety and enabling you to leverage specific methods or properties of the bounding class. This is particularly useful when you need to work with a variety of related types but require a common ancestor.

Let us illustrate this with an example, working with comparable objects. Suppose you need to write a generic method to find the maximum element in a collection. You can use an upper bound with a comparable interface.

Consider the following method **fetchMaxElement:**

```
public static <T extends Comparable<T>> T fetchMaxElement(List<T> list) {
  T max = list.get(0);
  for (T element : list) {
   if (element.compareTo(max) > 0) {
    max = element;
   }
  }
  return max;
}
```

In the above example, **<T extends Comparable<T>>** ensures that the type **T** must implement the comparable interface, and specifically, it must be comparable to itself. This allows us to use the **compareTo** method safely.

We can use the method given in the following:

```
List<String> listOfNames = Arrays.asList("Apple", "Carrot", "Grapes");
String maxName = fetchMaxElement(listOfNames);
List<Integer> listOfAges = Arrays.asList(25, 30, 20);
Integer maxAge = fetchMaxElement(listOfAges);
```

Both **String** and **Integer** implement the **Comparable** interface, hence both **maxName** and **maxAge** are valid.

The following are the key benefits of upper bounds:

- **Type safety:** Prevents passing incompatible types to generic methods or classes.
- **Code reusability:** Allows writing generic code that can work with a range of related types.
- **Access to methods:** Guarantees the availability of methods defined in the upper bound class or interface.

Lower bounds

Lower bounds on type parameters define a constraint based on a superclass and are defined using the **super** keyword. They specify that a type parameter must be a specific class or any of its ancestors in the inheritance hierarchy. These bounds are particularly useful when working with collections, allowing you to handle types at or above a certain level in the class hierarchy.

Think of it this way: **T super SomeClass** means that the type **T** can be **SomeClass** itself, or any of its superclasses (parent classes further up the inheritance tree). It sets a lower limit on the type.

Example 2.1: Consuming elements:

Imagine a method that adds elements to a collection. You might want to add objects of type **T** or any subtype of **T**. However, the collection itself might be able to hold objects of a supertype of **T**. Lower bounds allow you to express this.

Consider the following method, **addElements**:

```
public static <T> void addElements(List<? super T> list, T element) {
     list.add(element);
 }
```

Here, the **? super T** wildcard ensures that the list can accept **T** or any of its superclasses.

We can call this method as follows:

```
List<Object> objectList = new ArrayList<>();
addElements(objectList, new String("hello"));
addElements(objectList, new Integer(10));
```

The **addElements** method requires a list that can hold **T** or any of its supertypes.

Here, **objectList** is a **List<Object>**, and both **String** and **Integer** are subtypes of **Object**.

However, you cannot do the following:

```
List<String> stringList = new ArrayList<>();
// addElements(stringList, new Object());
```

This would result in a compile-time error because **stringList** is a **List<String>**, and **Object** is not a subtype of **String**. The **addElements** method expects to be able to add a **T** to the list. If **T** were a **String**, it should be able to add a **String**. It cannot add an **Object** to a **List<String>**.

Similarly, we cannot add a **Number** to a **List<Integer>** as shown in the following:

```
List<Integer> intList = new ArrayList<>();
// addElements(ints, new Number());
```

This would also result in a compile-time error because **intList** is a **List<Integer>**, and **Number** is not a subtype of **Integer**.

Example 2.2: Working with hierarchies:

Lower bounds are helpful when dealing with class hierarchies where you need to process elements at a certain level or above. For instance, you might have a hierarchy of shapes (for example, shape, circle, rectangle) and a method that operates on any shape or its ancestors.

For instance, consider you have an abstract class **AnyShape**, which serves as the base class for different shapes.

```
abstract class AnyShape {
abstract void drawShape();
}
```

Two concrete subclasses extend the **AnyShape** class.

```
class CircleShape extends AnyShape {
@Override
void drawShape() {
System.out.println("Drawing a Circle");
}
}
class RectangleShape extends AnyShape {
@Override
void drawShape() {
System.out.println("Drawing a Rectangle");
}
}
```

Now consider a method **drawShapes** as follows:

```
public static void drawShapes(List<? super CircleShape> shapes) {
  shapes.add(new CircleShape());
  for (Object shape : shapes) {
   System.out.println("Processing shape: " + shape.getClass().
```

```
getSimpleName());
   }
 }
```

The method accepts a list where the elements are of type **CircleShape** or any of its superclasses (**AnyShape,   Object**). This means you cannot pass **List<RectangleShape>** because **RectangleShape** is not related to **CircleShape**.

Fcr example, you cannot do this:

```
shapes.add(new Shape());
```

or

```
shapes.add(new Rectangle());
```

Example 2.3: Method return types (less common):

While less frequent, lower bounds can also be used in return types. This can be useful in situations where you want to return a value that is at least a certain type but could be a supertype as well.

Let us consider the method **getNumberList()** as follows:

```
public static List<? super Integer> getNumberList() {
        List<Number> numbers = new ArrayList<>();
        numbers.add(10);
        numbers.add(20.5);
        return numbers;
    }
```

The method returns a **List<? super Integer>**, that means, the returned list contains elements that are at least Integer but could also be of a supertype (Number, Object).

To the returned list, we can add integer values like the following:

```
List<? super Integer> list = getNumberList();
list.add(30);
```

Since the exact type is unknown, we can only retrieve elements as objects, not integers directly.

The following line would lead to a compilation error:

```
Integer num = list.get(0);  // Compilation error
```

However, we can retrieve elements as objects:

```
Object obj = list.get(0);
```

Key differences between upper and lower bounds

The following table highlights the key differences between upper bounds and lower bounds in generics, explaining their usage, constraints, and practical implications. Understanding these distinctions helps in writing more flexible and type-safe generic code:

Feature	Upper bounds	Lower bounds
Keyword used	**extends**	**super**
Constraint	Type or subtype	Type or supertype
Use case	Restricting to specific types or subtypes	Allowing flexibility for consuming/producing, working with hierarchies
Usage in collections	Typically used for reading from a collection.	Typically used for writing into a collection.

Table 2.1: *Differences between upper and lower bounds*

Wildcards

When working with generics, you often encounter situations where you need to handle unknown types while preserving type safety. Wildcards provide the solution, enabling you to work with a range of related types without sacrificing the benefits of generics. Using upper and lower bounds with wildcards further enhances this control. A helpful mnemonic for remembering how to use these bounds is the **producer extends, consumer super (PECS)** rule. This rule summarizes the best practices for using wildcards with upper and lower bounds.

Before exploring the different types of wildcards, it is essential to understand a fundamental property of Java generics: **invariance**.

Invariance means that even if **TypeA** is a subtype of **TypeB**, **List<TypeA>** is not considered a subtype of **List<TypeB>**. For instance, **List<Integer>** is not a subtype of **List<Number>**, even though Integer is a subtype of Number.

Hence, the following is not allowed:

```
List<Number> numbers = new ArrayList<Integer>(); // Compilation error
```

This invariance is by design to preserve type safety. For example, if the assignment above were allowed, one could add a double to numbers, which internally is an **ArrayList<Integer>**, leading to a runtime **ClassCastException**.

To safely enable polymorphic behavior with generics, Java provides wildcards.

This limitation highlights the necessity of wildcards, which offer a controlled mechanism for achieving flexibility in generic programming. Wildcards allow developers to express relationships among various generic types while maintaining type safety. By doing so, they enable code to operate over a broader range of types, effectively overcoming the constraints introduced by invariance.

The following is a breakdown of the three forms of wildcards:

- **Unbounded wildcard: ?:** The simplest wildcard, **?**, represents any type. It is useful when you want to write code that can work with any generic type, but you do not need to know the specific type. For example, if you have a method that simply prints the elements of a collection, regardless of the element type, you could use an unbounded wildcard.

  The following is the sample code:

  ```
  public static void printElements(Collection<?> anyCollection) {
      for (Object theObject : anyCollection) {
          System.out.println(theObject);
      }
  }
  ```

  The method **printElements** simply accepts any collection and prints its elements. It is not restricted to any one type of collection.

- **Upper bounded wildcard: ? extends Type:** As we have already seen in this chapter, upper bounded wildcard, **? extends Type**, restricts the unknown type to be either **Type** itself or any subtype of **Type**. This is useful when you want to work with a range of related types, typically when you want to read elements from a collection (such as when you are a producer of elements). Following the PECS rule (producer extends), if you are producing values from a parameterized type, use extends.

  For example, if you have a hierarchy of shapes and you want to process any collection of shapes or their subtypes:

  ```
  public static void drawShapes(List<? extends Shape> shapesList) {
    for (Shape eachShape : shapesList) {
     eachShape.drawShape();
    }
  }
  ```

  Here, shapes can be a **List<Shape>**, a **List<Circle>**, a **List<Rectangle>**, or any other list whose element type is a subtype of **Shape**. This is often referred to as covariance. It is safe to read a **Shape** because you know everything in the list is at least a **Shape**.

- **Lower bounded wildcard: ? super Type:** A lower bounded wildcard, **? super Type**, restricts the unknown type to be either **Type** itself or any supertype of **Type**. This is typically used when you want to add elements to a collection (such as when you are a consumer of elements). Following the PECS rule (consumer super), if you are consuming values from a parameterized type, use **super**.

For example, if you want to add **Circle** objects to a list that can hold **Circles** or any of their supertypes:

```
public static void addCircles(List<? super Circle> circles) {
  circles.add(new Circle());
}
```

Here, **circles** can be a **List<Circle>**, a **List<Shape>**, a **List<Object>**, etc. It is safe to add a **Circle** because you know the list can hold at least **Circle** objects.

The reason you cannot add a **Shape** to a **List<? super Circle>** is not because **Shape** is a superclass of **Circle**. It is because of the wildcard **? super Circle** represents a *specific*, but *unknown*, supertype of **Circle**. It is crucial to understand that **? super Circle** does *not* mean any supertype of **Circle**. It means a *specific* supertype of **Circle**, which is unknown to the compiler.

Imagine you have a basket labeled *Things that are at least Apples*. You can safely put an apple in it. However, if you have a basket labeled *Things that are at least Apples*, you *cannot* necessarily put a fruit in it. The basket might actually be a basket specifically for apples. The label only guarantees that the basket can hold apples, but it might not be able to hold all fruits.

Similarly, **List<? super Circle>** means a list of some *specific* type that is at least a **Circle**. The compiler does not know what that specific type is, so it cannot be sure that adding a **Shape** (which is a fruit in our analogy) is always safe.

Best practice

Prefer bounded wildcards for method parameters.

When designing methods that accept generic types, it is recommended to use bounded wildcards (**? extends T** or **? super T**) in method parameters rather than exact type parameters (**T**).

This enhances the flexibility and reusability of your APIs without compromising type safety. For instance, a method accepting **List<? extends Number>** can work with **List<Integer>**, **List<Double>**, and so on, whereas **List<Number>** would reject those.

This approach follows the PECS principle:

- Use **extends** when the generic type produces data (you only read from it).
- Use **super** when the type **b** data (you write to it).

This principle helps in writing more general and robust code when working with collections and other parameterized types.

Therefore, wildcards provide flexibility while maintaining type safety. The PECS rule is a crucial guideline for using wildcards effectively. Understanding when to use each type of wildcard, especially in conjunction with upper and lower bounds, is essential for effective generic programming in Java.

Bounded type parameters

A bounded type parameter restricts the type argument to match a specific range of types. This helps in creating methods or classes that are both flexible and constrained. Bounded type parameters are essential for expressing relationships between types and ensuring type safety when working with generics.

Having explored upper and lower bounds in detail, we now summarize their function as bounded type parameters. The following reiterates the key points:

- **Upper bounds (extends):** Restrict a type parameter to a specific type or its subtypes. They are commonly used when you need to produce values of a certain type or when you want to ensure that a type parameter supports specific operations (for example, methods defined in an interface or superclass). Think of it as saying, *This type must be at least this specific type.*

- **Lower bounds (super):** Restrict a type parameter to a specific type or its supertypes. They are typically used when you need to consume or add value to a collection. They ensure that the collection can hold objects of the specified type or any of its subtypes. Think of it as saying, *This type can hold at least this specific type.*

- **Importance of bounded type parameters:** Bounded type parameters allow you to write generic code that is both type-safe and flexible. They prevent you from accidentally using incompatible types and enable you to work with a range of related types. The PECS mnemonic is a valuable tool for remembering how to use upper and lower bounds effectively.

By using bounded type parameters strategically, you can design robust and reusable generic classes and methods that work seamlessly with various types within a defined hierarchy.

Examples of bounded types in practice

We have seen that bounded type parameters are essential in ensuring type safety and flexibility in generic programming. The following examples illustrate their practical applications across various domains:

- **Processing financial transactions:** Imagine you are building a financial system that needs to process various types of transactions, such as deposits and withdrawals. Each transaction type might have its own specific logic, but they all share some common properties, like the amount. We can use a bounded type parameter to create a generic method that can process any type of transaction while ensuring type safety.

The following is how:

```java
import java.util.Arrays;
import java.util.List;
abstract class Transaction {
    private double amount;
    public Transaction(double amount) {
        this.amount = amount;
    }
    public double getAmount() {
        return amount;
    }
    public abstract String getType(); // Different transaction types
    @Override
    public String toString() {
        return "Transaction{" +
                "amount=" + amount +
                ", type='" + getType() + '\'' +
                '}';
    }
}
class Deposit extends Transaction {
    public Deposit(double amount) {
        super(amount);
    }
    @Override
    public String getType() {
        return "Deposit";
    }
}
class Withdrawal extends Transaction {
    public Withdrawal(double amount) {
        super(amount);
    }
    @Override
    public String getType() {
        return "Withdrawal";
```

```
        }
    }
    public class TransactionProcessor {
        public static <T extends Transaction> void
    processTransactions(List<T> transactions) {
            for (T transaction : transactions) {
                System.out.println("Processing " + transaction);
                // Perform specific actions based on transaction type (e.g.,
    update balances)
                if (transaction instanceof Deposit) {
                    // ... handle deposit-specific logic
                } else if (transaction instanceof Withdrawal) {
                    // ... handle withdrawal-specific logic
                }
            }
        }
        public static void main(String[] args) {
            List<Deposit> deposits = Arrays.asList(new Deposit(100), new
    Deposit(50));
            processTransactions(deposits); // Works: Deposit extends
    Transaction
            List<Withdrawal> withdrawals = Arrays.asList(new Withdrawal(20),
    new Withdrawal(75));
            processTransactions(withdrawals); // Works: Withdrawal extends
    Transaction
            List<Transaction> allTransactions = Arrays.asList(new
    Deposit(100), new Withdrawal(20));
            processTransactions(allTransactions); // Works: Transaction is a
    Transaction
            // List<String> strings = Arrays.asList("a", "b");
            // processTransactions(strings); // Compile-time error: String
    is not a Transaction
        }
}
```

We define an abstract **Transaction** class that represents the common properties of all transactions. **Deposit** and **Withdrawal** are concrete subclasses that represent specific transaction types. They inherit the amount property and the **getAmount()** method from **Transaction**, but provide their own implementation of the **getType()** method.

The **processTransactions** method is generic, using the type parameter **<T extends Transaction>**. This bond is crucial. It means that **T** can be any type that is a transaction or a subtype of transaction. This allows the method to work with lists of deposits, withdrawals, transactions, or any other future transaction type we might add.

Inside the method, we iterate through the list of transactions. This is because of the **<T extends Transaction>** bound; we are guaranteed that every transaction object in the list is *at least* a transaction. This means we can safely call methods like **transaction. getAmount()** and **transaction.getType()**.

The main method demonstrates how we can call **processTransactions** with lists of different transaction types. The compiler ensures that we cannot pass a list of, say, String objects to the method because the string is not a transaction or a subtype of transaction. This is the type of safety that bounded type parameters provide. They ensure that our **processTransactions** method only works with valid transaction types.

- **Generic repository interface:** Data access is a common task in software development. A repository pattern is often used to abstract the details of data storage. We can use generics to create a type-safe and reusable repository interface. Furthermore, we might need specialized repositories for entities that have specific functionalities, like searching. Bounded-type parameters can help us express these relationships.

  Consider the following example, which demonstrates a generic **Repository** interface, a **Searchable** interface for entities that can be searched, and a **SearchableRepository** interface that extends both:

```
import java.util.List;
public class RepositoryProcessor {
 public static void main(String args[]) {
   SearchableRepository<Product> productRepository = new
SearchableProductRepository();
   List<Product> products = productRepository.search("Laptop");
   System.out.println(products);
 }
}
interface Repository<T> {
 T findById(Long id);
 List<T> findAll();
 void save(T entity);
 void delete(Long id);
}
class ProductRepository implements Repository<Product> {
```

```
  // ... implementation for Product entities
}
// Bounded type parameter for more specialized repository operations
interface SearchableRepository<T extends Searchable> extends
Repository<T> {
  List<T> search(String keyword);
}
interface Searchable {
  boolean matches(String keyword);
}
class SearchableProductRepository extends ProductRepository implements
SearchableRepository<Product> {

  // ... implementation for Product entities, including search
}
```

The **Repository<T>** interface defines basic data access operations for entities of type T, such as finding by ID, finding all, saving, and deleting. Specific repository implementations, like **ProductRepository**, would provide concrete implementations for these methods, working with **Product** entities.

The **Searchable** interface defines a matches method, which allows an entity to be checked against a **search** keyword. The product class now implements this interface, providing a concrete implementation of the matches method for products.

The **SearchableRepository<T extends Searchable>** interface extends both **Repository<T>** and adds the search method. The crucial part here is that the bound T extends **Searchable**. This ensures that any repository that implements **SearchableRepository** must work with entities that also implement the **Searchable** interface. This is how we enforce the relationship; only searchable entities can have a searchable repository.

The **SearchableProductRepository** class extends **ProductRepository** (and implicitly implements **Repository<Product>**) and implements **SearchableRepository<Product>**. This is important because the **SearchableRepository** itself extends the repository.

By extending **ProductRepository**, we do not have to rewrite the basic repository methods. The **SearchableProductRepository** provides the specific search implementation, leveraging the matches method of the product class.

In the main method, we create a **SearchableRepository<Product>** and use it to search for products.

It is because the product implements searchable, and **SearchableProductRepository** works with product entities, the type constraints are satisfied, and the code compiles and runs correctly. This example clearly demonstrates how bounded type parameters, combined with interface inheritance, ensure type safety and code reusability when working with different types of entities and specialized repository operations.

- **Implementing a comparable interface:** Sometimes, you need to create generic classes that can be compared to each other. For example, you might want to create a generic **SampleBox** class that can hold any comparable type and then compare **SampleBox** instances based on the values they contain. Bounded type parameters, combined with the comparable interface, make this possible.

The following is how:

```java
class SampleBox<T extends Comparable<T>> implements
Comparable<SampleBox<T>> {
 private T value;
 public SampleBox(T value) {
  this.value = value;
 }
 public T getValue() {
  return value;
 }
 @Override
 public int compareTo(SampleBox<T> other) {
  return this.value.compareTo(other.value);
 }
 public static void main(String[] args) {
  SampleBox<Integer> box1 = new SampleBox<>(10);
  SampleBox<Integer> box2 = new SampleBox<>(20);
  int comparison = box1.compareTo(box2); // Comparing Integer values
  SampleBox<String> box3 = new SampleBox<>("apple");
  SampleBox<String> box4 = new SampleBox<>("banana");
  int stringComparison = box3.compareTo(box4); // Comparing String
values
  System.out.println("Integer comparison: " + comparison);
  System.out.println("String comparison: " + stringComparison);
 }
}
```

In this example, we define a generic **SampleBox** class that holds a value of type T. The crucial part is the declaration **SampleBox<T extends Comparable<T>>**. This bound has two important effects:

- **T extends Comparable<T>:** This means that the type parameter T must implement the **Comparable<T>** interface. This is essential because we want to be able to compare **SampleBox** instances.

  The **Comparable<T>** interface defines the **compareTo** method, which is used for comparisons. This bound ensures that we can call the **compareTo** method on the value field.

- **Implements comparable<SampleBox<T>>:** This means that the **SampleBox** class itself implements the comparable interface. Specifically, a **SampleBox<T>** can be compared to another **SampleBox<T>**. This allows us to compare **SampleBox** objects based on the values they contain.

  Inside the **compareTo** method of the **SampleBox** class, we simply delegate the comparison to the **compareTo** method of the underlying value (which we know exists because the **T extends Comparable<T>** bound).

  The main method demonstrates how we can create **SampleBox** objects of different comparable types, such as Integer and String. This is because both integer and string implement comparable, we can create **SampleBox<Integer>** and **SampleBox<String>** objects and compare them using the **compareTo** method. The compiler ensures that we cannot create a **SampleBox** of a non-comparable type. This is the power of bounded type parameters; they enforce type constraints that are necessary for our logic to work correctly.

  These examples demonstrate the power and versatility of bounded type parameters in Java generics. By constraining type parameters to specific ranges, you can create type-safe and reusable code that works seamlessly with related types. Bounded types are essential for building robust and flexible generic classes and methods.

Conclusion

This chapter has provided a comprehensive overview of the key features of generics, including type parameters, wildcards, and bounded types. By using generics effectively, you can catch type errors at compile time, write code that is more adaptable to different data types, and avoid the overhead of runtime casts.

The next chapter explores how generics are used in the Java Collections Framework, where they play a crucial role in making your code cleaner and more reliable. We will see how generics help you work with collections more effectively.

Exercise

1. **What is the purpose of a bounded type parameter in Java generics?**

   a. To allow the use of primitive types in generic classes.

   b. To restrict the type argument to a specific range of types.

   c. To improve the runtime performance of generic code.

   d. To simplify the syntax for declaring generic methods.

2. **Which keyword is used to specify an upper bound for a type parameter?**

   a. super

   b. extends

   c. implements

   d. within

3. **Which keyword is used to specify a lower bound for a type parameter?**

   a. super

   b. extends

   c. implements

   d. within

4. **What does the upper bound <T extends Number> mean?**

   a. T can be any type.

   b. T can be a number or any supertype of a number.

   c. T can be a number or any subtype of number.

   d. T must be exactly the number.

5. **What does the lower bound <T super Comparable<T>> mean?**

   a. T can be any type that implements comparable.

   b. T can be comparable or any supertype of comparable.

   c. T can be comparable or any subtype of comparable.

   d. T must be exactly comparable.

6. **When is it appropriate to use an upper bounded wildcard (? extends Type)?**

   a. When you want to add elements to a collection.

   b. When you want to read elements from a collection.

   c. When you want to define a generic class.

   d. When you want to specify a lower bound for a type parameter.

7. **When is it appropriate to use a lower bounded wildcard (? super Type)?**
    a. When you want to read elements from a collection.
    b. When you want to add elements to a collection.
    c. When you want to define a generic interface.
    d. When you want to specify an upper bound for a type parameter.

8. **Which of the following is a correct way to declare a method that accepts a list of numbers or their subtypes?**
    a. public void processNumbers(List<Number> numbers)
    b. public void processNumbers(List<? extends Number> numbers)
    c. public void processNumbers(List<? super Number> numbers)
    d. public void processNumbers(List<T extends Number> numbers)

9. **Which of the following is a correct way to declare a method that can add Integers to a list that can hold Integers or their supertypes?**
    a. public void addIntegers(List<Integer> list)
    b. public void addIntegers(List<? extends Integer> list)
    c. public void addIntegers(List<? super Integer> list)
    d. public void addIntegers(List<T super Integer> list)

10. **What is the PECS principle?**
    a. A rule for defining generic classes.
    b. A mnemonic for remembering when to use extends and super with wildcards.
    c. A set of rules for converting primitive types to wrapper types.
    d. A guideline for improving the performance of generic code.

Answers

1. a

    Explanation: Bounded type parameters restrict the types that can be used as type arguments, enabling type safety and allowing you to work with a range of related types.

2. b

    Explanation: The extends keyword is used to define an upper bound, limiting the type parameter to a specific type or its subtypes.

3. a

    Explanation: The super keyword is used to define a lower bound, restricting the type parameter to a specific type or its supertypes.

4. c

   Explanation: <T extends Number> means T can be Number itself, or any class that inherits from Number (for example, integer, double).

5. b

   Explanation: <T super Comparable<T>> means T can be Comparable itself, or any interface/class that Comparable is a supertype of.

6. b

   Explanation: Upper bounded wildcards are typically used when you are producing values from a collection (reading), as they ensure that you will get at least the specified type.

7. b

   Explanation: Lower bounded wildcards are commonly used when you are consuming values (adding) to a collection, ensuring the collection can accept elements of at least the specified type.

8. b

   Explanation: List<? extends Number> allows the method to accept lists of Number, Integer, Double, etc.

9. c

   Explanation: List<? super Integer> allows the method to accept lists of Integer, Number, Object, etc., and you can safely add Integers to any of these lists.

10. b

    Explanation: **Producer extends, consumer super (PECS)** is a helpful mnemonic to remember when to use extends (for producing or reading) and super (for consuming or writing) with wildcards.

Join our Discord space

Join our Discord workspace for latest updates, offers, tech happenings around the world, new releases, and sessions with the authors:

https://discord.bpbonline.com

CHAPTER 3
Generics in Collections

Introduction

The Java Collections Framework provides a set of well-structured interfaces and classes for managing groups of objects efficiently. Before the introduction of generics, collections operated on raw types, which allowed insertion of any object type and required explicit casting when retrieving elements. This often led to runtime ClassCastExceptions and made the code verbose and error-prone. Generics addressed these issues by enforcing type safety at compile time, eliminating the need for explicit casting and enabling early detection of type-related errors. This significantly improved code reliability. In this chapter, we will explore how generics are applied to different collection types and understand their advantages in improving code readability, maintainability, and performance.

Structure

The chapter covers the following topics:

- Overview of Java Collections Framework
- Applying generics to List<T>
- Applying generics to Set<T>
- Applying generics to Map<K, V>

- Common pitfalls and best practices
- Type erasure in generics

Objectives

By the end of this chapter, you will understand how Java's Collections Framework integrates with generics to provide type-safe and reusable data structures. You will learn how generics are applied to common collections like **List<T>**, **Set<T>**, and **Map<K, V>**, along with best practices to avoid pitfalls when working with them. Additionally, you will explore type erasure and its impact on generics in collections. *Exercises* at the end of this chapter will reinforce your understanding through practical implementation.

Overview of Java Collections Framework

The **Java Collections Framework (JCF)** is a unified architecture for handling and manipulating collections in Java. It includes interfaces and classes for various data structures, such as Lists, Sets, Maps, etc. The framework provides efficient and flexible ways to store, retrieve, and process objects.

Before exploring the application of generics in the Java Collections Framework, it is helpful to understand the core collection interfaces.

The following table provides an overview of the main collection types and their primary characteristics:

Interface	Description
List<T>	An ordered collection that allows duplicates (for example, ArrayList, LinkedList).
Set<T>	A collection that does not allow duplicates and is not ordered (for example, HashSet, TreeSet).
Queue<T>	A collection designed typically for **first-in-first-out** (FIFO) operations (for example, PriorityQueue).
Map<K, V>	A collection that stores key-value pairs (for example, HashMap, TreeMap).

Table 3.1: Core interfaces in Java Collections Framework

Understanding these collection types and their characteristics lays the foundation for effectively using generics with them. Generics enhance the type safety and flexibility of collections, allowing you to work with strongly typed data structures while avoiding unnecessary type casting and runtime errors.

In the following sections, we will explore how generics are applied to List, Set, and Map, along with best practices to ensure type safety and maintainability in your code. We will explore the

Collections Framework in depth in *Chapter 4, Introduction to Collections Framework*.

While generics are primarily known for enhancing type safety and readability, they also contribute to performance improvements. In pre-generic code, collections stored elements as raw **Object** types, requiring frequent casting and introducing the risk of **ClassCastException** at runtime. Generics eliminate the need for such casts, enabling more efficient and safer bytecode.

Moreover, generics reduce the overhead associated with boxing and unboxing when working with wrapper types, especially in collections like **List<Integer>**. Although Java does not yet include primitive-specialized collections (e.g., **IntList**) in the core library, generics with wrapper types provide a cleaner and more performant alternative to unchecked operations.

This compile-time type enforcement ensures cleaner code execution paths and allows tools like the **Java Virtual Machine (JVM)** and **just-in-time compiler (JIT compiler)** to optimize bytecode more effectively.

Consider the following example:

```
// Without generics (pre-Java 5)
List numbers = new ArrayList();
numbers.add(10);                      // Autoboxed to Integer
int n = (Integer) numbers.get(0);     // Requires explicit cast
// With generics
List<Integer> numbersGen = new ArrayList<>();
numbersGen.add(10);                   // Still autoboxed
int m = numbersGen.get(0);            // No cast needed
```

The second example avoids the need for explicit casting and allows the compiler to perform type checks during compilation. This not only improves safety but also enables better runtime optimization.

Applying generics to List<T>

The **List<T>** interface in Java represents an ordered collection of elements, allowing duplicates and providing positional access. Generics enhance lists by enforcing type safety, preventing runtime **ClassCastException** by ensuring that only elements of a specified type are stored in the list.

Before generics were introduced, Java collections stored elements of type object, meaning different types of objects could be added to the same list. However, this led to unsafe type conversions, requiring explicit casting when retrieving elements.

Consider the following example of a non-generic list implementation:

```java
import java.util.ArrayList;
import java.util.List;
public class NonGenericListExample {
 public static void main(String[] args) {
  List nonGenericList = new ArrayList(); // Raw type List
  nonGenericList.add("Java"); // String added
  nonGenericList.add(100); // Integer added (no compile-time error)
  fetchItems(nonGenericList);
 }
 public static void fetchItems(List nonGenericListItems) {
  String item1 = (String) nonGenericListItems.get(0); // Explicit casting (safe)
          String      item2      =      (String)      nonGenericListItems.
get(1); // Runtime error! ClassCastException
  System.out.println(item1);
  System.out.println(item2); // This will cause an error
 }
}
```

In this example, the list **nonGenericList** is created without specifying a type. We add a string and an integer to the same list. When retrieving elements, Java treats them as **Object**. In the method, **fetchItems(List nonGenericListItems)**, when fetching the second item (which is an integer), we can avoid compile-time error with explicit casting (**(String) list.get(1);**). However, at runtime, this would lead to a **ClassCastException** as an Integer cannot be casted to a **String**.

This is the reason to introduce generics, as they enforce type safety at compile time.

By specifying a **type parameter (<T>)**, we restrict the list to store only one type of element.

Let us write the same example with generics:

```java
import java.util.ArrayList;
import java.util.List;
public class GenericListExample {
 public static void main(String[] args) {
  List<String> genericList = new ArrayList<>(); // Type-safe list
  genericList.add("Java");
  // genericList.add(100); // Compilation error - only Strings allowed
  String item1 = genericList.get(0); // No explicit casting needed
  System.out.println(item1); // Output: Java
```

```
    }
}
```

Here, **List<String>** ensures only string elements can be stored. Trying to add 100 (an integer) would cause a compilation error. When retrieving the elements, no explicit casting is needed. The code is safer and cleaner with generics.

Wildcards in generic lists

While generics enforce strict type safety, there are scenarios where we want flexibility in working with unknown or related types. For example, we might want a method to process a list containing elements of different but related types.

Consider the following code:

```
public void printNames(List<? extends Person> people) {
    for (Person p : people) {
        System.out.println(p.getName());
    }
}
```

In the above code, the **printNames** method accepts a list of any type that is a subtype of **Person** (e.g., Employee, Student, etc.), allowing flexibility while still preserving type safety. Without wildcards, you would need a separate method for each specific subtype.

This is where wildcards (**?**) come in. Wildcards allow us to create more generalized methods that work with a range of generic types while still maintaining type safety. Let us explore the different types of wildcards and how they can be used effectively:

- **Unbounded wildcards (?)**: Sometimes, we need to write methods that can accept lists of any type without being restricted to a specific generic type parameter. This is especially useful when we are only reading data from the list and do not need to modify it.

  By using an unbounded wildcard (**?**), we indicate that the method can accept a list of any type, but we treat the elements as objects since we do not know their exact type. Let us look at an example:

  ```
  import java.util.List;
  import java.util.Arrays;
  public class UnboundedWildcardListExample {
      public static void printList(List<?> unboundedList) {
          for (Object eachItem : unboundedList) {
              System.out.println(eachItem);
          }
  ```

```
    }
    public static void main(String[] args) {
        List<String> stringList = Arrays.asList("A", "B", "C");
        List<Integer> intList = Arrays.asList(1, 2, 3);
        printList(stringList); // Works for any type
        printList(intList);
    }
}
```

In this example, any list type (**List<String>**, **List<Integer>**, etc.) can be passed to **printList** method. We cannot add new elements to **List<?>** because the exact type is unknown. The following line would lead to a compile-time error:

```
unboundedList.add("Hello");
```

- **Upper bounded wildcards (? extends Type) in lists**: When dealing with lists in generics, upper bounded wildcards (**? extends T**) allow us to work with collections that contain elements of a specific type or any of its subclasses. This is useful when we want to read data from a list without worrying about its exact type, if it is within the specified bounds.

Since the list can hold elements of various subtypes, we can safely retrieve elements, but we cannot add new elements to the list (except null) because we do not know the exact type at runtime. Let us explore this with the following example:

```
import java.util.List;
public class UpperBoundedWildcardListExample {
 public static double sumOfNumbers(List<? extends Number>
 upperBoundedNumberList) {
  double sum = 0;
  for (Number num : upperBoundedNumberList) {
   sum += num.doubleValue(); // Safe because Number has doubleValue()
  }
  return sum;
 }
 public static void main(String[] args) {
  List<Integer> intList = List.of(1, 2, 3);
  List<Double> doubleList = List.of(1.5, 2.5, 3.5);
  System.out.println(sumOfNumbers(intList)); // Output: 6.0
  System.out.println(sumOfNumbers(doubleList)); // Output: 7.5
 }
}
```

The method **sumOfNumbers(List<? extends Number> upperBoundedNumberList)** takes a list of any subclass of Number (Integer, Double, etc.). It iterates through the list and sums up the values using **doubleValue()**, which is available for all number types. This ensures that we can pass lists of integers, doubles, floats, etc.

We can retrieve elements as Number because we are sure they extend Number, but we cannot add new elements to numbers (except null).

- **Lower bounded wildcards (? super Type) in lists:** Lower bounded wildcards allow us to work with collections that can accept elements of a specific type or any of its supertypes. This is particularly useful when we want to add elements to a collection while maintaining type safety.

Unlike upper bounded wildcards, where we could only read elements, lower bounded wildcards allow safe addition but restrict retrieval to **Object** (since we do not know the specific type). Let us explore this with the following example:

```
import java.util.List;
import java.util.ArrayList;
public class LowerBoundedWildcardListExample {
 public static void addIntegers(List<? super Integer> lowerBoundedList)
{
  lowerBoundedList.add(10);
  lowerBoundedList.add(20);
  lowerBoundedList.add(30);
  // numbers.add(3.14); // Compilation error! Cannot add Double
  System.out.println("List after adding integers: " + lowerBoundedList);
 }
 public static void main(String[] args) {
  List<Number> numberList = new ArrayList<>();
  List<Object> objectList = new ArrayList<>();
  addIntegers(numberList);
  addIntegers(objectList);
  System.out.println(numberList); // Output: [10, 20, 30]
  System.out.println(objectList); // Output: [10, 20, 30]
 }
}
```

Method **addIntegers(List<? super Integer> numbers)** takes a list of integers or any of their supertypes (Number, Object). It safely adds integers (10, 20, 30) because Integer is the lower bound. It cannot add a Double or a String because those are not subtypes of an integer.

We can add elements of type integer or its subclasses. We cannot retrieve elements as integers, only as objects, because the list might be a **List<Number>** or **List<Object>**:

```
Integer num = numbers.get(0);   // Compilation error! Type mismatch
Object obj = numbers.get(0);    // Allowed
```

Lower bounds in lists are best suited for writing operations, such as adding values to a collection.

Applying generics to Set<T>

Generics enhance type safety and flexibility in Java's Set interface. By applying generics to sets, you can ensure that all elements belong to a specific type while benefiting from compile-time checks. This section explores how generics work with sets, including wildcard usage, upper, and lower bounds.

Set<T> is a collection that does not allow duplicate elements. By specifying a generic type **T**, you can create strongly typed sets that prevent accidental type mismatches.

Let us start by looking at a simple example of a generic set:

```
import java.util.Set;
import java.util.HashSet;
public class GenericSetExample {
 public static void main(String[] args) {
  Set<String> stringSet = new HashSet<>();
  stringSet.add("item1");
  stringSet.add("item2");
  stringSet.add("item3");
  for (String item : stringSet) {
   System.out.println(item);
  }
 }
}
```

The **Set<String>** ensures that only **String** elements can be stored in the set. Trying to add an Integer would result in a compile-time error. The **for** loop iterates safely without requiring explicit type casting.

Wildcards in generic sets

Wildcards allow for greater flexibility when working with sets containing unknown or related types. Let us understand this with examples:

- **Unbounded wildcards (Set<?>):** Unbounded wildcards (**?**) are useful when the exact type of elements in the set is unknown, but we still need to read from it. This is often used in generic methods that operate on sets of various types without modifying them.

Consider the following example.

```java
import java.util.Set;
public class UnboundedWildcardSetExample {
 public static void printSet(Set<?> unboundedSet) {
  for (Object element : unboundedSet) {
    System.out.println(element);
  }
 }
}
```

The method accepts any set, regardless of its element type. Since the type is unknown, you cannot add new elements to the set within the method. Iteration works using an object, ensuring type safety while reading values.

- **Upper bounded wildcards (Set<? extends T>):** Upper bounded wildcards allow a set to hold elements that are of a specific type or its subclasses. This is useful when working with collections that store a hierarchy of objects. Let us see how this works in practice:

```java
import java.util.Set;
public class UpperBoundedWildcardSetExample {
 public static void printAnimalSounds(Set<? extends Animal>
upperBoundedSet)
 {
  for (Animal animal : upperBoundedSet) {
    animal.animalSound();
  }
 }
}
class Animal {
 void animalSound() {
  System.out.println("Some general animal sound");
 }
}
class Dog extends Animal {
```

```
@Override
void animalSound() {
 System.out.println("Bark");
 }
}
```

The wildcard **?** **extends** **Animal** ensures that the set contains elements that are animals or any subclass (Dog, Cat, etc.). The method iterates over the set and calls **animalSound()**, ensuring correct behaviour for each subclass. You cannot add new elements inside the method because the exact subtype is unknown at runtime.

- **Lower bounded wildcards (Set<? super T>)**: Lower bounded wildcards allow sets to contain elements of a specified type or any of its super classes. This is particularly useful when you need to add elements while ensuring a minimum type constraint. Let us explore this with an example:

```
import java.util.Set;
public class LowerBoundedWildCardsetExample {
 public static void addEmployees(Set<? super Manager> employeeSet) {
  employeeSet.add(new Manager("Manager1"));
  employeeSet.add(new Manager("Manager2"));
 }
}
```

The wildcard **?** **super** **Manager** ensures the set can hold a **Manager** or any superclass (Employee, Person). You can add **Manager** elements since it is a valid subtype. Retrieving elements is limited since the exact type is unknown beyond the object.

Applying generics to Map<K,V>

Generics significantly improve type safety and flexibility when working with Java's **Map** interface. By applying generics to maps, we ensure that both keys and values conform to specific types, reducing runtime errors and unnecessary casting. This section explores how generics work with maps, including wildcard usage, upper and lower bounds

Map<K, V> associates keys of type **K** with values of type **V**. By specifying generic types, we create strongly typed maps that prevent accidental type mismatches.

Let us start by looking at a simple example of a generic **Map**:

```
import java.util.Map;
import java.util.HashMap;
public class GenericMapExample {
```

```
public static void main(String[] args) {
  Map<Integer, String> genericEmployeeMap = new HashMap<>();
  genericEmployeeMap.put(101, "Employee1");
  genericEmployeeMap.put(102, "Employee2");
  genericEmployeeMap.put(103, "Employee3");
  for (Map.Entry<Integer, String> entry : genericEmployeeMap.entrySet()) {
    System.out.println("ID: " + entry.getKey() + ", Name: " + entry.
getValue());
  }
 }
}
```

The **Map<Integer, String>** ensures that only **Integer** keys and **String** values can be stored. Using generics prevents accidental type mismatches when inserting or retrieving elements. The **for** loop iterates through the entries safely without requiring explicit type casting.

Wildcards in generic maps

Wildcards make maps more flexible when handling various types. Let us understand this with examples:

- **Unbounded wildcards (Map<?, ?>)**: Unbounded wildcards (**?**) allow a map to store any key-value pair without specifying exact types. This is useful for read-only operations where we do not modify the map:

```
import java.util.Map;
public class UnboundedWildcardMapExample {

    public static void printMap(Map<?, ?> unboundedGenericMap) {
        for (Map.Entry<?, ?> entry : unboundedGenericMap.entrySet()) {
            System.out.println("Key: " + entry.getKey() + ", Value: " +
entry.getValue());
        }
    }
}
```

The method **printMap** accepts any map, regardless of key or value types. Since the exact types are unknown, adding new elements is not allowed. Iteration works using an object, ensuring type safety while reading values.

- **Upper bounded wildcards (Map<? extends K, ? extends V>):** Upper bounded wildcards allow maps to hold elements that belong to a specific type or its subclasses. This is useful when working with class hierarchies.

Let us understand this with an example:

```
import java.util.HashMap;
import java.util.Map;
public class UpperBoundedWildcardMapExample {
 public static void printEmployees(Map<? extends Number, ? extends Employee>
employeeMap) {
   for (Map.Entry<? extends Number, ? extends Employee> entry :
employeeMap.entrySet()) {
     System.out.println("ID: " + entry.getKey() + ", Name: " +
entry.getValue().empName);
   }
// Note: We cannot add entries to employeeMap here because the exact t
ypes //of the key and value are unknown
// For example, the below is not allowed.
//employeeMap.put(3, new Employee("NewEmp", 3));

 }
 public static void main(String[] args) {
  Map<Integer, Employee> employees = new HashMap<>();
  employees.put(1, new Employee("Employee1", 1));
  employees.put(2, new ProgramManager("Employee2", 2));
// ProgramManager is a subclass of Employee
  printEmployees(employees);
 }
}
class Employee {
 String empName;
 int empId;
 Employee(String name, int id) {
  this.empName = name;
  this.empId = id;
```

```
   }
}
class ProgramManager extends Employee {
 ProgramManager(String name, int id) {
  super(name, id);
 }
}
```

The wildcard **? extends Number** ensures that keys are of type **Number** or its subclasses. The wildcard **? extends Employee** ensures that values are **Employee** or any subclass (**Manager**). You cannot insert new elements inside the method, as the exact subtype is unknown at runtime.

The main method demonstrates how to create a **Map<Integer, Employee>** and pass it to **printEmployees**.

- **Lower bounded wildcards (Map<? super K, ? super V>):** Lower bounded wildcards allow maps to store elements of a specified type or any of its super classes. This is useful when adding new elements while ensuring a minimum type constraint:

```
import java.util.Map;
import java.util.HashMap;
public class LowerBoundedWildcardMapExample {
 public static void addEmployees(Map<? super Integer, ? super Employee>
employeeMap) {
  employeeMap.put(201, new Employee("Employee1", 201));
  employeeMap.put(202, new ProgramManager("Employee2", 202));
 }
 public static void main(String[] args) {
  Map<Number, Object> employees = new HashMap<>();
  addEmployees(employees);
  for (Map.Entry<Number, Object> entry : employees.entrySet()) {
   System.out.println("ID: " + entry.getKey() + ", Value: " +
entry.getValue());
  }
 }
}
```

The wildcard **? super Integer** ensures the map can accept **Integer** or any superclass (like **Number, Object**). The wildcard **? super Employee** ensures that values are

Employee or any superclass. You can add elements, but retrieving values requires casting since the exact type is unknown beyond object.

The main method demonstrates how a **Map<Number, Object>** is used to call **addEmployees**.

Common pitfalls and best practices

When using generics with Java collections (**List**, **Set**, and **Map**), it is crucial to follow best practices to ensure type safety and prevent runtime errors. Misusing generics can lead to issues like compilation errors, class cast exceptions, and unexpected behaviour.

In the following, we will discuss some common pitfalls and how to avoid them with best practices:

- **Using raw types instead of parameterized types:**
  - **Pitfall:** Using raw types (i.e., collections without generic parameters) removes compile-time type checking, increasing the risk of **ClassCastException** at runtime:

    ```
    List namesList = new ArrayList(); // Raw type, no type safety
    namesList.
    add(10); // Allowed, but incorrect if expecting only Strings
    String name = (String) namesList.
    get(0); // Throws ClassCastException
    ```

  - **Best practice:** To enforce type safety, always specify the generic type when declaring collections. This ensures that only compatible objects are added, preventing runtime errors:

    ```
    List<String> namesList = new ArrayList<>(); // Type-safe collection
    namesList.add("Name1"); // Allowed
    namesList.add("Name2"); // Allowed
    String name = namesList.get(0); // No casting needed
    ```

- **Adding elements to collections with wildcards:**
  - **Pitfall:** When using upper bounded wildcards (**? extends T**), the compiler prevents modifications because it cannot determine the exact subtype, leading to compilation errors:

    ```
    List<? extends Number> numbers = new ArrayList<Integer>();
    numbers.add(10); // Compilation error: Can't add elements
    ```

  - **Best practice:** Use lower bounded wildcards (**? super T**) when you need to add elements, ensuring that the collection can accept the expected type safely:

```
List<? super Integer> numbers = new ArrayList<>();
numbers.add(10); // Allowed
numbers.add(20); // Allowed
```

From this, a clear guideline emerges for reading from and writing to collections with wildcards:

- Use **? extends T** when **reading** elements (ensures you can retrieve values safely).

- Use **? super T** when **writing** elements (ensures you can insert values safely).

- **Misusing upper and lower bounded wildcards:**

  - **Pitfall:** Using **? extends T** incorrectly can lead to situations where adding elements is disallowed.
    ```
    List<? extends Animal> animals = new ArrayList<Dog>();
    animals.add(new Dog()); // Compilation error
    ```

  - **Best practice:** If you need to modify a collection, use a lower bounded wildcard (**? super T**) to allow inserting elements safely.
    ```
    List<? super Dog> animals = new ArrayList<Animal>();
    animals.add(new Dog()); // Allowed
    animals.add(new Bulldog()); // Allowed if Bulldog extends Dog
    ```

    This leads to a helpful rule of thumb when working with generics and wildcards:

    - Use **? extends T** for reading values, but avoid modifying the collection.
    - Use **? super T** for adding elements while restricting the types that can be retrieved.

- **Using unbounded wildcards (?) for modification operations:**

  - **Pitfall:** An unbounded wildcard (**?**) makes a collection completely type-agnostic, which means we cannot add any elements to it.
    ```
    Set<?> set = new HashSet<Integer>();
    set.add(5); // Compilation error: Cannot add to a wildcard
    collection
    ```

  - **Best practice:** Unbounded wildcards (**?**) should be used for read-only operations, such as printing or iterating through collections, where modification is not required.

    Use **?** when you only need to read from a collection and do not need to modify it. If modification is required, use a specific type or **? super T** instead:

```
public static void printCollection(Set<?> set) {
    for (Object element : set) {
        System.out.println(element); // Reading is allowed
    }
}
```

This gives rise to a simple guideline when using unbounded wildcards:

- Use **?** when you only need to read from a collection and do not need to modify it.
- If modification is required, use a specific type or **? super T** instead.

- **Using generics in maps incorrectly:**

  o **Pitfall:** Incorrectly specifying key-value types in generic maps can lead to type mismatch errors:

  ```
  Map<Object, String> map = new HashMap<Integer, String>(); //
  Compilation error
  ```

  o **Best practice:** Always declare **Map<K, V>** correctly to maintain type safety and avoid mismatches:

  ```
  Map<Integer, String> employeeMap = new HashMap<>();
  employeeMap.put(101, "Employee1");
  employeeMap.put(102, "Employee2");
  ```

  This leads to a general principle for reading from and writing to generic maps safely:

  - When reading values from a generic map, use **Map<?, ?>** to allow different key-value types without modification.
  - When writing values, use **Map<? super K, ? super V>** to allow type-safe insertions.

- **Misunderstanding invariance:**

  o **Pitfall:** A common misconception in Java generics is assuming that subtyping relationships between classes carry over to generic types. However, Java generics are invariant, meaning that **List<Integer>** is not a subtype of **List<Number>**, even though **Integer** is a subtype of **Number**:

  ```
  List<Number> numbers = new ArrayList<Integer>(); // Compilation
  error
  ```

  o **Best practice:** Always declare **Map<K, V>** correctly to maintain type safety and avoid mismatches:

  ```
  Map<Integer, String> employeeMap = new HashMap<>();
  ```

```
employeeMap.put(101, "Employee1");
employeeMap.put(102, "Employee2");
```

This leads to a general principle for reading from and writing to generic maps safely:

- When **reading** values from a generic map, use `Map<?, ?>` to allow different key-value types without modification.
- When **writing** values, use `Map<? super K, ? super V>` to allow type-safe insertions.

Type erasure in generics

Type erasure is the process by which the Java compiler removes generic type parameters and replaces them with their bound type (or object if no bound is specified). Generics in Java provide compile-time type safety but do not exist at runtime due to type erasure. This means that all generic type information is removed during compilation, and only raw types remain. While this allows backward compatibility with older Java versions, it also introduces certain limitations and pitfalls.

Let us understand how type erasure works, its impact, and how to handle its limitations effectively.

Consider the following example of a generic class:

```
public class TypeEraserExample<T> {
 private T value;
 public void set(T value) {
  this.value = value;
 }
 public T get() {
  return value;
 }
}
```

After compilation, type erasure removes the generic type and transforms it into:

```
public class TypeEraserExample {
 private Object value;
 public void set(Object value) {
  this.value = value;
 }
 public Object get() {
```

```
    return value;
  }
}
```

This means that at runtime, generic type parameters do not exist, everything is treated as an object, and type safety is enforced only at compile-time.

Impact of type erasure

Since type information is erased at runtime, several limitations arise. Let us understand these limitations in detail:

- **Loss of type information:** At runtime, all instances of a generic type look the same. For example:

```
List<String> stringList = new ArrayList<>();
List<Integer> intList = new ArrayList<>();
System.out.println(stringList.getClass() == intList.getClass()); // true
```

  Both lists appear to be instances of **ArrayList** without any distinction in type.

- **Restrictions on instanceof:** Since type parameters do not exist at runtime, using **instanceof** with generic types is not allowed. For example:

```
if (value instanceof List<String>) {   // Compilation error
    System.out.println("This is a list of strings");
}
```

  Instead, you must use wildcard types:

```
if (value instanceof List<?>) {
    System.out.println("This is a list");
}
```

- **Generic arrays are not allowed:** This is because type information is erased. Java does not allow the creation of generic arrays:

```
T[] array = new T[10]; // Compilation error
```

  This restriction exists because arrays in Java enforce runtime type safety, whereas generics do not retain type information after compilation. To work around this, you can use reflection:

```
T[] array = (T[]) Array.newInstance(clazz, 10);
```

  Here, **clazz** is an instance of **Class<T>**, which represents the type at runtime. It allows the creation of an array of the correct type, even though generics lose their type information due to erasure.

Alternatively, instead of arrays, you can use a **List<T>**:

```
List<T> list = new ArrayList<>();
```

- **Method overloading issues:** Methods differing only by generic type parameters are considered identical after type erasure, leading to compilation errors. For example:

```
public void process(List<String> list) { }

public void process(List<Integer> list) { } // Compilation error
```

To resolve this, you can use different method names:

```
public void processStrings(List<String> list) { }

public void processIntegers(List<Integer> list) { }
```

You can also use wildcards to handle multiple types in one method, as shown in the following:

```
public void process(List<?> list) {
    System.out.println("Processing list: " + list);
}
```

Conclusion

In this chapter, we explored the intricacies of Java generics and their impact on type safety, code reusability, and runtime behaviour. We examined how generics enhance collections like lists, sets, and maps, ensuring compile-time checks and preventing unsafe operations. Along the way, we discussed common pitfalls, such as using raw types, misusing wildcards, and the limitations introduced by type erasure. By adopting best practices, like handling wildcards carefully and understanding how type erasure works, developers can write more flexible and maintainable code.

Understanding generics lays a strong foundation for working with Java's powerful collection classes. In the next chapter, we will begin our exploration of the JCF, learning how it simplifies data manipulation and provides essential structures for organizing and managing data.

Exercise

1. **Which of the following is a correct way to declare a type-safe List in Java?**
    a. List list = new ArrayList();
    b. List<Object> list = new ArrayList();
    c. List<String> list = new ArrayList<>();
    d. List<?> list = new ArrayList<String>();

2. **What will be the output of the following code?**

```
public <T extends Number> void print(T t) {
        System.out.println(t.intValue());
        }
   print(5.5);
```

   a. 5

   b. 5.5

   c. Compile error

   d. Runtime error

3. **Which wildcard should you use when you only need to read elements from a collection?**

   a. ? super T

   b. ? extends T

   c. ?

   d. T

4. **What will be the output of the following code?**

```
List<String> list1 = new ArrayList<>();
List<Integer> list2 = new ArrayList<>(); System.out.println(list1.
getClass() == list2.getClass());
```

   a. true

   b. false

   c. Compile-time error

   d. Runtime exception

5. **Which of the following declarations allows adding elements to a collection?**

   a. List<? extends Number> list = new ArrayList<Integer>();

   b. List<?> list = new ArrayList<String>();

   c. List<? super Integer> list = new ArrayList<Number>();

   d. List list = new ArrayList();

6. **What is the result of this code?**

```
List<String>[] arr = new ArrayList<String>[10];
```

   a. Compiles successfully

   b. Compile error

    c.   Runtime error

    d.   Work with warning

7. **Which keyword is used to declare a lower bounded wildcard in Java?**

    a.   extends

    b.   super

    c.   implements

    d.   wildcard

8. **What is a common pitfall of using raw types in Java collections?**

    a.   Increased runtime performance.

    b.   Reduced memory usage.

    c.   Loss of compile-time type safety and potential ClassCastException.

    d.   Simplified syntax for method declarations.

9. **How can you safely check if an object is a List of any type?**

    a.   if(obj instanceof List<String>)

    b.   if(obj instanceof List<?>)

    c.   if(obj instanceof List<T>)

    d.   if(obj instanceof ArrayList<String>)

10. **Which method signature is valid for processing collections of any type?**

    a.   public <T> void process(List<T> list)

    b.   public void process(List<?> list)

    c.   public void process(List<Object> list)

    d.   public void process(List list)

Answers

1. c

    Explanation: Declaring List<String> ensures type safety, so only String elements can be added to the list, preventing runtime ClassCastException.

2. b

    Explanation: The method print(T t) accepts any type that extends Number. 5.5 is a double, which is a subtype of Number, so it's valid. t.intValue() returns the integer part of the double, which is 5. Hence, the output is 5.

3. b

   Explanation: The ? extends T wildcard is used for reading elements. It ensures you can retrieve values safely but prevents adding new elements (except null).

4. a

   Explanation: Due to type erasure, generic type information is removed at runtime in Java. So both List<String> and List<Integer> become just List. Therefore, their runtime classes are the same, and list1.getClass() == list2.getClass() returns true.

5. c

   Explanation: Using ? super Integer allows adding Integer or its subtypes to the list, as it accepts elements that are Integer or a superclass of Integer.

6. b

   Explanation: You cannot create generic arrays in Java directly due to type erasure. This line List<String>[] arr = new ArrayList<String>[10]; produces a compile-time error, because generic array creation is not allowed.

7. b

   Explanation: The 'super' keyword defines a lower bounded wildcard, meaning the collection can accept elements of a specified type or its subtypes.

8. c

   Explanation: Using raw types removes compile-time type checks, making it possible to insert incompatible elements and leading to runtime ClassCastException errors.

9. b

   Explanation: Since generic type information is erased at runtime, you cannot check for specific types with instanceof. Using List<?> allows a safe type check.

10. b

    Explanation: Using List<?> as a method parameter allows the method to accept a list of any type, without knowing its specific type. It supports flexibility while still being type-safe for read-only operations.

Join our Discord space

Join our Discord workspace for latest updates, offers, tech happenings around the world, new releases, and sessions with the authors:

https://discord.bpbonline.com

CHAPTER 4

Introduction to Collections Framework

Introduction

The Collections Framework in Java is a powerful and essential part of the **Java Development Kit (JDK)**. It provides a unified architecture for representing and manipulating groups of objects. Before the Collections Framework, developers had to rely on ad-hoc data structures like arrays, which often led to code that was difficult to maintain and extend.

Consider organizing a library without a structured system. The books would be scattered, making it extremely difficult to locate specific titles. The Collections Framework serves as an organized library system, providing a variety of pre-implemented data structures with well-defined interfaces, facilitating efficient data management and manipulation.

Structure

The chapter covers the following topics:

- Overview of Java Collections Framework
- Collections hierarchy
- Collection interface
- Key methods in collections

- Iterable interface and iterators
- Nested classes in collections
- Wrapper class

Objectives

By the end of this chapter, you will have a comprehensive understanding of the JCF, including its architecture, core interfaces, and the relationships between them. This foundational knowledge will enable you to effectively work with different collection types and understand their strengths and trade-offs. In subsequent chapters, we will discuss the detailed implementations of List, Set, and Map, providing you with practical insights for real-world Java development.

Overview of Java Collections Framework

The JCF is a set of interfaces and classes that provide a unified architecture for storing and processing collections of objects. It eliminates the need for developers to create custom data structures, allowing them to leverage pre-built, optimized implementations.

Before Java 2, developers used arrays and other manual data structures to store and manage data. However, arrays have several limitations:

- Fixed size (cannot grow dynamically)
- No built-in sorting or searching algorithms
- Lack of flexibility in adding or removing elements

To overcome these issues, JCF provides resizable and efficient data structures, making operations like searching, sorting, and iteration easier.

Collections hierarchy

The JCF is built around a set of interfaces and abstract classes. The following figure represents its hierarchy:

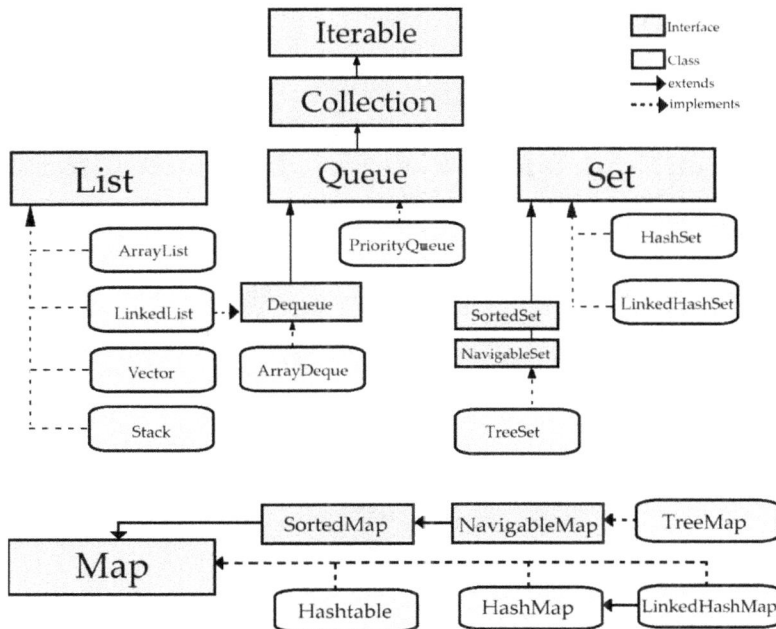

Figure 4.1: *Collections hierarchy*

The key interfaces of the collection hierarchy are:

- **Collection**: The root interface for all collection types.
- **List**: An ordered collection that allows duplicates (ArrayList, LinkedList).
- **Set**: A collection that does not allow duplicate elements (HashSet, TreeSet).
- **Queue**: A collection that follows FIFO (PriorityQueue).
- **Map**: A collection of key-value pairs (Hashtable, HashMap, TreeMap).

Each interface has different implementations optimized for specific use cases.

Collection interface

The collection interface is the root interface of the JCF. It represents a group of objects, known as elements, and is the parent interface of more specialized collection types like List, Set, and Queue.

However, we often confuse *collection* with *collections,* which are two distinct concepts in Java. Understanding this distinction is essential, as it helps avoid common mistakes when working with the Java Collections Framework.

The following table shows the difference between collection and collections:

Aspect	Collection	Collections
Type	Interface	Utility class
Package	`java.util.Collection`	`java.util.Collection`
Purpose	Represents a group of objects	Provides static methods for collection manipulation
Key methods	`add()`, `remove()`, `size()`, `iterator()`	`sort()`, `reverse()`, `shuffle()`, `min()`
Inheritance	Extended by List, Set, Queue	No inheritance. It is purely a helper class.
Example	`Collection<String> names = new ArrayList<>(); names. add("Ryan"); names.add("Roger");`	`Collections.sort((List<String>) names);`

Table 4.1: Collections and collection differences

Key methods in the collection interface

The collection interface provides several essential methods for managing and manipulating elements. Let us explore the most used ones, with examples:

- **add(E element)**: Adds an element to the collection. Returns true if the collection changed because of the operation.

  The **add(E element)** method attempts to insert the specified element into the collection and returns true if the collection was modified. The following example demonstrates this behavior:

```
import java.util.ArrayList;
import java.util.Collection;
public class AddElementExample {
 public static void main(String[] args) {
   Collection<String> names = new ArrayList<>();
   names.add("Ryan");
   names.add("Roger");
   boolean checkAddReturn = names.add("Royce");
   System.out.println(checkAddReturn);// Output: true
   System.out.println(names); // Output: [Ryan, Roger, Roger]
 }
}
```

In the above example, the **checkAddReturn** has a true value as the collection got changed after the add operation.

- **addAll(Collection<? extends E> c)**: Adds all elements from a specified collection to the current collection.

The following example shows how using the **add(E element)** method updates the collection and returns a Boolean indicating whether the collection was modified:

```java
import java.util.ArrayList;
import java.util.Collection;
public class AddAllExample {
 public static void main(String[] args) {
  Collection<String> firstCollection = new ArrayList<>();
  firstCollection.add("Ryan");
  Collection<String> secondCollection = new ArrayList<>();
  secondCollection.add("Roger");
  secondCollection.add("Royce");
  firstCollection.addAll(secondCollection);
  System.out.println(firstCollection); // Output: [Ryan, Roger, Royce]
  System.out.println(secondCollection); // Output: [Ryan, Royce]
 }
}
```

In the above example, we created two collections and added **secondCollection** to **firstCollection** using the **addAll** method.

- **remove(Object element)**: Removes a single instance of the specified element, if present. If the element is not present, the method returns false.

The following example illustrates how the **remove(Object element)** method behaves when the specified element is present in the collection and when it is not:

```java
import java.util.ArrayList;
import java.util.Collection;
public class RemoveExample {
    public static void main(String[] args) {
        Collection<String> names = new ArrayList<>();
        names.add("Ryan");
        names.add("Roger");
        names.add("Royce");
        System.out.println(names); // Output: [Ryan, Roger, Royce]
```

```
        names.remove("Ryan");
        System.out.println(names); // Output: [Roger, Royce]
        boolean result = names.remove("Roy");
        System.out.println(result); // Output: false
        System.out.println(names); // Output: [Roger, Royce]
    }
}
```

The above example shows that the output of the **remove(Object element)** method is false when the specified element is not found in the collection. It is important to note that the matching of the specified element within the collection is determined by the **equals()** method. The collection iterates through its elements and uses the **equals()** method to check for equality. If no match is found, the method returns false. Understanding this behavior helps avoid unexpected results, especially when working with custom objects. In such cases, it may be necessary to override the **equals()** method to define what constitutes a match.

Additionally, for hash-based collections like **HashMap**, proper functioning relies on both **equals()** and **hashCode()**. We will explore this in more detail in the upcoming chapter on **Maps**, *Chapter 6, Map Interface and Implementations.*

- **contains(Object element):** Checks if the collection contains a specific element.

The following example demonstrates how the **contains(Object element)** method checks for the presence of an element in the collection using the **equals()** method:

```
import java.util.ArrayList;
import java.util.Collection;
public class ContainsExample {
    public static void main(String[] args) {
        Collection<String> names = new ArrayList<>();
        names.add("Ryan");
        names.add("Royce");
        System.out.println(names.contains("Ryan")); // Output: true
        System.out.println(names.contains("Roger")); // Output: false
    }
}
```

In the above example, **names.contains(Roger)** returns false because the name does not exist in the collection. Like the remove method, the contains method checks for element equality using the **equals()** method. If no element in the collection matches the specified element according to **equals()**, the method returns false. Some other fundamental methods of the collection interface are:

o **int size();**: Returns the number of elements

o **void clear();**: Removes all elements

o **boolean isEmpty();**: Checks if collection is empty

These methods form the backbone of working with data structures, letting you add, remove, and traverse elements effortlessly. In later chapters, we will explore how these methods behave in specific collection types like List, Set, and Map, each of which offers unique capabilities and optimizations.

Key methods in collections

We have already explored the fundamental methods of the **Collection** interface, which help manage elements in collections (like add, remove, contains, and size). Now, let us discuss the key methods in the **Collections** class, a utility class that provides static methods to operate on or return collections.

The **Collections** class contains various static methods for tasks like sorting, searching, finding min/max elements, and more. These methods simplify complex operations, saving developers from writing custom algorithms. Let us break down some of the most commonly used methods with examples:

- **Sorting a list:** Sorting is one of the most frequent operations on collections. The **Collections.sort()** method sorts elements in their natural order (for example, alphabetically for strings or ascending order for numbers).

  All elements in the list must implement the **Comparable** interface to define their natural ordering. If elements do not implement **Comparable**, attempting to sort the list will result in a **ClassCastException**. For primitive types, Java uses their wrapper classes (like Integer or Double), which already implement **Comparable**, allowing them to be sorted seamlessly. We will explore wrapper classes in more detail in the following section.

  Consider the following example:

```
import java.util.ArrayList;
import java.util.Collections;
import java.util.List;
public class SortExample {
    public static void main(String[] args) {
        List<String> names = new ArrayList<>();
        names.add("Ryan");
        names.add("Zane");
        names.add("Aiden");
        Collections.sort(names);
```

```
        System.out.println(names); // Output: [Aiden, Ryan, Zane]
    }
}
```

Here, we created a list of names and used **Collections.sort()** to sort them alphabetically. The sorted list is printed as **[Aiden, Ryan, Zane]**. If case-insensitive sorting is needed, use **String.CASE_INSENSITIVE_ORDER** as shown in the following:

```
Collections.sort(names, String.CASE_INSENSITIVE_ORDER);
```

String.CASE_INSENSITIVE_ORDER is a built-in **Comparator<String>** that compares strings ignoring case.

Case-insensitive reverse order can be achieved as shown in the following:

```
Collections.sort(names, String.CASE_INSENSITIVE_ORDER.reversed());
```

Sorting helps organize data, making it easier to search or display in a structured format.

- **Finding the maximum and minimum elements:** The **Collections.max()** and **Collections.min()** methods help you find the largest and smallest elements in a collection, based on their natural ordering.

  Consider the following example:

```
import java.util.Arrays;
import java.util.Collections;
import java.util.List;
public class MaxMinExample {
    public static void main(String[] args) {
        List<Integer> scores = Arrays.asList(85, 90, 78, 88);
        int maxScore = Collections.max(scores);
        int minScore = Collections.min(scores);
        System.out.println("Highest Score: " + maxScore); // Output: 90
        System.out.println("Lowest Score: " + minScore);   // Output: 78
    }
}
```

  We created a list of scores and used **Collections.max()** and **Collections.min()** to find the highest and lowest scores. These methods are useful when you need to quickly determine boundary values in a collection.

- **Shuffling elements randomly:** The **Collections.shuffle()** method randomly rearranges the elements in a list. This is helpful for scenarios like games or simulations where random order is necessary:

```java
import java.util.ArrayList;
import java.util.Collections;
import java.util.List;
public class ShuffleExample {
    public static void main(String[] args) {
        List<String> names = new ArrayList<>();
        names.add("Ryan");
        names.add("Roger");
        names.add("Royce");
        Collections.shuffle(names);
        System.out.println(names); // Output: Random order of [Roger,
Ryan, Royce]
    }
}
```

In this example, we added three names to a list and used **Collections.shuffle()** to randomly reorder the elements. Every time you run the program, the order will be different. This is perfect for scenarios like creating card games or randomly selecting elements from a list.

- **Reversing a list:** The **Collections.reverse()** method reverses the order of elements in a list. This can be useful when you want to iterate through elements in reverse sequence.

Consider the following example:

```java
import java.util.ArrayList;
import java.util.Collections;
import java.util.List;
public class ReverseExample {
    public static void main(String[] args) {
        List<String> names = new ArrayList<>();
        names.add("Ryan");
        names.add("Roger");
        names.add("Royce");
        System.out.println(names); // Output: [Ryan, Roger, Royce]
        Collections.reverse(names);
        System.out.println(names); // Output: [Royce, Roger, Ryan]
    }
}
```

Here, **Collections.reverse()** flips the order of elements. The original list **[Ryan, Roger, Royce]** becomes **[Royce, Roger, Ryan]** after reversal. This is useful when you need to process elements in reverse order or create a simple undo feature.

- **Filling a list with a specific element**: The **Collections.fill()** method replaces all elements in a list with a specified value.

For example:

```
package com.meennu.javabook.chap4;
import java.util.ArrayList;
import java.util.Collections;
import java.util.List;
public class FillExample {
    public static void main(String[] args) {
        List<String> names = new ArrayList<>();
        names.add("Ryan");
        names.add("Roger");
        names.add("Royce");
        System.out.println(names); // Output: [Ryan, Roger, Royce]
        Collections.fill(names, "Unknown");
        System.out.println(names); // Output: [Unknown, Unknown, Unknown]
    }
}
```

In this example, **Collections.fill()** replaces every element in the list with the value **"Unknown"**. This can be useful when resetting a collection or initializing elements with a default value.

Understanding the **Collections** class is essential because it provides ready-to-use algorithms that save time and reduce code complexity. These methods abstract away the implementation details, allowing you to focus on solving higher-level problems.

These key methods in the **Collections** class help you handle complex data manipulation tasks with ease. However, working with collections often involves accessing elements one by one, which is where iterators come into play.

The following table provides a quick reference to the most commonly used methods from the **Collection** interface and the **Collections** utility class. It summarizes their purpose, mutability effects, and common usage scenarios, helping you decide which method to use in different contexts:

Method	Belongs to	Description	Modifies collection?	Common use case
`add(E e)`	Collection	Adds the specified element to the collection (if possible).	Yes	Adding a new element to a list, set, or other collection
`remove(Object o)`	Collection	Removes a single instance of the specified element.	Yes	Removing a matching element from a collection
`contains(Object o)`	Collection	Checks if the collection contains the specified element.	No	Validating the presence of an element
`size()`	Collection	Returns the number of elements in the collection.	No	Getting the count of elements
`isEmpty()`	Collection	Checks if the collection has no elements.	No	Performing conditional logic if a collection is empty
`clear()`	Collection	Removes all elements from the collection.	Yes	Resetting a collection
`sort(List<T> list)`	Collections	Sorts elements in their natural order.	Yes	Organizing data for search or display
`sort(List<T> list, Comparator<? super T> c)`	Collections	Sorts elements using a custom comparator.	Yes	Custom ordering, such as case-insensitive sorting
`max(Collection<? extends T> coll)`	Collections	Returns the largest element based on natural ordering.	No	Finding the highest score or maximum value
`min(Collection<? extends T> coll)`	Collections	Returns the smallest element based on natural ordering.	No	Finding the lowest score or minimum value
`shuffle(List<?> list)`	Collections	Randomly rearranges elements in a list.	Yes	Randomizing order for games or simulations
`reverse(List<?> list)`	Collections	Reverses the order of elements in a list.	Yes	Processing elements in reverse order
`fill(List<? super T> list, T obj)`	Collections	Replaces all elements in the list with the specified value.	Yes	Initializing or resetting all list values

Table 4.2: *Summary of key methods in the collection interface and the collections utility class*

In the next section, we will explore the iterable interface and how iterators provide a powerful way to traverse collections, bridging the gap between collection manipulation and iteration.

Iterable interface and iterators

We use collections to organize data and iterators to process that data. The iterable interface is the root interface for all collection classes in Java. It represents a collection of elements that can be traversed one by one. Almost all collection classes in Java implement this interface, allowing you to use for-each loops and iterators to navigate through elements.

The iterable interface provides the **iterator()** method, which returns an **Iterator** object to step through elements in the collection.

Understanding iterators ensures you can:

- **Access elements sequentially:** Move through elements one at a time.
- **Modify collections safely:** Remove elements without causing **ConcurrentModificationException**.
- **Work with various collection types uniformly:** Use a single approach to iterate over Lists, Sets, or Queues.

The **Iterable** interface contains only one method, as shown in the following:

```
public interface Iterable<T> {
    Iterator<T> iterator();
}
```

This method returns an **Iterator** object, which provides several useful methods to traverse the collection. An **Iterator** provides methods to iterate through a collection without exposing its internal structure.

Iterator interface

The **Iterator** interface provides three primary methods for navigating through a collection:

- **hasNext():** Returns true if the collection has more elements.
- **next():** Returns the next element in the collection.
- **remove():** Removes the last element returned by the **next()** method.

Let us understand iteration with the following example:

```
import java.util.ArrayList;
import java.util.Iterator;
import java.util.List;
public class IteratorExample {
```

```java
public static void main(String[] args) {
    List<String> names = new ArrayList<>();
    names.add("Ryan");
    names.add("Roger");
    names.add("Royce");
    Iterator<String> iterator = names.iterator();
    System.out.println("Iterating through the list:");
    while (iterator.hasNext()) {
        String name = iterator.next();
        System.out.println(name);
        // Removing an element during iteration
        if (name.equals("Ryan")) {
            iterator.remove();
        }
    }
    System.out.println("\nList after removal: " + names);
}
}
```

The following is the output:

Iterating through the list:

Ryan

Roger

Royce

List after removal: [Roger, Royce]

In this example:

- We use an iterator to walk through the list of names.

- The **remove()** method safely deletes **Raju** during iteration, which would throw a **ConcurrentModificationException** if done directly on the list.

Understanding the enhanced for loop in Java

The enhanced for loop, also known as the for-each loop, provides a simpler way to iterate over arrays and collections in Java.

Since Java 5, collections implementing **Iterable** can be iterated using a for-each loop, for example:

```
for (String name : names) {
    System.out.println(name);
}
```

While the for-each loop is more convenient, iterators offer greater control, especially when modifying collections.

While collection classes provide ways to store and organize data, iterators give you a systematic way to access and traverse elements without exposing the underlying structure. This becomes especially useful for operations like element removal during iteration or working with complex, nested collections.

Using Lambdas for iteration

From Java 8 onward, the **Iterable** interface has **forEach** as a default method. This method allows you to iterate through the collection using a Lambda expression, making the code even cleaner and more concise.

The same for-each loop can be written using a Lambda expression as:

```
names.forEach(name -> System.out.println(name));
```

Lambda expressions simplify iteration by reducing boilerplate code.

We can use an even more compact way to print elements or other operations using a method reference as follows:

```
names.forEach(System.out::println);
```

Nested classes in collections

The JCF includes several nested classes that help you work with collections more effectively. These classes are usually static inner classes that provide additional functionalities, such as creating unmodifiable views, empty collections, or singleton collections.

Understanding these nested classes is valuable, as they help manage various collection-related scenarios without the need for additional custom code. Let us explore each type of nested class and examine how they contribute to handling collections effectively.

Empty collections

Sometimes, you need to return an empty collection instead of null to avoid a **NullPointerException**. Java provides methods to create immutable empty collections:

- **Collections.emptyList()**
- **Collections.emptySet()**
- **Collections.emptyMap()**

Let us look at an example to understand how to create an empty list:

```
import java.util.Collections;
import java.util.List;
public class EmptyCollectionExample {
    public static void main(String[] args) {
        List<String> emptyList = Collections.emptyList();
        System.out.println("Empty List: " + emptyList);//Output: Empty List: []
    }
}
```

With empty collections, we can avoid null checks. They are immutable, preventing accidental modification. Any attempt to add elements will throw **UnsupportedOperationException**. Empty collections are useful when you want to return an empty list without allocating a new object.

Singleton collections

When you need a collection with only one element, we can use a singleton collection:

- **singleton(T element)**: Creates an immutable set with one element.
- **Collections.singletonList(T element)**: Creates an immutable list with one element.

Let us see an example to create a singleton set:

```
import java.util.Collections;
import java.util.Set;
public class SingletonExample {
    public static void main(String[] args) {
        Set<String> singletonSet = Collections.singleton("Ryan");
        System.out.println("Singleton Set: " + singletonSet);
        //Output: Singleton Set: [Ryan]
        // singletonSet.add("Roger");
    }
}
```

We create a singleton set with an element. If you try to add another element to this collection, it will lead to **UnsupportedOperationException**.

Singleton collections can be used when you want to represent a single item as a collection. It is useful for default values or constant elements.

Synchronized collections

If you are working in a multithreaded environment, collections are not thread-safe by default. The collections class provides methods to wrap collections in synchronized views:

- **Collections.synchronizedList(List<T> list)**
- **Collections.synchronizedSet(Set<T> set)**
- **Collections.synchronizedMap(Map<K, V> map)**

The following is an example of creating a synchronized list:

```java
import java.util.ArrayList;
import java.util.Collections;
import java.util.List;
public class SynchronizedExample {
    public static void main(String[] args) {
        List<String> names = Collections.synchronizedList(new ArrayList<>());
        names.add("Ryan");
        names.add("Roger");
        names.add("Royce");
        // Synchronize during iteration
        synchronized (names) {
            for (String name : names) {
                System.out.println(name);
            }
        }
        /*Output:
        Ryan
        Roger
        Royce*/
    }
}
```

Synchronized collections are used to prevent race conditions in multi-threaded applications and protect against concurrent modification errors.

> Note: **You still need to manually synchronize iteration (like using the synchronized block above).**

Checked collections

Checked collections enforce type safety at runtime. This helps catch **ClassCastException** early, especially when dealing with raw types.

Let us try creating a checklist:

```java
import java.util.ArrayList;
import java.util.Collections;
import java.util.List;
public class CheckedCollectionExample {
    public static void main(String[] args) {
        List<String> names = Collections.checkedList(new ArrayList<>(), String.class);
        names.add("Ryan");
        // Trying to add a wrong type will cause a runtime error
        // names.add(100); // This will throw ClassCastException
        System.out.println("Checked List: " + names);
    //Output: Checked List: [Ryan]
    }
}
```

Checked collections add a runtime safety check and help catch type-mismatch bugs early in development.

Immutable collections

From Java 9, you can create immutable collections directly:

- **List.of()**
- **Set.of()**
- **Map.of()**

The following is an example of creating an immutable list:

```java
import java.util.List;
public class ImmutableCollectionExample {
    public static void main(String[] args) {
        List<String> names = List.of("Ryan", "Roger", "Royce");
        System.out.println("Immutable List: " + names);
        //Output: Immutable List: [Ryan, Roger, Royce]
        // Trying to add a wrong type will cause a runtime error
```

```
    //names.add("Zane"); // This will throw UnsupportedOperationException
  }
}
```

Immutable collections are thread-safe, as no modifications are allowed. They are ideal for constant data or read-only views.

Nested classes in the collections utility class save time and reduce complexity. Instead of manually writing logic for empty, singleton, or synchronized collections, you can leverage these built-in methods to:

- Handle edge cases (like empty results or single items).
- Improve performance (by preventing unnecessary modifications).
- Enhance safety (with checked collections and immutable views).

The following table summarizes the key nested classes and factory methods in the collections utility class, highlighting their mutability, thread safety, exception behavior, and typical use cases. Use this as a quick reference when deciding which type of collection wrapper or view to apply in different scenarios.

Category	Factory method(s)	Modifi-able	Thread-safe	Throws Un-supportedO-perationEx-ception on modification	Usage
Empty collections	`Collections. emptyList(), Collections.emp-tySet(),Collec-tions.emptyMap()`	No	Yes (immutable)	Yes	When you want to re-turn an emp-ty collection instead of null to avoid a NullPoint-erException.
Singleton collections	`Collections. singleton(T element),Collec-tions.singleton-List(T element), Collections. singletonMap(K key, V value)`	No	Yes (immutable)	Yes	When you need a collection with exactly one element (e.g., default values, con-stants).

Synchro-nized col-lections	`Collections. synchro-nizedList(list), Collections. synchronized-Set(set),Collec-tions.synchro-nizedMap(map)`	Yes	Yes (for single op-erations; iteration still needs manual synchronization)	No	When mul-tiple threads access and modify a collection.
Checked collec-tions	`Collec-tions.check-edList(list, type), Collec-tions.checked-Set(set, type), Collections. checkedMap(map, keyType, value-Type)`	Yes	No (wrap with synchronized if needed)	No	When you want runtime type checking to prevent ClassCastEx-ception.
Im-mutable collec-tions (Java 9+)	`List.of(...), Set.of(...),Map. of(...)`	No	Yes (immutable)	Yes	For creating unmodifiable collections directly with fixed content.

Table 4.3: Summary of nested classes and factory methods

Wrapper class

In Java, primitive data types (like int, char, and double) are not objects. The Collections Framework, however, works with objects rather than primitives. This is where wrapper classes come in. They provide a way to represent primitive values as objects so they can be used in collections.

Wrapper classes are part of **java.lang** package and offer a convenient way to work with primitives in a fully object-oriented manner.

The benefits of wrapper classes include:

- **Compatibility with collections**: Collections only work with objects, not primitives.
- **Utility methods**: Wrapper classes provide useful methods for parsing, comparison, and more.

- **Immutability**: Wrapper objects are immutable, making them safer to use in concurrent programming.

- **Autoboxing and unboxing**: Java automatically converts primitives to wrapper objects (and vice versa).

The following table shows the list of wrapper classes in Java:

Primitive type	Wrapper class
byte	Byte
short	Short
int	Integer
long	Long
float	Float
double	Double
char	Character
boolean	Boolean

Table 4.4: Wrapper classes

Let us look at an example to understand this better:

```java
import java.util.ArrayList;
import java.util.List;
public class WrapperClassExample {
    public static void main(String[] args) {
        // Creating a list of integers (using the Integer wrapper class)
        List<Integer> numberList = new ArrayList<>();
        // Autoboxing: Primitive int to Integer object
        numberList.add(10);
        numberList.add(20);
        numberList.add(30);
        // Accessing elements with unboxing
        int firstNumber = numberList.get(0); // Unboxing: Integer to int
        System.out.println("List of numbers: " + numberList);
        //Output: List of numbers: [10, 20, 30]
        System.out.println("First number: " + firstNumber);
        //Output: First number: 10
    }
}
```

As we can see, Java automatically converts 10, 20, and 30 (primitive int) into Integer objects. When accessing elements, Java automatically converts the Integer object back to a primitive int.

Wrapper classes come with useful methods for parsing, comparison, and conversions. Let us see that in an example:

```java
public class WrapperClassMethods {
    public static void main(String[] args) {
        // Parsing a string to an integer
        int number = Integer.parseInt("100");
        // Converting primitive to string
        String numStr = Integer.toString(200);
        // Comparing two wrapper objects
        Integer a = 10;
        Integer b = 20;
        int comparison = a.compareTo(b);
        System.out.println("Parsed number: " + number);
        System.out.println("Number as string: " + numStr);
        System.out.println("Comparison result: " + comparison);
        /*
         * Output:
         * Parsed number: 100
    Number as string: 200
    Comparison result: -1
         * */
    }
}
```

In the following:

- **parseInt()**: Converts a string to an integer.
- **toString()**: Converts an integer to a string.
- **compareTo()**: Compares two wrapper objects (returns negative, zero, or positive).

While wrapper classes are powerful, they come with some overhead:

- **Memory usage**: Wrapper classes consume more memory than primitives.
- **Null values**: Wrapper classes can be null, which adds flexibility but also the risk of `NullPointerException`.

In most cases, the benefits outweigh these costs, especially when working with collections.

Wrapper classes bridge the gap between primitive types and the object-oriented nature of Java. They enable primitives to be used in collections and provide useful utility methods. Understanding wrapper classes is essential for mastering Java collections, as they appear frequently in real-world applications.

Conclusion

In this chapter, we explored the JCF, understanding its architecture, core interfaces, and essential methods. We learned how collections simplify data management, providing flexible ways to store, manipulate, and iterate through objects.

We discussed the difference between collection and collections, the role of the Iterable interface, and the importance of iterators for accessing elements. Nested classes and wrapper classes further extended the framework's capabilities, enhancing functionality and compatibility.

In the next chapters, we will take a closer look at individual collection types, starting with list, set, and map implementations. We will understand their unique behaviors, practical applications, and how to choose the right collection for a given scenario.

Exercise

1. **Which of the following is the root interface in the Java Collections Framework?**
   a. List
   b. Collection
   c. Iterable
   d. Map

2. **What is the main purpose of the Java Collections Framework?**
   a. To handle file input and output operations
   b. To provide a standardized architecture for handling collections of objects
   c. To manage threads and concurrency
   d. To create graphical user interfaces

3. **Which collection type does not allow duplicate elements?**
   a. List
   b. Queue
   c. Set
   d. Map

4. **What is the difference between collection and collections in Java?**
   a. Collection is a class, and collections is an interface
   b. Collection is an interface, and collections is a utility class

c. They are both interfaces

d. They are both utility classes

5. **Which of the following methods is part of the collection interface?**

   a. sort()

   b. add()

   c. shuffle()

   d. reverse()

6. **How can you iterate through a collection using an iterator?**

   a. By calling the iterator() method and using a for loop

   b. Using the get() method directly

   c. Using the iterator keyword

   d. By converting the collection to an array first

7. **What happens if you try to add elements to a List created with List.of()?**

   a. Elements are added successfully

   b. A runtime exception is thrown

   c. The list resizes dynamically

   d. The list ignores the new elements

8. **Which collection is best suited for storing elements in a sorted order?**

   a. ArrayList

   b. LinkedList

   c. HashSet

   d. TreeSet

9. **What is the purpose of the iterator.remove() method?**

   a. To clear all elements in the collection

   b. To remove the last element returned by the iterator

   c. To remove a random element from the collection

   d. To remove elements based on a condition

10. **Which interface must a collection implement to be used with an enhanced for loop?**

    a. Collection

    b. Iterable

    c. List

    d. Comparator

Answers

1. c

   Explanation: The Iterable interface is the root interface in the Java Collections Framework. It provides the ability to iterate over elements using an iterator or enhanced for-loop.

2. b

   Explanation: The Java Collections Framework provides a unified architecture for manipulating and handling groups of objects, making data storage, retrieval, and manipulation easier.

3. c

   Explanation: The Set interface does not allow duplicate elements. It is useful when you want to maintain a collection of unique elements.

4. b

   Explanation: Collection is the root interface for most collection types, while Collections is a utility class that provides static methods for manipulating collections.

5. b

   Explanation: The add() method is part of the collection interface and is used to insert elements into a collection.

6. a

   Explanation: You can use the iterator() method to get an iterator object, then use its hasNext() and next() methods to iterate through elements.

7. b

   Explanation: Lists created with List.of() are immutable, meaning any attempt to add, remove, or modify elements will throw an UnsupportedOperationException.

8. d

   Explanation: TreeSet maintains elements in sorted order and does not allow duplicates. It is useful for scenarios where ordering matters.

9. b

   Explanation: The iterator.remove() method removes the last element returned by the iterator. It must be called after next(), or it throws an exception.

10. b

    Explanation: A collection must implement the Iterable interface to be used with an enhanced for loop, as it provides the iterator() method for element traversal.

CHAPTER 5
List Interface and Implementations

Introduction

The List interface in Java is a part of the JCF and represents an ordered collection of elements. Unlike sets, lists allow duplicate elements and provide positional access to elements. Lists are widely used in applications where elements need to be stored, retrieved, and manipulated in a specific sequence.

This chapter explores the List interface and its key implementations, like ArrayList, LinkedList, and Vector. It also covers list synchronization, immutable lists, and checked collections. Additionally, we will look at internal implementations, compare different list types, and implement custom list behaviours.

Structure

The chapter covers the following topics:

- List interface
- ArrayList implementation
- LinkedList implementation
- Vector implementation

- Synchronization in lists
- Unmodifiable collections
- Checked collections

Objectives

This chapter aims to provide a comprehensive understanding of the List interface in Java, its key implementations, and how they function internally. By the end of this chapter, you will have a clear understanding of how **ArrayList**, **LinkedList**, and **Vector** differ in terms of performance, memory usage, and practical applications. You will also learn about synchronization mechanisms for thread safety, creating immutable lists, and ensuring type safety using checked collections. Additionally, this chapter will include hands-on examples and custom implementations to solidify your understanding of how lists work in real-world applications.

List interface

The List interface extends the collection interface and represents an ordered collection of elements. It allows duplicate values and provides indexed access to elements.

The following are the key characteristics of Lists:

- **Ordered collection**: Elements are stored in the order they were added.
- **Allows duplicates**: Unlike sets, a list can contain multiple occurrences of the same element.
- **Indexed access**: Elements can be accessed, modified, or removed using their index.
- **Supports iteration**: Lists support various iteration mechanisms, including iterator, for-each, and stream-based iteration.

The List interface has several implementations in Java, each with different characteristics. Implementations include **ArrayList**, **LinkedList**, and **Vector**.

The following figure is the representation of the List interface and its implementations:

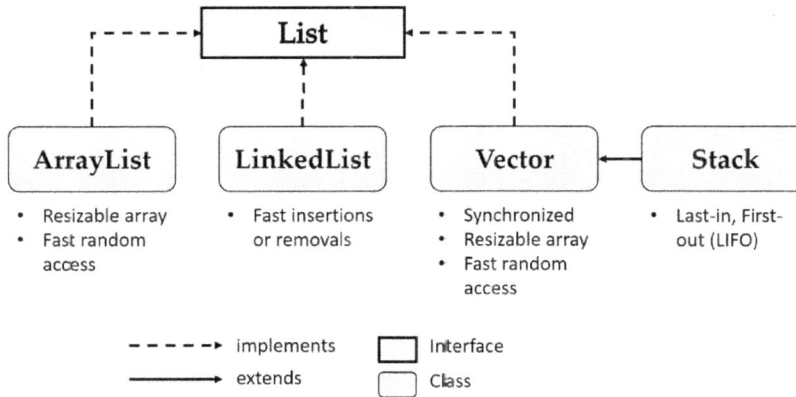

Figure 5.1: *List interface and implementations*

The List interface extends the collection interface and introduces several additional methods:

Method	Description
`add(E e)`	Appends the specified element to the end of the list.
`add(int index, E element)`	Inserts the specified element at the specified position.
`get(int index)`	Returns the element at the specified index.
`set(int index, E element)`	Replaces the element at the specified position.
`remove(int index)`	Removes the element at the specified index.
`indexOf(Object o)`	Returns the index of the first occurrence of the specified element.

Table 5.1: *Additional methods in List interface*

To understand how the List interface works in Java, let us consider an example where we create and manipulate a List of student names:

```java
import java.util.ArrayList;
import java.util.List;
public class ListExample {
    public static void main(String[] args) {
        // Creating a List of student names
        List<String> studentNames = new ArrayList<>();
        // Adding elements to the List
        studentNames.add("Ryan");
        studentNames.add("Roger");
        studentNames.add("Royce");
```

```
        // Accessing elements using index
        System.out.println("First Student: " + studentNames.get(0));
        // Iterating through the List, this will print elements in the order
they were added
        System.out.println("All Students:");
        for (String name : studentNames) {
            System.out.println(name);
        }
        // Checking if an element exists
        System.out.println("Is Ryan in the list? " + studentNames.contains("Ryan"));
        // Removing an element
        studentNames.remove("Roger");
        System.out.println("After removing Roger: " + studentNames);
    }
}
```

The following is the output:

First Student: Ryan

All Students:

Ryan

Roger

Royce

Is Ryan in the list? true

After removing Roger: [Ryan, Royce]

This example demonstrates key operations such as adding, accessing, iterating, checking, and removing elements in a List. We use an **ArrayList**, which is a common implementation of the **List** interface, to store and manipulate student names. The **add()** method inserts elements, **get(index)** retrieves them, and the **contains()** method checks if a specific element exists in the list. The **remove()** method deletes an element, and iterating over the list allows us to print all stored names. Since **ArrayList** maintains insertion order, the output reflects the order in which elements were added.

We will learn more about **ArrayList** in detail in the next section, including its internal implementation and performance characteristics.

ArrayList implementation

ArrayList is one of the most widely used implementations of the List interface in Java. It is part of **java.util** package provides a **dynamic array** that grows as needed, unlike regular arrays, which have a fixed size. Internally, **ArrayList** maintains an array (**Object[] elementData**) that expands when it reaches its capacity.

The following is the internal structure of **ArrayList**:

- **ArrayList** begins with an initial capacity.
- In Java 8 and earlier, this default capacity is ten.
- From Java 9 onward, **ArrayList** starts with an empty array, and the internal array is only allocated when the first element is added (lazy initialization).
- The elements are stored in an internal array called **Object[] elementData**.
- As elements are added, they are placed into this array sequentially.
- When the array becomes full, **ArrayList** creates a new array with a larger capacity and copies all existing elements into this new array.
- The new capacity is typically calculated as follows:
  - In JDK 1.6, *newCapacity = (oldCapacity * 3/2) + 1*

    For example: *10 | 16 | 25 | 38 | ...*
  - From JDK 1.7 onwards, the formula was simplified and optimized for performance: *newCapacity = oldCapacity + (oldCapacity >> 1)*
  - This is a 50% increase, computed using a bitwise right shift.

    For example: *10 | 15 | 22 | 33 | 49 | 73 | ...*

When working with collections in Java, understanding how they manage memory and resize themselves is crucial for writing efficient code.

Let us consider an **ArrayList** of integers and observe how it grows dynamically. Follow these steps:

1. **Creating an empty ArrayList:**

   a. **List<Integer> numbers = new ArrayList<>();** an array of default capacity (ten) is created.

   b. It is initially empty, meaning all positions are null.

   Note: **In Java 9+, ArrayList starts with an empty array (elementData = {}) and defers allocation until the first element is added.**

Index	0	1	2	3	4	5	6	7	8	9
Value										

2. **Adding elements (within initial capacity):**

```
numbers.add(10);
numbers.add(20);
numbers.add(30);
numbers.add(40);
numbers.add(50);
numbers.add(60);
numbers.add(70);
numbers.add(80);
numbers.add(90);
numbers.add(100);
```

Internal array (after ten elements are added):

Index	0	1	2	3	4	5	6	7	8	9
Value	10	20	30	40	50	60	70	80	90	100

The array is now full because it has reached its initial capacity of 10.

3. **Adding the 11th element (Triggers resizing):**

```
numbers.add(110); // Triggers resizing
```

As we continue adding elements, the **ArrayList** eventually reaches its capacity. Let us observe what happens internally when the 11th element is added; it triggers resizing.

   a. Since the array is full, **ArrayList** creates a new array with almost 50% more capacity.

   b. The new capacity is $10 + (10 >> 1) = $ *In binary* $->$ $(00001010 + 00000101) = (10 + 5) = 15$.

   c. A new array of size 15 is created, and all existing elements are copied into it.

   After resizing and adding the new element (*Capacity* = 15):

Index	0	1	2	3	4	5	6	7	8	9	10	11	12	13	14
Value	10	20	30	40	50	60	70	80	90	100	110				

   d. Resizing is an expensive operation because all elements must be copied.

Use cases for ArrayList

ArrayList is best suited for scenarios where fast random access and frequent traversal are needed, and where insertions or deletions in the middle of the list are less frequent. Common use cases include:

- **Storing a dynamic list of items**: When the number of elements is not known in advance and can change over time (e.g., a list of online users in a chat application).

- **Random access operations**: When you need to quickly access elements by index, as **ArrayList** provides O(1) time complexity for **get()** and **set()** operations.

- **Read-heavy collections**: When most operations involve reading data rather than inserting or removing elements in the middle of the list.

- **Maintaining insertion order**: When it is important to preserve the order in which elements are added, such as maintaining a list of tasks in sequence.

- **Temporary storage for computation**: When you need a resizable data structure to temporarily store data for processing (e.g., collecting results before writing them to a file or database).

- **Small to medium datasets**: When working with data sizes that do not cause frequent costly resizes or memory overhead issues.

Performance considerations

While **ArrayList** provides fast random access (O(1) for get operations), its resizing behaviour introduces performance trade-offs. Let us examine them in detail:

- **Growth and resizing overhead:**

  - **ArrayList growth:** The internal array grows dynamically when it reaches its capacity.

  - **Resizing:** It involves:

    - Creating a new array with a larger capacity.

    - Copying all existing elements from the old array to the new one.

- **Time complexity:** $O(n)$ (where n is the number of elements copied).

- **Optimization tip:** If you know the expected size of the list in advance, use:

  ```
  List<Integer> numbers = new ArrayList<>(100);
  ```

  This avoids multiple resizings, improving performance.

- **Insertions at the end (best case):**

  - Adding an element at the end of the list (when capacity is not exceeded) takes O(1) (amortized) time.

  - If resizing is required, the cost is O(n) due to copying.

  - The optimization tip is that if frequent additions are expected in the middle, consider **LinkedList** instead. We shall discuss **LinkedList** in the later sections.

- **Insertions at the beginning or middle (worst case):**
  - Adding an element at the beginning or middle shifts all subsequent elements to the right.
  - To understand the cost of insertions at the beginning or middle, consider the following example where we insert an element at index 0.

    ```
    numbers.add(0, 100); // Inserts at index 0, shifting all elements
    ```

    When you insert an element at index 0, all existing elements in the **ArrayList** are shifted one position to the right to make space. This shifting operation takes linear time, O(n), because every affected element must be moved individually. This is considered the worst case.
  - If frequent middle insertions are required, **LinkedList** is a better choice.

- **Deletions and their cost:**
  - Removing the last element (**remove(size - 1)**) | *O(1)* (no shifting needed).
  - Removing from the middle or beginning (**remove(index)**) | *O(n)* (all elements shift left).
  - The optimization tip is that if the order does not matter, swap the element with the last element and then remove it:

    ```
    numbers.set(index, numbers.get(numbers.size() - 1)); // Swap with last
    ```

    ```
    numbers.remove(numbers.size() - 1); // Remove last element
    ```
  - This reduces shifting cost from *O(n)* to *O(1)*.

- **Memory consumption:**
  - **ArrayList** pre-allocates extra space to reduce the number of resizings.
  - If an **ArrayList** has significantly fewer elements than its capacity, it wastes memory.
  - The optimization tip is that if an **ArrayList** will not grow further, trim unused capacity:

    ```
    numbers.trimToSize();
    ```
  - This releases excess memory.

- **Synchronization and thread safety:**
  - **ArrayList** is not thread-safe.
  - If multiple threads modify a list concurrently, use:

    ```
    List<Integer> syncList = Collections.synchronizedList(new
    ArrayList<>());
    ```

However, **CopyOnWriteArrayList** is a better choice for concurrent reads and occasional writes. This makes reads fast (O(1)) but adds overhead to writes (O(n)). It is useful when reads are frequent but writes are rare, such as in caching or event listener lists. We will see an example of **CopyOnWriteArrayList** in a later section.

Custom implementation of ArrayList

To better understand **ArrayList**, let us implement a simplified version of it.

The following are the points to consider:

- **Internal storage**: We can use an integer array (data) to store elements.
- **Dynamic expansion**: If the array is full when adding a new element, we can give a resizing logic by doubling the capacity and copying existing elements.
- **Retrieval**: To retrieve the elements, we can have a get(index) method. We can add validation to ensure the index is within bounds before returning the element.
- **Size tracking:** We can track the size of the array with the help of a size variable. This variable keeps track of the number of elements added.

The following is the sample code for the custom **ArrayList**:

```
class CustomArrayList {
    private int[] data;
    private int size;
    private int capacity;
    public CustomArrayList(int initialCapacity) {
        this.capacity = initialCapacity;
        this.data = new int[capacity];
        this.size = 0;
    }
    public void add(int element) {
        if (size == capacity) {
            expandCapacity();
        }
        data[size++] = element;
    }
    private void expandCapacity() {
        capacity *= 2; // Double the capacity
        int[] newData = new int[capacity];
```

```
        System.arraycopy(data, 0, newData, 0, size);
        data = newData;
    }
    public int get(int index) {
        if (index < 0 || index >= size) {
            throw new IndexOutOfBoundsException("Index out of bounds");
        }
        return data[index];
    }
    public int size() {
        return size;
    }
    public static void main(String[] args) {
        CustomArrayList list = new CustomArrayList(2);
        list.add(10);
        list.add(20);
        list.add(30); // Triggers capacity expansion
        System.out.println("Element at index 1: " + list.
get(1)); // Output: 20
        System.out.println("List size: " + list.size()); // Output: 3
    }
}
```

In the above example:

- We initialized the list with a capacity of 2.
- Adding a third element triggers resizing (from size 2 to 4).
- We retrieve an element using get(1), which returns 20.

Note: In this custom implementation, we did not implement the List interface. The focus was on demonstrating the internal working of a dynamic array, such as resizing logic and element addition. Implementing the full List interface would require a comprehensive implementation of all its methods, which is beyond the scope of this example.

LinkedList implementation

Unlike **ArrayList**, which is backed by a dynamic array, **LinkedList** is implemented as a doubly linked list. Each element is called a *node*. A node contains:

- **Data**: The actual value stored.
- **A reference to the next node**: Points to the next element.
- **A reference to the previous node**: Points to the previous element.

This structure allows fast insertions and deletions, since modifying references is quicker than shifting elements (as in **ArrayList**). However, accessing elements by index is slower because traversal is required.

Internal structure of LinkedList

A **LinkedList** consists of nodes where each node points to the next and previous nodes. It internally uses a static nested class **Node<E>**. The following is a simplified version of its internal structure:

```
private static class Node<E> {
    E item;
    Node<E> next;
    Node<E> prev;
    Node(Node<E> prev, E element, Node<E> next) {
        this.item = element;
        this.next = next;
        this.prev = prev;
    }
}
```

Each node stores:

- **Item**: The data
- **Next**: Reference to the next node
- **Prev**: Reference to the previous node

Let us understand this with an example. Consider the following code.

```
LinkedList<Integer> list = new LinkedList<>();
list.add(10);
list.add(20);
list.add(30);
list.add(40);
```

This creates the following structure in memory:

1. **Initially, the list is empty**:

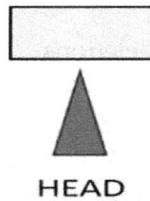

Figure 5.2: Initial LinkedList

2. **Adding 10**:

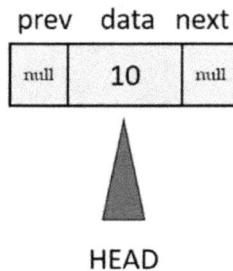

Figure 5.3: LinkedList after adding 10

Since this is the first element, both next and previous are null.

3. **Adding 20**:

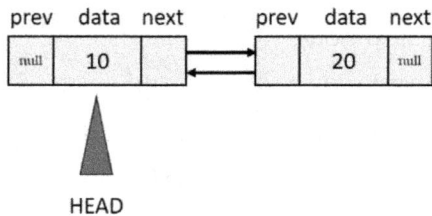

Figure 5.4: LinkedList after adding 20

Once 20 is added, here is what happens:

- **10 next**: Points to 20
- **20 prev**: Points to 10

4. **Adding 30**:

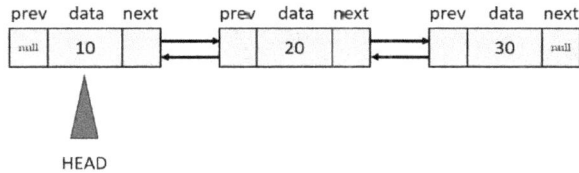

Figure 5.5: *LinkedList after adding 30*

After we add 30, the elements now link as follows:

- **20 next**: Points to 30
- **30 prev:** Points to 20

5. **Adding 40:**

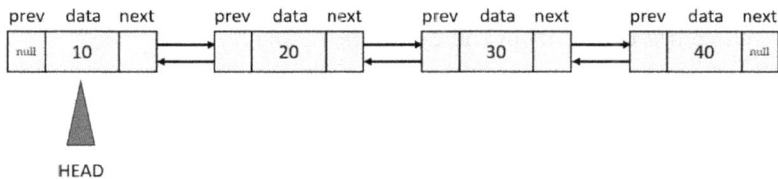

Figure 5.6: *LinkedList after adding 40*

Once 40 is added, it is linked as follows:

- **30 next**: Points to 40
- **40 prev**: Points to 30

To summarize the structure, each node stores two references (next and prev). The head always points to the first node. The tail (last node) points to null.

In case of removal of elements, only references are updated.

Let us say we remove 20 using:

```
list.remove(Integer.valueOf(20));
```

Now, the structure is updated to:

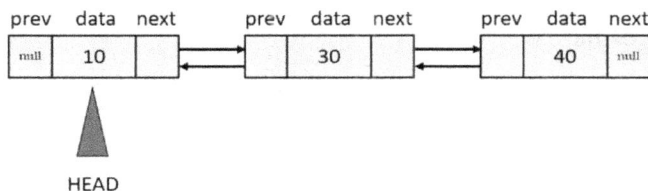

Figure 5.7: *LinkedList after removing 20*

After removing 20, the elements are now connected as follows:

- 10 next now points to 30 (skipping 20)
- 30 prev now points to 10

Performance considerations for LinkedList

Understanding the performance characteristics of **LinkedList** is crucial when deciding whether to use it over **ArrayList**. While **LinkedList** offers efficient insertions and deletions, it has trade-offs in terms of memory usage and element access speed. Let us explore the following key performance aspects:

- **Insertions and deletions:**
  - **Efficient insertions or deletions at the beginning or end:** Unlike **ArrayList**, **LinkedList** does not require shifting elements when inserting or deleting. Updating the previous and next references in nodes is enough, making adding or removing elements at the head or tail O(1).
  - **Middle insertions or deletions require traversal:** If an element is inserted or deleted in the middle, we need to traverse the list to find the correct position, making it O(n) in the worst case.

- **Element access:**
  - Unlike **ArrayList**, **LinkedList** does not support O(1) random access because it does not use an index-based structure.
  - Accessing an element by index requires traversal from the head or tail, making it O(n) in the worst case.
  - If accessing elements sequentially, iteration is slower than **ArrayList** due to a lack of contiguous memory storage.

- **Memory overhead:**
  - **Higher memory usage:** Each node in **LinkedList** stores both data and two references (previous and next), increasing memory consumption compared to **ArrayList**, which stores only elements.
  - **Garbage collection overhead:** Frequent insertions and deletions lead to more object creations and removals, which can impact garbage collection performance.

- **Iteration performance:**
  - **Forward and backward traversal: LinkedList** supports efficient iteration in both directions using **ListIterator**, but it is still O(n).
  - **Poor cache locality:** Since elements are scattered in memory, accessing them requires additional pointer dereferencing, making iteration slower compared to **ArrayList**.

- **Use cases where LinkedList performs better:**
  - **Frequent insertions or deletions:** If you often insert or remove elements at the beginning or middle of the list, **LinkedList** performs better than **ArrayList**.
  - **Queue and stack implementations: LinkedList** is ideal when used as a queue, FIFO, or stack, **last in first out (LIFO)**, because insertions and deletions are efficient.

Custom LinkedList implementation

To understand **LinkedList** deeply, let us implement our own custom **LinkedList**.

Let us create a **Node** class that contains:

- The data (actual value).
- A reference to the next node.
- A reference to the previous node (since it is a doubly linked list).

The following is an example of a **Node** class:

```
class Node<T> {
    T data;
    Node<T> next;
    Node<T> prev;
    public Node(T data) {
        this.data = data;
        this.next = null;
        this.prev = null;
    }
}
```

The linked list maintains references to the head (first node) and tail (last node). It also tracks the size of the list:

```
class CustomLinkedList<T> {
    private Node<T> head;
    private Node<T> tail;
    private int size;
    public CustomLinkedList() {
        this.head = null;
        this.tail = null;
        this.size = 0;
    }
}
```

To add new elements, we can create an add method. It appends the new element at the end by updating the **next** and **prev** references:

```java
public void add(T data) {
        Node<T> newNode = new Node<>(data);
        if (head == null) {  // If list is empty
            head = newNode;
            tail = newNode;
        } else {
            tail.next = newNode;
            newNode.prev = tail;
            tail = newNode;
        }
        size++;
    }
```

In the above code:

- If the list is **empty**, the new node becomes both head and tail.

- Otherwise, we update **tail.next** to point to the new node and **newNode.prev** to point back to the old tail.

To remove an element, we just need to update the references to skip the node:

```java
public boolean remove(T data) {
  if (head == null)
   return false; // Empty list
  Node<T> current = head;
  while (current != null) {
   if (current.data.equals(data)) {
    if (current == head) { // Removing head
     head = head.next;
     if (head != null)
      head.prev = null;
    } else if (current == tail) { // Removing tail
     tail = tail.prev;
     if (tail != null)
      tail.next = null;
    } else { // Removing from middle
     current.prev.next = current.next;
```

```
      current.next.prev = current.prev;
    }
    size--;
    return true;
  }
  current = current.next;
}
return false; // Element not found
}
```

In the above example:

- If the **head** matches, the next node becomes the new head, and its **prev** is set to null.
- If the **tail** matches, the previous node becomes the new tail, and its **next** is set to null.
- If an element is in the **middle**, the surrounding nodes are linked directly to each other, bypassing the removed node.

Unlike **ArrayList**, **LinkedList** does not have direct indexing. We need to traverse the list to find an element. We can do this with the get method as follows:

```
public T get(int index) {
  if (index < 0 || index >= size) {
    throw new IndexOutOfBoundsException("Index: " + index);
  }
  Node<T> current;
  if (index < size / 2) { // Traverse from head
    current = head;
    for (int i = 0; i < index; i++) {
      current = current.next;
    }
  } else { // Traverse from tail
    current = tail;
    for (int i = size - 1; i > index; i--) {
      current = current.prev;
    }
  }
  return current.data;
}
```

In the above example:

- If the index is in the **first half**, traversal starts from the head.

- If it is in the **second half**, traversal starts from the tail, reducing the number of steps.

Let us add a display method to visualize how the elements are stored in the list:

```
public void display() {
  Node<T> current = head;
  while (current != null) {
   System.out.print(current.data + " => ");
   current = current.next;
  }
  System.out.println("null");
 }
```

Now, let us create a sample code to test this **CustomLinkedList**:

```
public class LinkedListDemo {
 public static void main(String[] args) {
  CustomLinkedList<Integer> list = new CustomLinkedList<>();
  list.add(10);
  list.add(20);
  list.add(30);
  list.add(40);
  list.display(); // Output: 10 => 20 => 30 => 40 => null
  list.remove(20);
  list.display(); // Output: 10 => 30 => 40 => null
  System.out.println("Element at index 1: " + list.get(1)); // Output: 30
 }
}
```

We add the elements and call the **display()** method. The output shows that they are added sequentially. We can also access any element using the index as shown above.

Vector implementation

Vectors in Java are part of the **java.util** package and provide a dynamic array-like structure like **ArrayList**. However, unlike **ArrayList**, **Vector** is synchronized, making it thread-safe but potentially slower due to synchronization overhead. In this section, we will explore the internal implementation, storage mechanism, and performance considerations of **Vector**.

The following is the internal structure of **Vector**:

- Vector is internally backed by an array, just like **ArrayList**.
- When elements are added beyond the initial capacity, the array grows automatically.
- Unlike **ArrayList**, which grows by 50% when full, **Vector** doubles its size when resizing.
- It implements the List interface and allows duplicate elements while maintaining insertion order.

Let us consider an example of how to create and use a **Vector**:

```java
import java.util.Vector;
public class VectorExample {
 public static void main(String[] args) {
  // Creating a Vector of integers
  Vector<Integer> numbers = new Vector<>();
  // Adding elements
  numbers.add(10);
  numbers.add(20);
  numbers.add(30);
  numbers.add(40);
  // Accessing elements
  System.out.println("First Element: " + numbers.firstElement());
  System.out.println("Last Element: " + numbers.lastElement());
  // Removing an element
  numbers.remove(2); // Removes 30
  // Displaying the Vector
  System.out.println("Updated Vector: " + numbers);
 }
}
```

The following is the output:

First element: 10
Last element: 40
Updated Vector: [10, 20, 40]

Like an **ArrayList**:

- When the **Vector** reaches its capacity, it increases its size by doubling.
- For example, if the initial capacity is 4, then when the 5th element is added, it increases its size to 8.

- This doubling behavior ensures fewer resizes but may lead to higher memory consumption.

The following are the performance considerations:

- `Vector` is synchronized, meaning multiple threads can safely modify it. However, this comes at the cost of performance.

- Since synchronization is applied on every method, operations like `add()`, `remove()`, and `get()` are slower compared to `ArrayList`.

- If synchronization is not required, `ArrayList` is preferred.

- Vector is suitable when multiple threads access and modify the collection concurrently.

When deciding between `ArrayList`, `LinkedList`, and `Vector`, it is important to understand the key differences in terms of performance, synchronization, and usage. The following table summarizes the main features and characteristics of each to help you make an informed choice based on your specific needs:

Feature	ArrayList	LinkedList	Vector
Underlying data structure	Dynamic array	Doubly LinkedList	Dynamic array
Access time (Random access)	Constant time (O(1))	Linear time (O(n))	Constant time (O(1))
Insertion or deletion time	Linear time (O(n)) for middle insertions	Constant time (O(1)) for insertions at ends	Linear time (O(n)) for insertions
Memory usage	Less memory overhead	More memory overhead due to pointers	Like ArrayList, but with more memory for resizing
Synchronization	Not synchronized	Not synchronized	Synchronized by default
Thread-safety	Not thread-safe	Not thread-safe	Thread-safe
Resizing	Automatically resizes when full	No resizing; elements are linked	Automatically resizes when full
Null elements	Supports null elements	Supports null elements	Supports null elements
Use case	Best for frequent access, less modification	Best for frequent insertions and deletions	Suitable for legacy systems needing thread-safety

Table 5.2: Comparison of ArrayList, LinkedList, and Vector

Synchronization in lists

In a multi-threaded environment, multiple threads may attempt to read from or write to a list at the same time. Without proper synchronization, this can lead to race conditions, data inconsistencies, or even runtime exceptions like **ConcurrentModificationException**. To maintain data integrity and ensure thread safety, it is essential to use synchronized list implementations or wrap existing lists with synchronization mechanisms.

Some classes, like **Vector**, are synchronized by default, meaning all their methods are thread-safe. However, they come with performance trade-offs in single-threaded or read-heavy environments. On the other hand, commonly used collections like **ArrayList** and **LinkedList** are not thread-safe and require explicit synchronization when accessed by multiple threads concurrently.

Collections.synchronizedList()

The **Collections.synchronizedList()** method provides a synchronized wrapper around a list. Let us see its usage with the help of an example:

```
import java.util.List;
import java.util.Collections;
import java.util.ArrayList;
public class SynchronizedListExample {
 public static void main(String[] args) {
// Create a thread-safe (synchronized) list using Collections.
synchronizedList()
   List<Integer> list = Collections.synchronizedList(new ArrayList<>());
   list.add(10);
   list.add(20);
   list.add(30);
/*
* Even though the list is synchronized for individual operations
* (like add, remove, get), we still need to explicitly synchronize
* when iterating over it to avoid ConcurrentModificationException
* if other threads modify it during iteration.
*/
   synchronized (list) {
    for (Integer num : list) {
     System.out.println(num);
    }
```

```
    }
   }
}
```

Output:

```
10
20
30
```

`Collections.synchronizedList()` ensures that all individual operations on the list are thread-safe. However, iteration is not automatically synchronized; we need to manually synchronize on the list object to make the iteration block thread-safe.

Note: **A synchronized block is only required when iterating over the list. Other methods like `add()`, `remove()`, or `get()` are already synchronized internally when using `Collections.synchronizedList()`. However, iteration must be done within a synchronized block to avoid `ConcurrentModificationException`.**

CopyOnWriteArrayList

Java provides **CopyOnWriteArrayList**, a thread-safe list where all write operations create a new copy of the list. Let us see its usage with an example:

```java
import java.util.concurrent.CopyOnWriteArrayList;
public class CopyOnWriteArrayListExample {
    public static void main(String[] args) {
        CopyOnWriteArrayList<String> list = new CopyOnWriteArrayList<>();
        list.add("Java");
        list.add("Python");
        list.add("C++");
        for (String language : list) {
            System.out.println(language);
        }
    }
}
```

The following is the output:

```
Java
Python
C++
```

Since **CopyOnWriteArrayList** does not allow modifications to affect ongoing iterations, it prevents **ConcurrentModificationException**, but consumes more memory.

Unlike a **synchronizedList()**, it does not require an explicit synchronization for iteration. It is suitable for read-heavy operations, but inefficient for frequent writes due to copying overhead.

Unmodifiable collections

In Java, sometimes we need to create read-only collections to ensure that the data remains unchanged after initialization. The collections class provides methods to create unmodifiable versions of Lists, Sets, and Maps.

This is particularly useful when exposing collections from APIs where we want to prevent accidental modifications by the caller.

For example, in a role-based access control system, an API might return a list of user roles that should not be altered by the client. Making the collection unmodifiable ensures data integrity and prevents unintended modifications. Additionally, unmodifiable collections help improve thread safety by eliminating synchronization issues related to modifications.

Let us understand this with an example:

```
List<String> names = new ArrayList<>();
names.add("Ryan");
names.add("Roger");


List<String> unmodifiableNames = Collections.unmodifiableList(names);
unmodifiableNames.add("Royce"); // Throws UnsupportedOperationException
```

In the above example:

- The **unmodifiableList()** method wraps the original list and prevents modifications.
- If an attempt is made to modify the list, an **UnsupportedOperationException** is thrown.

Note: **If the original list (names) is modified, those changes will be reflected in the unmodifiable list. To create a truly immutable list, Java 9+ provides the List.of() method, which prevents both modifications and updates to the underlying collection.**

The following is an example of **List.of()** usage:

```
List<String> immutableNames = List.of("Ryan", "Roger", "Royce");
// immutableNames.add("Zane"); // Throws UnsupportedOperationException
```

It creates an immutable list that cannot be modified after creation. Any attempt to add, remove, or change elements will result in an **UnsupportedOperationException**.

Checked collections

In Java, the checked collections class, part of the **java.util.Collections** utility class is used to ensure that elements in a collection adhere to a specified type at runtime. This is particularly useful when working with generic collections where type safety is important but cannot be enforced at compile time due to certain constraints, such as when collections are created dynamically or passed around without explicit type parameters.

The **Collections.checkedCollection()**, **checkedList()**, **checkedSet()**, and **checkedMap()** methods allow you to wrap a collection in a checked version, enforcing that all elements conform to the specified type. If an element of an incompatible type is added to the collection, a **ClassCastException** will be thrown. This helps catch type errors earlier during runtime rather than at a later stage, enhancing reliability and maintainability.

Let us understand this with an example:

```
List rawList = new ArrayList(); // raw type
List<String> checkedList = Collections.checkedList(rawList, String.class);
checkedList.add("Hello");  // Valid
rawList.add(10);                // Compiles, but will cause a runtime error
System.out.println(checkedList.get(1)); // Throws ClassCastException
```

Collections.checkedList() wraps the original raw list into a checked list that enforces type safety at runtime. Adding **Hello** is allowed, but when an integer (10) is added directly to the raw list, it bypasses compile-time checks. However, accessing it through **checkedList** causes a **ClassCastException**, because the wrapper ensures that only **String** objects are treated as valid elements at runtime.

Advantages of using checked collections

When working with collections in Java, ensuring type safety at runtime becomes critical, especially in dynamic environments. Checked collections offer several benefits:

- **Type safety**: Checked collections enforce that only elements of the specified type can be added, which helps prevent runtime errors that can be tricky to debug.

- **Legacy support**: They are invaluable when integrating older, non-generic collections with newer, generic-based collections, ensuring type safety without requiring a major refactor.

- **Enhanced reliability**: By applying runtime type checks, they provide a safeguard against introducing invalid data, especially when collections are used with external sources or dynamic inputs.

This makes checked collections a useful tool for improving code reliability and managing data consistency across various parts of an application.

Conclusion

In this chapter, we explored the List interface and its various implementations, including ArrayList, LinkedList, and Vector. We examined the internal structure and dynamic behavior of each implementation, along with its performance considerations. Additionally, we covered synchronization in lists, the synchronized collections class, and unmodifiable collections to help ensure data integrity and security in multi-threaded environments. We also explored checked collections for type safety in runtime operations.

By understanding these different implementations, their internal workings, and associated methods, you are better equipped to make informed decisions about which List implementation to use in various real-world scenarios. Each collection type has its strengths and weaknesses, and by considering factors like performance, thread-safety, and data immutability, you can optimize the performance of your Java applications.

In the next chapter, we will discuss Maps, exploring their unique properties, use cases, and implementations.

Exercise

1. **Which of the following correctly instantiates an ArrayList?**
   a.   List<int> list = new ArrayList<>();
   b.   List<String> list = new ArrayList<>();
   c.   ArrayList list = new List<>();
   d.   List list = new ArrayList<String>();

2. **What is the default initial capacity of an ArrayList in Java?**
   a.   5
   b.   10
   c.   16
   d.   20

3. **How does ArrayList dynamically increase its size when full?**
   a.   It creates a new array with double the size and copies elements into it.
   b.   It creates a new array 1.5 times the size and copies elements into it.
   c.   It extends the existing array in memory without copying elements.
   d.   It does not increase size dynamically; the user must manually create a new array.

4. **What is the time complexity of adding an element at the end of an ArrayList?**
    a. O(1) in most cases
    b. O(n)
    c. O(log n)
    d. O(n^2)

5. **Which data structure is internally used by LinkedList in Java?**
    a. Dynamic array
    b. Doubly linked list
    c. Singly linked list
    d. Hash table

6. **Which of the following is true about Vector in Java?**
    a. It is synchronized
    b. It dynamically grows by doubling its size
    c. It is preferred over ArrayList in multi-threaded applications
    d. All of the above

7. **Which method is used to obtain a synchronized version of an ArrayList?**
    a. Collections.synchronizedList()
    b. Collections.synchronizedArrayList()
    c. Arrays.synchronizedList()
    d. synchronized(new ArrayList<>())

8. **Which class should be used to create an unmodifiable list in Java?**
    a. Collections.unmodifiableList()
    b. List.unmodifiable()
    c. Arrays.unmodifiableList()
    d. Collections.synchronizedList()

9. **What is the purpose of checked collections in Java?**
    a. To prevent adding null values
    b. To ensure type safety at runtime
    c. To allow concurrent modifications
    d. To improve performance

10. **Which list implementation is most suitable when frequent insertions and deletions are required?**

   a. ArrayList

   b. Vector

   c. LinkedList

   d. UnmodifiableList

Answers

1. b

   Explanation: Java generics do not support primitive types, so List<int> is invalid. Correct usage requires specifying a valid generic type, such as String.

2. b

   Explanation: The default initial capacity of an ArrayList is 10 when created with the default constructor.

3. b

   Explanation: When an ArrayList reaches its capacity, it dynamically grows by 1.5 times its previous size (in most Java implementations, such as OpenJDK). A new array is created, elements are copied into it, and the reference is updated, allowing dynamic expansion.

4. a

   Explanation: Adding an element at the end of an ArrayList is usually O(1), except when resizing occurs, which makes it O(n) occasionally.

5. b

   Explanation: LinkedList in Java is implemented as a doubly linked list, where each node contains references to both the previous and next nodes.

6. d

   Explanation: Vector is synchronized, grows by doubling its size when full, and is used in multi-threaded environments where thread safety is required.

7. a

   Explanation: The Collections.synchronizedList() method returns a synchronized version of the given list.

8. a

   Explanation: The Collections.unmodifiableList() method returns an unmodifiable version of the given list, preventing modifications.

9. b

    Explanation: Checked collections help enforce type safety at runtime by wrapping collections with type validation.

10. c

    Explanation: LinkedList is preferred for frequent insertions and deletions as it uses a doubly linked list structure, making such operations efficient.

Join our Discord space

Join our Discord workspace for latest updates, offers, tech happenings around the world, new releases, and sessions with the authors:

https://discord.bpbonline.com

CHAPTER 6

Map Interface and Implementations

Introduction

In Java, a Map is a data structure that stores key-value pairs, where each key is unique and maps to a specific value. Unlike collections such as List or Set that focus on individual elements, Map emphasizes efficient association and retrieval based on keys. It is commonly used in applications like caching, configuration management, frequency counting, and database-like lookups.

Java provides several implementations of the Map interface, each with different internal structures and performance characteristics. These include HashMap, LinkedHashMap, TreeMap, and Hashtable, each suited for different use cases depending on ordering, synchronization, and sorting requirements.

In this chapter, we will explore the fundamental concepts of the Map interface, its primary implementations, and their internal mechanics. We will also look at performance considerations, common use cases, synchronization strategies, and the use of generic algorithms with Maps.

Structure

The chapter covers the following topics:

- Map interface

- HashMap implementation
- LinkedHashMap implementation
- TreeMap implementation
- Hashtable implementation
- Performance considerations
- Common use cases for Maps
- Synchronization in Maps
- Generic algorithms for Maps

Objectives

By the end of this chapter, you will understand how the Map interface works in Java, including its core purpose of storing key-value pairs with unique keys. You will explore the primary Map implementations like HashMap, LinkedHashMap, TreeMap, and Hashtable, and understand how they differ in terms of ordering, synchronization, and performance. You will also gain a deeper understanding of the internal data structures that power these implementations, such as hash tables, linked lists, and red-black trees. Additionally, you will learn when to choose each implementation based on specific use cases, how to handle thread safety with maps, and how to use generic algorithms to process map data effectively. This knowledge will enable you to write cleaner, more efficient, and maintainable Java code involving key-value associations.

Map interface

The Map interface in Java defines the contract for key-value pair mappings. It is part of `java.util` package and differs from other collection types like List or Set in that it is not a direct subtype of the Collection interface. The main purpose of a Map is to associate a unique key with a specific value. Each key is mapped to exactly one value, but the values themselves may be duplicated.

The following are the key characteristics of Maps:

- **Uniqueness of keys:** A Map does not allow duplicate keys, ensuring that each key is associated with only one value.

- **Null key/value handling:** Some Map implementations allow null keys and values, while others do not.

- **Basic operations:** The interface includes essential methods like `put()`, `get()`, `remove()`, and `containsKey()`, which help manage the data stored in the Map.

- **Iterators:** Maps offer iterators for keys, values, and entries, which makes it easy to traverse the data.

To better understand the functionality of the Map interface, here is a list of the commonly used methods, along with their descriptions. These methods provide essential operations for managing key-value mappings in a Map. Refer to the following table:

Method	Description
`put(K key, V value)`	Inserts a key-value pair into the map. If the key already exists, it updates the value associated with it
`get(Object key)`	Retrieves the value associated with the specified key, or returns null if the key does not exist in the map
`remove(Object key)`	Removes the key-value pair associated with the specified key. Returns the value if found, or null if the key does not exist
`containsKey(Object key)`	Returns true if the map contains a mapping for the specified key; otherwise, it returns false
`containsValue(Object value)`	Returns true if the map contains one or more keys mapped to the specified value; otherwise, it returns false
`keySet()`	Returns a Set view of the keys contained in the map
`values()`	Returns a Collection view of the values contained in the map
`entrySet()`	Returns a Set view of the key-value pairs (entries) contained in the map. Each entry is a **Map.Entry** object
`size()`	Returns the number of key-value pairs in the map
`isEmpty()`	Returns true if the map contains no key-value mappings; otherwise, it returns false
`clear()`	Removes all key-value mappings from the map
`putAll(Map<? extends K,? extends V> m)`	Copies all the mappings from the specified map to the current map
`equals(Object o)`	Compares the specified object with the map for equality, based on the key-value mappings
`hashCode()`	Returns the hash code value for the map, based on its key-value pairs
`forEach(BiConsumer<? super K,? super V> action)`	Performs the specified action for each key-value pair in the map

Table 6.1: Useful methods in the Map interface

Java provides several implementations of the Map interface, each optimized for specific use cases. The following figure is a visual overview of the primary classes that implement the Map interface:

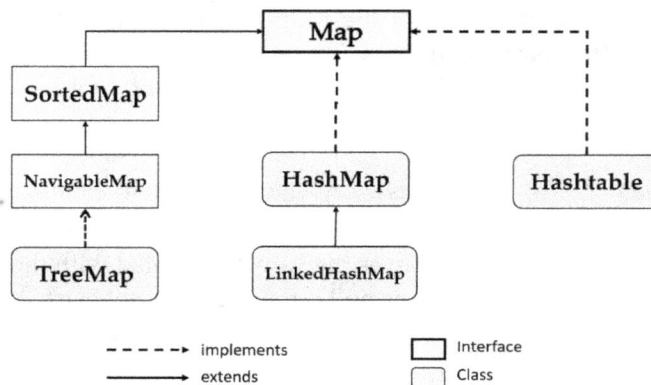

Figure 6.1: *Map interface and implementations*

HashMap implementation

HashMap is one of the most used implementations of the Map interface. It stores key-value pairs and offers constant-time performance for basic operations like **get()** and **put()** on average, making it an ideal choice for scenarios where fast access to data is crucial.

The following are the key characteristics:

- **Order**: HashMap does not guarantee any specific order of its elements. The order of keys and values can change over time, especially if entries are added or removed.

- **Null handling**: HashMap allows one null key and multiple null values, which is not allowed in all Map implementations.

- **Concurrency**: HashMap is not synchronized, meaning it is not thread-safe. If you need to use it in a concurrent environment, you might want to use **ConcurrentHashMap** or wrap it with **Collections.synchronizedMap()**.

Internal structure of HashMap

Internally, HashMap uses a hash table, where the keys are hashed, and the resulting hash code determines where the corresponding value is stored in the table. If two keys have the same hash code (a hash collision), HashMap uses a linked list (or a balanced tree in the case of many collisions) to store the values associated with those keys.

At its core, a HashMap stores key-value pairs in an array of buckets. Each bucket is essentially a linked list (or a balanced tree in certain scenarios) that holds entries with the same hash code.

Let us understand the key features of a HashMap:

- **Node<K,V> Class:** Internally, each key-value pair is represented by a static inner class called **Node<K,V>**, which implements the **Map.Entry<K,V>** interface. Here is a simplified version of its structure:

```
static class Node<K,V> implements Map.Entry<K,V> {
    final int hash;
    final K key;
    V value;
    Node<K,V> next;
    // Constructors and methods...
}
```

In this structure:

- o **hash**: The hash code of the key.
- o **key**: The key of the entry.
- o **value**: The value associated with the key.
- o **next**: A reference to the next node in the bucket (used in case of collisions).

- **Bucket array (table)**: The HashMap maintains an array called table, where each element is a reference to a **Node**. The default initial capacity of this array is 16, and it resizes dynamically as the number of entries increases.

This is represented in the following:

```
transient Node<K,V>[] table;
```

- **Hash function**: To determine the index of the bucket where a key-value pair should reside, HashMap uses a **hash** function. It computes the hash code of the key and then applies a supplemental **hash** function to reduce collisions. The following is the **hash** function that is used:

```
static final int hash(Object key) {
    int h;
    return (key == null) ? 0 : (h = key.hashCode()) ^ (h >>> 16);
}
```

This function takes the original hash code of the key and mixes its higher-order bits with the lower-order bits using an XOR operation. This helps in achieving a more uniform distribution of hash codes across the buckets, especially when the hash codes have patterns in the higher bits.

- **Index calculation**: Once the hash code is computed, the index for the bucket array is determined using the following formula:

```
index = (n - 1) & hash;
```

Here, n is the length of the bucket array (i.e., the capacity of the HashMap). The bitwise AND operation with **n - 1** ensures that the index falls within the bounds of the array. This method is efficient because it avoids the use of the modulo operator and works effectively when n is a power of two, which is always the case for HashMap capacities.

To understand this better, let us walk through the internal operations of some key methods in HashMap with an example.

Consider the following code:

```
Map<String, String> map = new HashMap<>();
map.put("Apple", "Fruit");
```

For the put method, Java internally calls:

```
int h = "Apple".hashCode();
```

Suppose this returns 63062875.

Then the supplemental hash is applied, $h = h \wedge (h >>> 16)$:

- **h**: *63062875 ^ (63062875 >>> 16)*

- **h**: *63062875 ^ 961* which gives a final *hash = 63061914*

HashMap's array length is always a power of 2. Initial capacity is 16. So the index is calculated as follows:

index: *(16 - 1) & 63061914 = 15 & 63061914*

This gives us an *index = 2*. So, the entry should be placed in bucket index 2.

Now, HashMap checks if there is already a node at index 2:

- If yes, it compares the keys using **equals()** to see if it is the same key. If the key is the same, it updates the old value with the new value.
- If not, it creates a new node and inserts it at that position.

In our example, it is empty, so it adds a new node as shown in the following:

```
Node<String, String> newNode = new Node<>(hash=63061914, key="Apple",
value="Fruit", next=null);
```

If we want to retrieve a value from the HashMap as shown in the following:

```
map.get("Apple");
```

The following is the sequence that is followed for the retrieval of values from the Map:

- Hash for *Apple* is computed, which gives us 63061914.
- The index is calculated, which gives us two, and then we go to bucket two to find the node.
- The keys are compared using the **equals()** method, and once the matching key is found, the value is returned. In this case, the value returned is *Fruit*.

In case of a collision, let us say **Orange** also hashes to index 2 (just hypothetically) in the following code:

```
map.put("Orange", "NotFruit");
```

It finds bucket two already has Apple and **Orange.equals(Apple)** is compared, which gives a false. This is a collision where two different keys lead to the same bucket. In this scenario, a new node is created and added to the bucket.

Now, the bucket with index 2 has two nodes, as shown in the following figure:

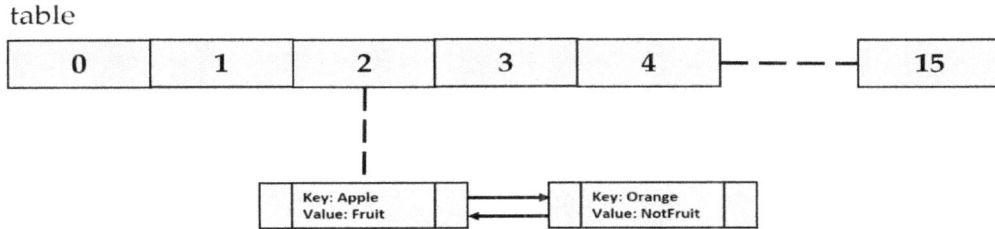

Figure 6.2: Hash collision in HashMap

If the bucket gets more than eight entries and the overall capacity is 64 or more, the list will be converted to a red-black tree for performance.

A HashMap resizes (doubles its capacity) when the number of entries exceeds the product of capacity and load factor (default 0.75), rehashing all existing entries.

Consider the following example:

```java
import java.util.HashMap;
public class HashMapResizeDemo {
    public static void main(String[] args) {
        HashMap<Integer, String> map = new HashMap<>(4, 0.75f);
 // small initial capacity to trigger resize
        for (int i = 1; i <= 10; i++) {
            map.put(i, "Value " + i);
            System.out.println("Added: " - i + " => map size: " + map.size());
        }
    }
}
```

The following is the output:

```
Added: 1 => map size: 1
Added: 2 => map size: 2
Added: 3 => map size: 3
```

```
Added: 4 => map size: 4
Added: 5 => map size: 5
Added: 6 => map size: 6
Added: 7 => map size: 7
Added: 8 => map size: 8
Added: 9 => map size: 9
Added: 10 => map size: 10
```

In the above example, the initial *capacity = 4*, *load factor = 0.75*. Resize will happen when *size > 4 * 0.75 = 3*. After inserting the 4th element, the HashMap will resize to a capacity of 8.

Another resize occurs when entries exceed *8 * 0.75 = 6* (at the 7th element), resulting in a new capacity of 16.

Note: **In a HashMap, the hashCode() and equals() methods play a critical role in ensuring that keys are stored and retrieved accurately and efficiently. If either method is not overridden correctly (especially in custom key classes), the HashMap may behave incorrectly, which could lead to failing to find keys, overwriting values, or duplicating entries.**

Constructors in HashMap

The HashMap class provides several constructors to create a map with different configurations:

- **HashMap()**: Creates an empty **HashMap** with an initial capacity of 16 and a load factor of 0.75. **HashMap** does not guarantee any specific iteration order of its elements.

- **HashMap(int initialCapacity)**: Creates an empty **HashMap** with the specified initial capacity and a load factor of 0.75. This constructor allows you to optimize memory usage by specifying the expected number of entries.

- **HashMap(int initialCapacity, float loadFactor)**: Creates an empty **HashMap** with the specified initial capacity and load factor. This gives more control over the resizing behavior of the map.

- **HashMap(Map<? extends K, ? extends V> m)**: Creates a new **HashMap** with the same mappings as the specified map **m**. This constructor copies the entries from another map and uses the default initial capacity and load factor.

LinkedHashMap implementation

A **LinkedHashMap** is a subclass of **HashMap** that maintains a doubly-linked list running through all its entries. This enables predictable iteration order, either by insertion order or access order, depending on the constructor used.

The following are the key characteristics of **LinkedHashMap**:

- Maintains a doubly-linked list of entries for predictable iteration order.
- Preserves insertion order by default.
- Can preserve access order if the **accessOrder** flag is set to true.
- Supports all operations of **HashMap** with a small performance overhead.
- Useful for caching and ordered iteration use cases.
- Slightly slower than **HashMap** due to linked list maintenance.
- Non-synchronized, like **HashMap**, must be synchronized externally for thread safety.

Internal structure of LinkedHashMap

Each entry in the map is represented by a specialized internal class, as shown in the following:

```
static class Entry<K,V> extends HashMap.Node<K,V> {
    Entry<K,V> before, after;
}
```

The map uses a standard hash table to store entries just like **HashMap**, enabling O(1) lookup time. Each bucket still contains a chain of nodes (via next pointer) for handling collisions.

In addition to this, each node also has two new pointers:

- **before**: Points to the previous entry in iteration order.
- **after**: Points to the next entry in iteration order.

A doubly-linked list connects all entries in insertion order (or access order, if configured). To understand the access order, consider the following example:

```
map.put("A", 1);
map.put("B", 2);
map.put("C", 3);
```

The Map looks like the following:

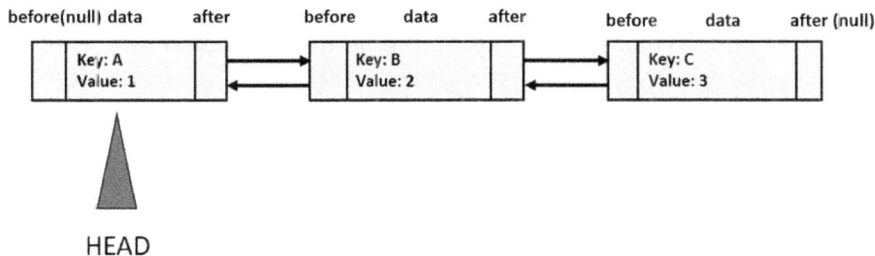

Figure 6.3: LinkedHashMap initial structure

If **accessOrder** is true and we do **map.get(B)**, **B** moves to the end, and now the **Map** would look like the following figure:

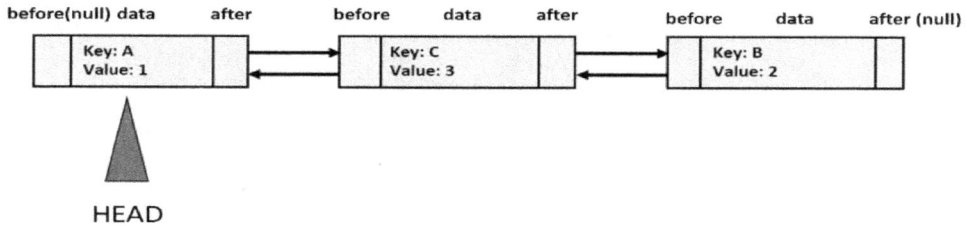

Figure 6.4: LinkedHashMap with accessOrder

Note: **The doubly linked list is independent of the hash table buckets. It is only used for iteration and not for searching or hashing. This adds slight overhead compared to HashMap, but gives you order preservation.**

Constructors in LinkedHashMap

The **LinkedHashMap** class provides several constructors to create a map with different configurations:

- **LinkedHashMap()**: Creates an empty **LinkedHashMap** with an initial capacity of 16 and a load factor of 0.75, maintaining the insertion order of entries.
- **LinkedHashMap(int initialCapacity)**: Creates an empty **LinkedHashMap** with the specified initial capacity and a load factor of 0.75, preserving insertion order.
- **LinkedHashMap(int initialCapacity, float loadFactor)**: Creates an empty **LinkedHashMap** with the specified initial capacity and load factor, maintaining insertion order.
- **LinkedHashMap(int initialCapacity, float loadFactor, boolean accessOrder)**: Creates an empty **LinkedHashMap** with the specified initial capacity, load factor, and iteration order.

If **accessOrder** is true, the map will be iterated in access order (most recently accessed entries will be moved to the end), which is useful for implementing **least recently used** (**LRU**) caches.

If **accessOrder** is false, the map will maintain insertion order.

TreeMap implementation

TreeMap is a **Map** implementation that stores its entries in a sorted order. It is based on a red-black tree, which is a self-balancing binary search tree. It ensures that the keys are always sorted according to their natural ordering or by a comparator provided at the time of creation.

The following are the key characteristics of **TreeMap**:

- **Sorted order**: **TreeMap** sorts the entries by key. By default, it uses the natural ordering of keys (if they implement comparable), or you can specify a custom comparator for sorting.

- **Null keys**: **TreeMap** does not allow null keys. However, it allows null values.

- **Performance**: The time complexity of the **get()**, **put()**, and **remove()** operations is O(log n) due to the underlying red-black tree structure.

- **Thread safety**: **TreeMap** is not synchronized. If thread-safety is required, external synchronization should be used, or consider using **Collections.synchronizedMap()**.

Internal structure of TreeMap

As mentioned earlier, **TreeMap** uses a red-black tree as its underlying data structure. This ensures that the map stays balanced and that operations like **get()**, **put()**, and **remove()** all have O(log n) time complexity. Here is a step-by-step breakdown of how it works:

1. **Red-black tree properties**:
   a. It is a type of self-balancing binary search tree.
   b. Each node in the tree has a color (either red or black) to maintain balance.
   c. The tree follows specific properties to ensure that it remains balanced, with key properties of red-black trees like:
      i. The root node is always black.
      ii. Red nodes cannot have red children.
      iii. Every path from a node to its descendant null nodes must have the same number of black nodes.

2. **Insertion**:
   a. When a key-value pair is inserted into the TreeMap, it is placed in the tree according to the natural ordering of the keys (or the comparator if provided).
   b. After insertion, the red-black tree might become unbalanced. If so, rotations and color flips are performed to restore balance.

3. **Searching**:
   a. When you search for a key in the TreeMap, the tree is traversed starting from the root. It checks the left or right child based on the key's comparison to the current node's key. This continues recursively, following the binary search tree logic.
   b. This is because the tree is balanced; the time complexity for searching is O(log n).

Here is a simple example demonstrating basic operations on a TreeMap in Java, including insertion, retrieval, update, deletion, and iteration:

```java
import java.util.TreeMap;
import java.util.Map;
public class TreeMapExample {
    public static void main(String[] args) {
        // Create a TreeMap
        TreeMap<Integer, String> studentMap = new TreeMap<>();
        // Add entries to the TreeMap
        studentMap.put(102, "Aaron");
        studentMap.put(101, "Bella");
        studentMap.put(103, "Chris");
        // TreeMap maintains ascending order of keys
        System.out.println("Initial TreeMap: " + studentMap);
        // Get a value by key
        System.out.println("Student with ID 101: " + studentMap.get(101));
        // Update a value
        studentMap.put(101, "Brian");
        System.out.println("After updating ID 101: " + studentMap);
        // Remove an entry
        studentMap.remove(102);
        System.out.println("After removing ID 102: " + studentMap);
        // Iterate over the TreeMap
        System.out.println("Iterating TreeMap:");
        for (Map.Entry<Integer, String> entry : studentMap.entrySet()) {
            System.out.println("ID: " + entry.getKey() + ", Name: " + entry.getValue());
        }
        // Other useful TreeMap operations
        System.out.println("First Entry: " + studentMap.firstEntry());
        System.out.println("Last Key: " + studentMap.lastKey());
        System.out.println("Ceiling Entry for 102: " + studentMap.ceilingEntry(102));
        System.out.println("Lower Key than 103: " + studentMap.lowerKey(103));
    }
}
```

The following is the output:

```
Initial TreeMap: {101=Bella, 102=Aaron, 103=Chris}
Student with ID 101: Bella
After updating ID 101: {101=Brian, 102=Aaron, 103=Chris}
After removing ID 102: {101=Brian, 103=Chris}
Iterating TreeMap:
ID: 101, Name: Brian
ID: 103, Name: Chris
First Entry: 101=Brian
Last Key: 103
Ceiling Entry for 102: 103=Chris
Lower Key than 103: 101
```

In the above example:

- **Insertion (put)**: Adds key-value pairs to the TreeMap. Keys must be unique and are automatically sorted.

  For example, **studentMap.put(102, "Aaron");** adds a student with ID 102 and name Aaron.

- **Retrieval (get)**: Fetches the value associated with a specific key.

  For example, **studentMap.get(101);** returns "**Bella**".

- **Update (put)**: If a key already exists, calling put again with the same key updates the value.

  For example, **studentMap.put(101, "Brian");** updates the name for ID 101.

- **Deletion (remove)**: Removes the entry associated with a specific key.

  For example, **studentMap.remove(102);** deletes the entry for ID 102.

- **Iteration (entrySet)**: Allows looping through all key-value pairs in sorted order.

  For example, a for-each loop prints all entries in increasing order of ID.

- **First and last Entry (firstEntry, lastKey)**: Retrieve the lowest and highest entries or keys. **firstEntry()** returns the entry with the smallest key. **lastKey()** returns the highest key.

- **Navigational methods**:
  - **ceilingEntry(102)**: Returns the entry with the least key greater than or equal to 102.
  - **lowerKey(103)**: Returns the greatest key strictly less than 103.

Constructors in TreeMap

The TreeMap class provides several constructors to create a map with different configurations:

- **TreeMap()**: Creates an empty **TreeMap** that sorts elements according to their natural ordering (i.e., using comparable).

- **TreeMap(Map<? extends K, ? extends V> m)**: Creates a new **TreeMap** containing the same mappings as the specified map m. The entries are sorted according to the natural ordering of the keys or a specified comparator.

- **TreeMap(Comparator<? super K> comparator)**: Creates an empty **TreeMap** that uses the specified comparator to order the keys. If the comparator is null, the map will use natural ordering.

- **TreeMap(SortedMap<K, ? extends V> m)**: Creates a new **TreeMap** containing the same mappings as the specified **SortedMap**. The entries are sorted according to the order of the **SortedMap**.

Common methods in TreeMap

The following table shows some common methods available in TreeMap:

Method	Description
firstKey()	Returns the first (lowest) key currently in the map
lastKey()	Returns the last (highest) key currently in the map
firstEntry()	Returns a key-value mapping associated with the lowest key
lastEntry()	Returns a key-value mapping associated with the highest key
ceilingKey(K key)	Returns the least key greater than or equal to the given key, or null if none
ceilingEntry(K key)	Returns the entry with the least key ≥ the given key
floorKey(K key)	Returns the greatest key less than or equal to the given key, or null if none
floorEntry(K key)	Returns the entry with the greatest key ≤ the given key
higherKey(K key)	Returns the least key strictly greater than the given key
higherEntry(K key)	Returns the entry with the least key > the given key
lowerKey(K key)	Returns the greatest key strictly less than the given key
lowerEntry(K key)	Returns the entry with the greatest key < the given key
pollFirstEntry()	Removes and returns the first entry (lowest key) from the map
pollLastEntry()	Removes and returns the last entry (highest key) from the map

Table 6.2: Additional methods in TreeMap

Hashtable implementation

Hashtable is a legacy class that implements the **Map** interface and was part of the original version of Java. It stores key-value pairs and ensures that keys are unique. Like **HashMap**, it uses hashing to store and retrieve elements efficiently.

However, unlike **HashMap**, **Hashtable** is synchronized, making it thread-safe for use in multithreaded environments, though this comes at the cost of performance.

The following are the key characteristics of a **Hashtable**:

- **Thread-safe**: All methods are synchronized.

- **No null keys or values**: A **Hashtable** does *not* allow null as a key or value.

- **Unordered**: It does not maintain insertion or sorted order.

- **Legacy class**: Considered outdated for most modern applications; **ConcurrentHashMap** or **Collections.synchronizedMap()** is preferred instead.

Internal working of Hashtable

Internally, **Hashtable** uses an array of buckets where each bucket is a linked list (or **Entry[]**) that stores key-value pairs. The hash code of the key determines the bucket index. When collisions occur (i.e., two keys hash to the same index), it resolves them using chaining.

This is represented as shown in the following:

```
public class Hashtable<K,V> extends Dictionary<K,V> implements Map<K,V>,
Cloneable, java.io.Serializable {
    private transient Entry<?,?>[] table;
    private int count;
    private int threshold;
    private float loadFactor;
    ...
}
```

Each **Entry** stores a key, a value, a hash code, and a pointer to the next **Entry** (for handling collisions).

Constructors in Hashtable

The **Hashtable** class provides several constructors to create a map with different initial settings:

- **Hashtable()**: Creates an empty **Hashtable** with a default initial capacity of 11 and a load factor of 0.75.

- **Hashtable(int initialCapacity)**: Constructs a `Hashtable` with the specified initial capacity and the default load factor (0.75).

- **Hashtable(int initialCapacity, float loadFactor)**: Creates a `Hashtable` with the given initial capacity and load factor.

- **Hashtable(Map<? extends K, ? extends V> t)**: Initializes the `Hashtable` with the mappings from the specified `Map`. The table's capacity will be enough to hold these mappings.

Consider a simple working example demonstrating how to use a `Hashtable` in Java:

```java
import java.util.Hashtable;
public class HashtableExample {
    public static void main(String[] args) {
        // Create a Hashtable with default capacity and load factor
        Hashtable<String, Integer> studentMarks = new Hashtable<>();
        // Adding key-value pairs
        studentMarks.put("Ray", 85);
        studentMarks.put("Sara", 92);
        studentMarks.put("Adam", 76);
        studentMarks.put("Grace", 88);
        // Retrieving a value
        System.out.println("Sara's marks: " + studentMarks.get("Sara"));
        // Iterating through Hashtable
        for (String name : studentMarks.keySet()) {
            System.out.println(name + " scored " + studentMarks.get(name));
        }
        // Removing a key
        studentMarks.remove("Adam");
        System.out.println("Updated Hashtable: " + studentMarks);
    }
}
```

The following is the output:

```
Sara's marks: 92
Grace scored 88
Adam scored 76
Ray scored 85
Sara scored 92
Updated Hashtable: {Grace=88, Ray=85, Sara=92}
```

Comparing Map implementations

As we explore different implementations of the `Map` interface, it is important to understand how they compare in terms of ordering, performance, thread safety, and internal structure. The following table summarizes the key differences between `HashMap`, `LinkedHashMap`, `TreeMap`, and `Hashtable`:

Feature	HashMap	LinkedHashMap	TreeMap	Hashtable
Ordering	No guaranteed order	Maintains insertion order	Sorted according to natural/comparator order	No guaranteed order
Null keys or values	Allows one null key and multiple null values	Allows one null key and multiple null values	Does not allow null keys, allows null values	Does not allow null keys or values
Thread safety	Not thread-safe	Not thread-safe	Not thread-safe	Thread-safe (synchronized methods)
Performance	Fastest (non-synchronized)	Slightly slower than HashMap due to order maintenance	Slower due to sorting	Slower due to synchronization
Internal data structure	An array of buckets with singly-linked lists or balanced trees (after threshold)	Same as HashMap and a doubly-linked list for order	Red-black tree (self-balancing BST)	An array of buckets (like an old HashMap)
Use case	General-purpose, non-threaded scenarios	When the order of insertion matters	When sorted keys are required	Legacy synchronized code
Introduced in	Java 1.2	Java 1.4	Java 1.2	Java 1.0
Null safety	Unsafe in a multithreaded environment	Unsafe in a multithreaded environment	Unsafe in a multithreaded environment	Safe for concurrent use
Fail-fast iterator	Yes	Yes	Yes	No (uses Enumerator, not Iterator)

Table 6.3: Comparison of HashMap, LinkedHashMap, TreeMap, and Hashtable

Performance considerations

Each implementation of the **Map** interface in Java offers different performance characteristics based on its underlying data structure:

- **HashMap** generally provides constant-time performance for basic operations like **get()**, **put()**, and **remove()**, assuming the hash function disperses elements properly. However, in the worst case, such as when many keys hash to the same bucket, these operations can degrade to linear time.

- **LinkedHashMap** maintains a doubly linked list to preserve insertion or access order, which adds a slight overhead compared to **HashMap**. However, its lookup and insertion times remain effectively constant under typical conditions.

- **TreeMap**, on the other hand, maintains a balanced binary search tree (specifically, a red-black tree), which guarantees O(log n) time for **get()**, **put()**, and **remove()** operations. This makes it slower than **HashMap** or **LinkedHashMap** for general use, but preferable when you need keys to be sorted.

- **Hashtable** is a legacy class that provides synchronized access, which introduces a performance hit in single-threaded contexts. Its basic operations are similar to those of **HashMap**, but the added synchronization overhead makes it less efficient in most modern applications.

The following table presents a concise comparison of the core operations and features of different **Map** implementations:

Feature	HashMap	LinkedHashMap	TreeMap	Hashtable
Time for get()/put()	O(1) average, O(n) worst	O(1) average (with insertion-order overhead)	O(log n)	O(1) average, O(n) worst
Time for remove()	O(1) average	O(1) average	O(log n)	O(1) average
Ordering	No ordering	Maintains insertion/ access order	Sorted by keys	No ordering
Thread safety	Not thread-safe	Not thread-safe	Not thread-safe	Thread-safe (via synchronization)
Memory usage	Low	Higher (due to linked list)	Moderate (tree nodes)	Higher (legacy synchronization)
Ideal use case	General-purpose map	When the order of entries matters	When sorted keys are needed	Legacy code needing thread safety

Table 6.4: Performance comparison between Map interface implementations

Generally, for unsorted, single-threaded use cases, **HashMap** is typically the best choice. When a predictable iteration order is required, **LinkedHashMap** is a better fit. If key ordering is important, **TreeMap** is the right tool. For thread-safe operations, prefer **ConcurrentHashMap** over **Hashtable**.

Common use cases for Maps

The Map interface is one of the most versatile data structures in Java, widely used in real-world applications. It provides an efficient way to associate keys with values, enabling quick lookups, updates, and deletions:

- A common use case is implementing caches, where keys are resource identifiers (like user IDs or URLs), and values are the associated data. For example, a **LinkedHashMap** with access-order enabled is ideal for building an LRU cache.

- Maps are also frequently used to maintain configurations and settings, where each key is a configuration name and the value is its setting. In data processing or analytics tasks, **Map** can serve as a frequency counter, mapping items to their number of occurrences.

- In applications involving routing or lookup services (like a dictionary or an address book), **Map** makes it easy to store and retrieve data based on a known key. Similarly, **TreeMap** is useful when keys need to be kept in sorted order, such as in scheduling applications or leaderboards.

Maps are foundational in frameworks as well, for example, storing HTTP headers, session attributes, or even binding form data in web applications. Whether maintaining object references, performing grouping operations, or representing relationships, Map remains an essential tool in a Java developer's toolkit.

Synchronization in Maps

By default, most commonly used Map implementations in Java, such as **HashMap**, **LinkedHashMap**, and **TreeMap**, are not thread-safe. This means that if multiple threads access a map concurrently and at least one thread modifies it, the map must be externally synchronized to prevent unpredictable behaviour.

For single-threaded environments or read-only access, no synchronization is required. However, in multi-threaded scenarios, Java provides several strategies to make map access safe:

- **Collections.synchronizedMap():** This utility method wraps any map with synchronized access. However, this locks the entire map for each operation, which may degrade performance in highly concurrent environments. This can be created as shown in the following:

```
Map<String, String> syncMap = Collections.synchronizedMap(new
HashMap<>());
```

- **ConcurrentHashMap**: For better concurrency, the **java.util.concurrent** package offers **ConcurrentHashMap**, which divides the map into segments to allow multiple threads to read and write without locking the entire map. This can be created as shown in the following:

```
Map<String, Integer> concurrentMap = new ConcurrentHashMap<>();
```

- **Immutable Maps:** If the map is only read after construction, you can use unmodifiable wrappers or factory methods from **Map.of()** to prevent changes. This is available from Java version 9 and above and can be used as shown in the following:

```
Map<String, String> readOnlyMap = Map.of("key", "value");
```

- **Synchronized Map – Hashtable**: Historically, **Hashtable** provided built-in synchronization. However, it synchronizes every method, making it less efficient and generally avoided in modern applications in favor of **ConcurrentHashMap**.

Choosing the right synchronization strategy depends on your specific use case, whether you prioritize safety, performance, or simplicity.

Generic algorithms for Maps

While the JCF provides direct support for many algorithms via utility classes like Collections and Arrays, Maps are not Collection types, so they are not directly compatible with all generic algorithms used for List, Set, etc. However, we can still apply a wide range of algorithmic operations to Map instances using their **keySet**, **values**, and **entrySet** views.

Here are some commonly used techniques and patterns:

- **Iterating over entries:** Use the **entrySet()** method to iterate over key-value pairs efficiently.

  The following is an example of using **entrySet()** for iteration:

```
for (Map.Entry<String, Integer> entry : map.entrySet()) {
    System.out.println(entry.getKey() + " -> " + entry.getValue());
}
```

- **Filtering values or keys:** Streams can be used to filter based on conditions, as shown in the following:

```
map.entrySet().stream()
    .filter(e -> e.getValue() > 10)
    .forEach(e -> System.out.println(e.getKey()));
```

- **Sorting a Map:** While **HashMap** does not maintain order, you can sort entries by keys or values using streams, as shown in the following:

```
map.entrySet().stream()
    .sorted(Map.Entry.comparingByValue())
    .forEach(System.out::println);
```

- **Transforming keys or values:** You can build new maps by applying transformations, as shown in the following:

```
Map<String, Integer> updated = map.entrySet().stream()
    .collect(Collectors.toMap(
        e -> e.getKey().toUpperCase(),
        e -> e.getValue() * 2
    ));
```

- **Grouping and counting:** Maps are integral in building groupings using **Collectors. groupingBy.** as shown in the following:

```
Map<String, Long> frequency = list.stream()
    .collect(Collectors.groupingBy(Function.identity(), Collectors.
counting()));
```

These algorithmic patterns let you handle complex data processing with ease. Though maps do not support direct algorithm calls like **Collections.sort()**, the flexibility of their views and Java streams enables robust, efficient operations on map data.

Conclusion

In this chapter, we explored the core Map interface and its primary implementations—HashMap, LinkedHashMap, TreeMap, and Hashtable. We discussed their internal workings, constructors, performance characteristics, and synchronization strategies. Additionally, we compared their strengths and limitations, outlined common use cases, and demonstrated how generic algorithms can be effectively applied to maps.

Understanding the nuances of each map implementation equips you to make the right choice based on performance requirements, ordering needs, and thread safety considerations, ultimately helping you write clean, scalable, and performant Java code.

In the next chapter, we will shift our focus to the Set interface, where we will examine how Java ensures uniqueness in collections through implementations like HashSet, LinkedHashSet, and TreeSet.

Exercise

1. **Which of these Map implementations is synchronized and does not allow null keys or values?**

    a. HashMap

    b. TreeMap

    c. Hashtable

    d. LinkedHashMap

2. **Which Map implementation maintains the insertion order of keys?**

    a. HashMap

    b. LinkedHashMap

    c. TreeMap

    d. Hashtable

3. **Which Map implementation keeps keys in a sorted order using their natural ordering or a comparator?**

    a. HashMap

    b. TreeMap

    c. Hashtable

    d. LinkedHashMap

4. **What is the average time complexity for put() and get() operations in a HashMap?**

    a. O(n)

    b. O(log n)

    c. O(1)

    d. O(n log n)

5. **What causes a HashMap to resize?**

    a. Reaching the maximum array size

    b. The number of keys exceeds the capacity

    c. Load factor threshold is breached

    d. EntrySet is empty

6. **Which of the following allows one null key and multiple null values?**

    a. Hashtable

    b. TreeMap

    c. HashMap

    d. None of the above

7. **Which Map implementation is best suited for concurrent access by multiple threads without external synchronization?**

    a. HashMap

    b. Hashtable

    c. TreeMap

    d. ConcurrentHashMap

8. **What happens when two keys in a HashMap return the same hash code?**

    a. Only one key is stored

    b. An exception is thrown

    c. A collision occurs, and both are stored using chaining

    d. The second key replaces the first one

9. **Which constructor is used to create a TreeMap with custom key sorting logic?**

    a. TreeMap(Collection c)

    b. TreeMap(SortedMap s)

    c. TreeMap()

    d. TreeMap(Comparator comparator)

10. **Which method should you override in a key class used in HashMap to ensure proper functioning?**

    a. compareTo()

    b. toString()

    c. equals() and hashCode()

    d. finalize()

Answers

1. c

    Explanation: A Hashtable is synchronized and does not permit null keys or values. All other implementations allow at least one null key or multiple null values.

2. b

    Explanation: LinkedHashMap maintains a doubly linked list to preserve the insertion order of entries.

3. b

    Explanation: TreeMap stores keys in a red-black tree structure and sorts them using natural ordering or a specified Comparator.

4. c

    Explanation: In the average case, HashMap provides constant time complexity for put() and get(), assuming a good hash function.

5. c

   Explanation: When the number of key-value pairs exceeds capacity * load factor, the map resizes to maintain performance.

6. c

   Explanation: HashMap allows one null key and any number of null values. TreeMap allows null values but not null keys (in natural ordering). Hashtable does not allow nulls at all.

7. d

   Explanation: ConcurrentHashMap is designed for thread-safe operations without locking the entire map, unlike Hashtable.

8. c

   Explanation: HashMap handles collisions by storing entries in a linked list or tree at the same bucket index.

9. d

   Explanation: This constructor allows you to define a custom Comparator for sorting the keys.

10. c

    Explanation: hashCode() is used to find the correct bucket, and equals() is used to check key equality within that bucket.

Join our Discord space

Join our Discord workspace for latest updates, offers, tech happenings around the world, new releases, and sessions with the authors:

https://discord.bpbonline.com

CHAPTER 7

Set Interface and Implementations

Introduction

In Java, a Set is a collection that contains no duplicate elements. Unlike List, which maintains the insertion order and allows duplicates, Set focuses on uniqueness and efficient lookups. Sets are commonly used when we want to store a group of distinct items, such as user IDs, unique tokens, or configuration keys. Java provides multiple implementations of the Set interface, each with different internal behaviors and performance characteristics.

In this chapter, we will explore the core concepts of the Set interface, its key implementations: HashSet, LinkedHashSet, and TreeSet, along with practical use cases, internal implementation details, custom implementation examples, and comparisons. We will also cover performance considerations, synchronization strategies, and the usage of generic algorithms specifically for Sets.

Structure

The chapter covers the following topics:

- Set interface
- HashSet implementation
- LinkedHashSet implementation

- TreeSet implementation
- Performance considerations
- Synchronization in Sets
- Generic algorithms for Sets

Objectives

By the end of this chapter, you will understand how the Set interface works in Java, including its primary implementations and how they differ from one another. You will gain insights into the internal data structures used by various Set types and when to use each based on your requirements. Additionally, you will learn how to create your own Set implementation, understand the nuances of thread safety, and explore how Java provides utilities to manipulate and process Sets effectively. This foundational knowledge will help you write more robust and efficient Java programs.

Set interface

The Set interface in Java is a part of the **java.util** package and extends the collection interface. It defines a collection that does not allow duplicate elements. If you try to add a duplicate, the set simply ignores it and retains only one instance.

Since Set is an interface, it cannot be instantiated directly. Instead, we use one of its concrete implementations, like HashSet, LinkedHashSet, or TreeSet.

The following are the key characteristics of Sets:

- **No duplicates:** Each element must be unique.

- **No guaranteed order:** In most implementations, like HashSet, the order of elements is not preserved.

- **Null element:** Most Set implementations allow a single null element.

The Set interface extends the collection interface and introduces several additional methods, as listed in the following table:

Method	Description
`add(E e)`	Adds an element if not already present
`addAll(Collection<? extends E> c)`	Adds all elements from another collection
`remove(Object o)`	Removes the specified element if it exists
`contains(Object o)`	Returns true if the element is present

`size()`	Returns the number of elements in the set
`isEmpty()`	Returns true if the set is empty
`clear()`	Removes all elements from the set
`iterator()`	Returns an iterator over the elements in the set

Table 7.1: *Additional methods in the Set interface*

The following figure is a visual overview of the primary classes that implement the Set interface:

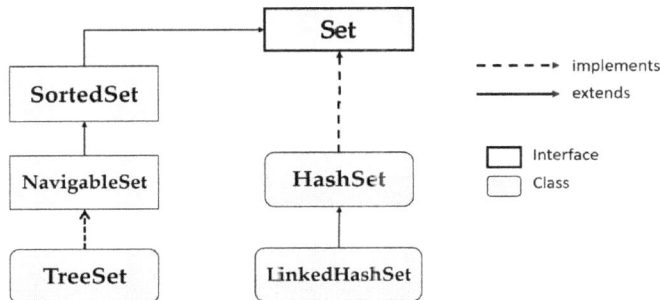

Figure 7.1: *Set interface and implementations*

HashSet implementation

HashSet is one of the most commonly used implementations of the Set interface. It is backed by a HashMap, meaning all operations like add, remove, and contains are internally delegated to the map structure.

The following are the key characteristics:

- Does not allow duplicate elements.
- Permits one null element.
- No guaranteed order of elements.
- Not synchronized.
- Allows constant-time performance for basic operations (add, remove, contains), assuming a good hash function.

Internal structure of HashSet

Internally, a HashSet is just a wrapper around a HashMap. When you add an element to the HashSet, it is stored as a key in the internal map, and a constant dummy value (like PRESENT) is used for all values.

Let us understand this with an example:

```
Set<String> set = new HashSet<>();
set.add("Apple");
set.add("Banana");
set.add("Apple"); // Duplicate, will be ignored
System.out.println(set); // Output might be [Apple, Banana] order can vary.
```

Internally, this is stored as the following:

```
Map<String, Object> map = new HashMap<>();
static final Object PRESENT = new Object();
map.put("Apple", PRESENT);
map.put("Banana", PRESENT);
map.put("Apple", PRESENT); // Overwrites the same key, no new entry added
```

When adding an element like "**Apple**", the HashMap computes a hash value using "**Apple**". **hashCode()** determines the appropriate bucket index and places the key-value pair accordingly. This mechanism is based on the hashing principles discussed in *Chapter 6, Map Interface and Implementations*. In case of duplicate elements, when you add an element to a HashSet, the hash value is calculated using the element's **hashCode()** method. This hash is used to find the bucket (index in the internal array). If that bucket already has an entry with the same hash, it checks equality using the **equals()** method. If both hash and **equals()** match, the new element is considered a duplicate and is not added.

Constructors in HashSet

Java provides several constructors in the HashSet class to offer flexibility in initialization, depending on the use case and performance needs:

- **HashSet():** Creates a new, empty HashSet with the default initial capacity (16) and load factor (0.75).

- **HashSet(int initialCapacity):** Creates a HashSet with the specified initial capacity. Useful when you know the number of elements in advance to reduce rehashing.

- **HashSet(int initialCapacity, float loadFactor):** Allows setting both the initial capacity and the load factor to fine-tune performance.

- **HashSet(Collection<? extends E> c):** Constructs a HashSet containing all elements from the given collection. Duplicate elements are automatically removed.

LinkedHashSet implementation

LinkedHashSet is a subclass of HashSet that maintains the insertion order of elements. Internally, it uses a doubly linked list along with a hash table. This combination ensures that the elements are stored in the order in which they were added, while still providing fast access.

Let us look at a simple example:

```
Set<String> names = new LinkedHashSet<>();
  names.add("Alex");
  names.add("Brian");
  names.add("Clara");
  System.out.println(names);    // Output: [Alex, Brian, Clara]
```

Even though it is a set and does not allow duplicates, it retains the order in which elements were inserted.

Internal structure of LinkedHashSet

LinkedHashSet maintains a linked list of entries in the order they were inserted. Internally, it is built on top of a LinkedHashMap, which combines:

- A hash table (for constant-time performance on basic operations like add, remove, and contains).
- A doubly linked list (to maintain insertion order).

Each element added to a LinkedHashSet is stored as a key in the internal LinkedHashMap. The value associated with each key is a constant dummy object (usually PRESENT).

When an element is added, the hash of the element is computed. If it is not already present, the hash is added to the hash table. A node is created that also links to the previous and next nodes in the insertion order.

Let us say you add elements in this order:

```
Set<String> items = new LinkedHashSet<>();
items.add("A");
items.add("B");
items.add("C");
```

Internally, the entries are linked in the order they were inserted using a doubly linked list. The structure maintains references to the first (head) entry, as shown in the following figure:

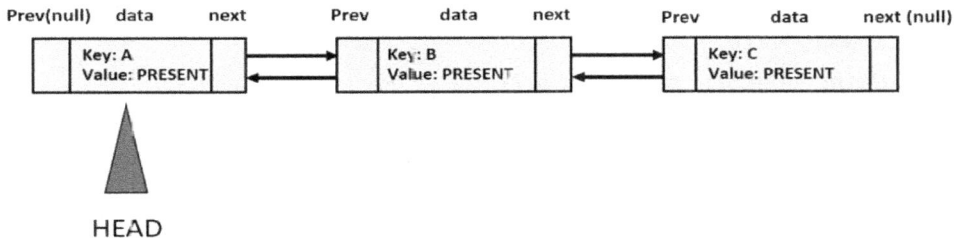

Figure 7.2: *LinkedHashSet internal structure*

Each entry points to the next and previous in insertion order. A LinkedHashSet has the benefits of fast lookup (like HashSet) and the predictability of ordered iteration (like a List).

Constructors in LinkedHashSet

The LinkedHashSet class provides several constructors that allow developers to create instances with different initial settings:

- **LinkedHashSet():** Creates an empty LinkedHashSet with the default initial capacity (16) and load factor (0.75).

- **LinkedHashSet(int initialCapacity):** Creates an empty LinkedHashSet with the specified initial capacity and the default load factor (0.75).

- **LinkedHashSet(int initialCapacity, float loadFactor):** Creates an empty LinkedHashSet with the specified initial capacity and load factor. This is useful if you want to optimize memory usage or performance for specific data sizes.

- **LinkedHashSet(Collection<? extends E> c):** Creates a LinkedHashSet containing the elements of the specified collection. The insertion order is preserved based on the collection passed.

Here is a simple example demonstrating different LinkedHashSet constructors:

```java
import java.util.*;
public class LinkedHashSetConstructorExamples {
    public static void main(String[] args) {
        // Using default constructor
        LinkedHashSet<String> set1 = new LinkedHashSet<>();
        set1.add("Apple");
        set1.add("Banana");
        // Using initial capacity constructor
        LinkedHashSet<String> set2 = new LinkedHashSet<>(20);
        set2.add("Cherry");
        // Using initial capacity and load factor
        LinkedHashSet<String> set3 = new LinkedHashSet<>(10, 0.5f);
        set3.add("Date");
        // Using constructor with a collection
        List<String> list = Arrays.asList("Sugarcane", "Fig", "Grape");
        LinkedHashSet<String> set4 = new LinkedHashSet<>(list);
        System.out.println("Set1: " + set1);
        System.out.println("Set2: " + set2);
        System.out.println("Set3: " + set3);
```

```
        System.out.println("Set4: " + set4);
    }
}
```

The output are:

Set1: [Apple, Banana]

Set2: [Cherry]

Set3: [Date]

Set4: [Sugarcane, Fig, Grape]

This example shows how all four constructors can be used, and as we can see, the insertion order is preserved.

TreeSet implementation

Unlike HashSet and LinkedHashSet, which use hashing for storing elements, TreeSet is a NavigableSet implementation based on a self-balancing binary search tree, like a red-black tree. This allows it to maintain elements in sorted (natural or custom-defined) order.

The following are the key characteristics:

- **Sorted order**: Elements are automatically sorted according to their natural ordering or by a comparator provided at the time of creation.
- **No duplicates**: Like all sets, TreeSet does not allow duplicate elements. If any duplicate elements are added, they will be ignored.
- **Performance**: `add()`, `remove()`, and `contains()` operations take O(log n) time due to tree balancing.
- **Null handling**: TreeSet does not allow null elements if using natural ordering (Comparable); doing so will result in a `NullPointerException`.
- **Not thread safe:** For concurrent access, it should be synchronized externally using `Collections.synchronizedSet()`.

Internal structure of TreeSet

TreeSet is an implementation of the Set interface that stores elements in sorted order. Internally, it is backed by a TreeMap, which means all the elements in the TreeSet are stored as keys in a TreeMap. The values in this map are just dummy objects.

To better understand how TreeSet works, consider a simple example as follows:

```
TreeSet<Integer> numbers = new TreeSet<>();

numbers.add(20);

numbers.add(10);

numbers.add(30);
```

When we create a **TreeSet<Integer>**, it internally creates a **TreeMap<Integer, Object>** as seen in the following:

```
private transient TreeMap<E,Object> map;

private static final Object PRESENT = new Object();
```

So, the TreeSet does not store the elements directly. Instead, it uses the keys of the TreeMap to store the elements, while assigning a dummy value (**PRESENT**) for all keys.

When we call **numbers.add(20);**, it internally calls **map.put(20, PRESENT)**. Since the map is empty, 20 is added as the root node of the underlying Red-Black tree. When we call **numbers. add(10);**, it compares ten with the root (20). Since 10 < 20, it is placed as the left child of 20. The tree may rebalance, but in this small example, rebalancing might not be needed. Finally, when **numbers.add(30);** is called, it compares 30 with 20. Since 30 > 20, it is placed as the right child of 20.

The underlying red-black tree now contains three nodes, as shown in the following figure:

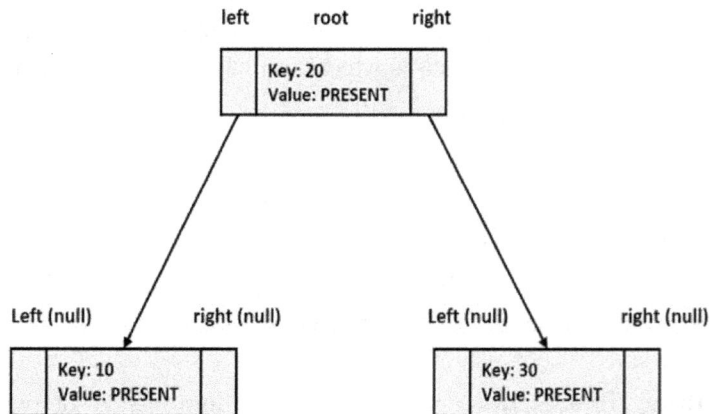

Figure 7.3 TreeSet internal representation

These elements are automatically sorted and balanced by the tree structure.

Eligibility requirements for elements in TreeSet

Before an element can be added to a TreeSet, it must satisfy certain criteria to ensure that the set maintains its sorted order and avoids inconsistencies, as mentioned in the following:

- **Must be comparable or provide a Comparator**: TreeSet sorts elements using natural ordering (Comparable) or a custom Comparator.

  The elements must either implement **Comparable<T>** or be inserted with a **Comparator<T>** passed to the constructor.

  If neither is provided, adding an element will result in:

```
java.lang.ClassCastException: class X cannot be cast to class java.lang.
Comparable
```

- **Must be mutually comparable**: All elements in the same TreeSet must be comparable with each other.

```
TreeSet<Object> set = new TreeSet<>();
set.add("abc");    // OK
set.add(100);      // Throws ClassCastException at runtime
```

- **Must not be null**: A TreeSet using natural ordering cannot contain null, as null is not comparable to non-null elements. Attempting to add null will throw a **NullPointerException**.

Constructors in TreeSet

The TreeSet class provides several constructors to create a sorted set in different ways:

- **TreeSet()**: Creates an empty TreeSet that sorts elements according to their natural ordering (i.e., using Comparable).

- **TreeSet(Collection<? extends E> c)**: Constructs a TreeSet containing the elements of the given collection, sorted by natural ordering.

- **TreeSet(Comparator<? super E> comparator)**: Creates an empty TreeSet that uses the specified Comparator for ordering.

- **TreeSet(SortedSet<E> s)**: Builds a TreeSet containing the same elements and order as the specified SortedSet.

Common methods in TreeSet

The following table shows some common methods available in TreeSet:

Method	Description
`first()`	Returns the lowest element (according to the set's sorting order).
`last()`	Returns the highest element.
`ceiling(E e)`	Returns the smallest element ≥ e, or null if no such element exists.
`floor(E e)`	Returns the largest element ≤ e, or null if no such element exists.
`higher(E e)`	Returns the least element > e, or null if no such element exists.

`lower(E e)`	Returns the greatest element < e, or null if no such element exists.
`pollFirst()`	Retrieves and removes the first (lowest) element.
`pollLast()`	Retrieves and removes the last (highest) element.
`descendingSet()`	Returns a reverse-order view of the elements.
`descendingIterator()`	Returns an iterator in reverse order.
`subSet(E from, E to)`	Returns a view of elements from from (inclusive) to to (exclusive).
`headSet(E to)`	Returns a view of elements less than to.
`tailSet(E from)`	Returns a view of elements greater than or equal to from.

Table 7.2: Additional methods in TreeSet

Comparison of HashSet, LinkedHashSet and TreeSet

Now that we have explored the major Set implementations individually, HashSet, LinkedHashSet, and TreeSet, let us compare them side by side. This comparison will highlight key differences such as ordering, performance, and internal structure, offering a clearer picture of when to use each implementation. Refer to the following table:

Feature	HashSet	LinkedHashSet	TreeSet
Ordering	No guaranteed order	Maintains insertion order	Maintains natural or specified order
Underlying data structure	Hash table	Hash table + linked list	Red-Black Tree (self-balancing BST)
Null elements	Allows one null	Allows one null	Does not allow null (throws NullPointerException for comparator-based sets)
Performance (Basic ops)	O(1) average time	O(1) average time	O(log n) time for add, remove, and contains
Sorted elements	No	No	Yes
Insertion order preserved	No	Yes	No (Sorted order instead)
Thread safety	Not thread-safe	Not thread-safe	Not thread-safe
Use case	When order does not matter	When the order of insertion matters	When sorted data is needed

Table 7.3: Comparison of HashSet, LinkedHashSet and TreeSet

Java 8 enhancements for the Set interface

Java 8 brought several important updates to the Set interface and its implementations, both in terms of API usability and performance improvements. The following are the enhancements made:

- **Default methods in the Set interface:** With Java 8, interfaces can have default and static methods.

  Set (and Collection, which it extends) now includes the following default methods:

  o **forEach(Consumer<? super E> action)**: This method can be used to iterate over elements using a lambda expression or method reference.

  ```
  Set<String> names = new HashSet<>();

  names.add("Alice");

  names.add("Bob");

  names.forEach(System.out::println);
  ```

  o **removeIf(Predicate<? super E> filter)**: Removes all elements that satisfy a given condition. For example: `names.removeIf(name -> name.startsWith("A"));`

  o **Stream API methods via Collection.stream() and Collection.parallelStream()**: These enable functional-style operations as shown below.

  ```
  names.stream()

      .filter(name -> name.length() > 3)

      .forEach(System.out::println);
  ```

- **Improved collision handling in HashSet**: HashSet in Java is backed by a HashMap, which stores elements in buckets based on their hash code. Sometimes, two or more elements may produce the same bucket index; this is called a hash collision.

  o **Before Java 8**: All elements in the same bucket were linked together in a singly linked list. In the worst case (when all elements land in the same bucket), lookups, insertions, and deletions degrade from O(1) average time to O(n).

  o **Java 8 improvement:** If a single bucket becomes too crowded (more than 8 elements), the linked list for that bucket is replaced with a balanced Red-Black tree. This process is called **treeification**. With treeification, worst-case lookup time improves from O(n) to O(log n), making performance more predictable even with many collisions.

- **Improved rehashing:** Java 8 optimized the rehashing process when resizing hash-based collections like HashSet.

  Instead of recomputing hash codes from scratch, it uses bitwise operations to redistribute elements more efficiently, improving performance during resize operations.

Performance considerations

Understanding the performance characteristics of different Set implementations is essential for choosing the right one based on an application's requirements. They are as follows:

- **HashSet**: Offers constant-time performance (O(1)) for basic operations like **add()**, **remove()**, and **contains()**, assuming the hash function disperses elements properly. Performance can degrade to O(n) in worst-case scenarios if hash collisions are high.

- **LinkedHashSet**: Has similar time complexity to HashSet but maintains insertion order, which slightly increases memory usage. Ideal when you need predictable iteration order with good performance.

- **TreeSet**: Backed by a TreeMap, it provides O(log n) time complexity for most operations (**add()**, **remove()**, **contains()**) because it uses a red-black tree. This makes it slower than HashSet, but it is suitable when an ordered arrangement is required.

- **Iteration**: Iterating over a HashSet or LinkedHashSet is generally faster than over a TreeSet due to the latter's need to maintain order.

- **Memory usage:** TreeSet consumes more memory than HashSet and LinkedHashSet because of the tree structure and additional pointers.

Synchronization in Sets

By default, implementations of the Set interface, like HashSet, LinkedHashSet, and TreeSet, are not thread-safe. This means if multiple threads access a set concurrently and at least one thread modifies it, you must synchronize it manually to avoid unpredictable behaviour.

To make a set synchronized, Java provides the utility method **synchronizedSet** in the Collections class, as shown in the following:

```
Set<String> set = Collections.synchronizedSet(new HashSet<>());
```

This wraps the original set with a thread-safe version. While operations like **add()** or **remove()** are synchronized, iteration over the set still requires a manual synchronized block, as shown in the following:

```
Set<String> set = Collections.synchronizedSet(new HashSet<>());
synchronized (set) {
    for (String item : set) {
        // safe iteration
    }
}
```

This is because the iterator itself is not synchronized. If not wrapped in a synchronized block, concurrent modifications can lead to a **ConcurrentModificationException**.

In modern concurrent environments (with multi-core processors), it is often necessary to choose set implementations that provide thread safety and scalability. Java offers specialized concurrent set implementations such as:

- **ConcurrentSkipListSet (a concurrent and sorted set):** A scalable, thread-safe alternative to TreeSet, internally based on a skip list.

- **CopyOnWriteArraySet:** Best suited for sets with frequent reads and infrequent writes. It creates a new copy of the underlying array on every modification.

Generic algorithms for Sets

Java provides a rich set of generic algorithms through the Collections utility class that can operate on any type of Set, making code more reusable and concise. These algorithms do not require any changes to the Set interface but offer powerful operations that can be applied directly to sets:

- **Collections.unmodifiableSet(Set<? extends T> s):** Creates a read-only view of the given set. Any attempt to modify the returned set results in an exception, as shown in the following:

```
Set<String> original = new HashSet<>();
original.add("apple");
Set<String> unmodifiable = Collections.unmodifiableSet(original);
unmodifiable.add("banana"); // Throws UnsupportedOperationException
```

This is useful when you want to share a set with other code without allowing modifications, such as exposing internal data from a class.

- **Collections.synchronizedSet(Set<T> s):** This wraps the given set with synchronization, making it safe to use across multiple threads as shown in the following:

```
Set<Integer> set = Collections.synchronizedSet(new HashSet<>());
set.add(1);
set.add(2);
```

Use this when you are accessing a set from multiple threads to avoid concurrency issues.

  Note: **You should still synchronize manually during iteration.**

- **Set operations using streams:** The Collectors class provides a **toSet()** method to collect the end result of a stream operation as a Set.

For example, common elements from two sets can be collected in a set, as shown in the following figure:

```
Set<Integer> set1 = new HashSet<>(List.of(1, 2, 3));
Set<Integer> set2 = new HashSet<>(List.of(2, 3, 4));
Set<Integer> intersection = set1.stream()
                                .filter(set2::contains)
                                .collect(Collectors.toSet());
```

This is useful for functional-style set operations without manual loops or conditionals.

Conclusion

In this chapter, we explored the core implementations of the Set interface: HashSet, LinkedHashSet, and TreeSet. Each implementation offers distinct advantages. HashSet provides fast performance for basic operations such as add, remove, and contains, but it does not maintain any order of elements. LinkedHashSet, on the other hand, preserves the insertion order while still offering relatively efficient operations with minimal overhead. TreeSet maintains elements in their natural or specified sorted order and supports efficient range-based operations, making it suitable for scenarios where ordered traversal or range queries are required.

We examined their internal structures, constructors, and performance considerations, and touched on aspects like synchronization and generic algorithms relevant to set operations.

A solid understanding of these implementations will help you choose the right data structure based on your specific needs in real-world applications.

In the next chapter, we will explore the queue and deque interfaces, where we will explore ordered processing, priority handling, and double-ended operations that are vital in concurrent and sequential task management scenarios.

Exercise

1. **Which of the following Set implementations maintains the insertion order?**
   a. HashSet
   b. LinkedHashSet
   c. TreeSet
   d. None of the above

2. **What will be the output of the following code?**
   ```
   Set<String> set = new HashSet<>();
   set.add("Book");
   set.add("Pen");
   ```

```
set.add("Book");
System.out.println(set.size());
```

    a. 2

    b. 3

    c. 1

    d. Compilation Error

3. **Which Set implementation keeps its elements sorted in natural order?**

    a. HashSet

    b. LinkedHashSet

    c. TreeSet

    d. All of the above

4. **What is the time complexity of the add() operation in HashSet?**

    a. $O(1)$

    b. $O(\log n)$

    c. $O(n)$

    d. $O(n \log n)$

5. **Which constructor of LinkedHashSet allows you to specify the initial capacity and load factor?**

    a. LinkedHashSet()

    b. LinkedHashSet(int initialCapacity)

    c. LinkedHashSet(int initialCapacity, float loadFactor)

    d. LinkedHashSet(Collection<? extends E> c)

6. **What happens if you try to insert a null element in a TreeSet?**

    a. It gets inserted at the beginning

    b. It gets inserted at the end

    c. It throws NullPointerException

    d. It is silently ignored

7. **How does LinkedHashSet internally maintain insertion order?**

    a. Tree structure

    b. Sorting on insertion

    c. Doubly linked list

    d. Binary search

8. **Which of the following is not true about HashSet?**
    a. It uses hashing for storing elements
    b. It allows one null element
    c. It maintains natural ordering
    d. It does not allow duplicates

9. **Choose the correct method to create an unmodifiable Set in Java 9+:**
    a. new HashSet<>()
    b. Set.unmodifiableSet(set)
    c. Collections.unmodifiableSet(set)
    d. Set.of("A", "B", "C")

10. **Which of these Set implementations is most suitable when you frequently need to access elements in sorted order?**
    a. HashSet
    b. LinkedHashSet
    c. TreeSet
    d. None

Answers

1. b

    Explanation: LinkedHashSet maintains insertion order by using a doubly linked list along with the hash table.

2. a

    Explanation: Sets do not allow duplicate elements. Apple is added only once.

3. c

    Explanation: TreeSet maintains elements in their natural sorted order using a red-black tree.

4. a

    Explanation: On average, HashSet provides constant-time performance for add, remove, and contains operations.

5. c

    Explanation: This constructor lets you control how the hash table is initialized and resized.

6. c

Explanation: TreeSet relies on comparison for ordering, and null cannot be compared, leading to a NullPointerException.

7. c

    Explanation: LinkedHashSet maintains a doubly linked list that records the order in which elements were inserted.

8. c

    Explanation: HashSet does not guarantee any specific order of its elements.

9. d

    Explanation: Set.of() creates an unmodifiable set directly in Java 9 and above.

10. c

    Explanation: TreeSet is backed by a NavigableMap and maintains elements in a sorted (ascending) order.

Join our Discord space

Join our Discord workspace for latest updates, offers, tech happenings around the world, new releases, and sessions with the authors:

https://discord.bpbonline.com

CHAPTER 8

Queue and Deque Interfaces

Introduction

In real-world applications, tasks are often processed in the order they arrive, just like people standing in a line to buy movie tickets or print jobs waiting to be processed by a printer. This natural *first-come, first-served* order is modelled in Java using the Queue interface. Additionally, for more flexible data management, Java provides the **double-ended queue (Deque)** interface, which allows insertion and removal from both ends.

This chapter explores these two fundamental interfaces in the JCF, their behaviour, typical use cases, and their major implementations. We will also explore internal structures, performance trade-offs, and concurrency-safe options.

Structure

The chapter covers the following topics:

- Queue interface
- PriorityQueue implementation
- Deque interface
- ArrayDeque implementation

- LinkedList as a Queue

- Synchronization in Queues and Deques

Objectives

By the end of this chapter, you will understand the fundamental differences and similarities between the Queue and Deque interfaces. They will be able to choose the right implementation based on insertion or removal order, performance requirements, and concurrency needs. Additionally, you will learn how internal structures such as heaps and circular buffers support these data structures and when to prefer one implementation over another in real-time applications.

Queue interface

The Queue interface in Java represents a collection designed for holding elements prior to processing. It follows the FIFO principle, which means elements are added at the end and removed from the front.

It is part of **java.util** package and extends the Collection interface as shown in the following:

```
public interface Queue<E> extends Collection<E>
```

Java provides multiple implementations of the Queue interface, each suited for different use cases:

- **LinkedList**: Implements Deque, and can be used as a queue or a stack. It allows null elements and is not thread-safe.

- **PriorityQueue**: Maintains elements in a sorted order (according to natural ordering or a custom comparator). It does not follow strict FIFO rules.

- **ArrayDeque**: A faster alternative to LinkedList for queue operations. It does not allow null elements.

- **ConcurrentLinkedQueue**: A thread-safe, lock-free implementation suitable for concurrent environments.

Characteristics of Queue interface

The following are some characteristics of a Queue that will help us understand it better:

- Elements are processed in the order they were added.

- It does not allow random access like a List.

- The head of the queue is the element that would be removed by a call to **remove()** or **poll()**.

- Tail of the queue is where new elements are added.

The Queue interface introduces several additional methods, as listed in the following table:

Method	Description
`add(E e)`	Inserts the specified element into the queue. Throws an exception if full.
`offer(E e)`	Inserts the element into the queue. Returns false if it fails, for example, if the queue is full.
`remove()`	Retrieves and removes the head. Throws an exception if empty.
`poll()`	Retrieves and removes the head. Returns null if empty.
`element()`	Retrieves (but does not remove) the head. Throws an exception if empty.
`peek()`	Retrieves (but does not remove) the head. Returns null if empty.

Table 8.1: Additional methods in the Queue interface

To understand how a queue behaves in Java, let us take a simple example using the Queue interface and its common implementation, LinkedList. This will help demonstrate the FIFO nature of queues. Consider the following code:

```
Queue<String> queue = new LinkedList<>();
queue.add("Apple");
queue.add("Banana");
queue.add("Cherry");

System.out.println(queue.poll());
System.out.println(queue.peek());
System.out.println(queue.poll());
```

The following is the output:

Apple

Banana

Banana

In this example:

- We are using the Queue interface with a LinkedList implementation. LinkedList is a commonly used class that implements Queue.
- **add("Apple")**, **add("Banana")**, and **add("Cherry")** insert elements into the queue in the order they arrive; this is the FIFO behavior.
- **poll()** retrieves and removes the head of the queue. Since "**Apple**" was added first, it was removed and printed.

- **peek()** retrieves but does not remove the head of the queue. Now, "**Banana**" is at the front, so it is shown.
- **poll()** retrieves and removes the head of the queue. Since "**Banana**" is at the front now, it has been removed and printed.

This example highlights the standard queue operations:

- **add()** to insert
- **poll()** to remove and return the front
- **peek()** to view the front without removing it

PriorityQueue implementation

The PriorityQueue is a part of the JCF and provides an efficient way to process elements based on priority rather than insertion order.

The following are the key characteristics of a PriorityQueue:

- **Not a FIFO queue**: The elements are ordered by their priority, not by the order in which they are added.
- **Duplicates allowed**: You can insert duplicate elements.

  Null elements are not allowed.
- **Not thread-safe**: Must be externally synchronized if used by multiple threads.
- **Unbounded queue**: Grows as needed and is constrained by system memory.

Internal structure of PriorityQueue

The PriorityQueue in Java is implemented using a binary heap, which is a type of complete binary tree. The elements are stored in an array (**Object[]** queue) that dynamically grows as needed.

A min-heap is the default behavior, meaning the smallest element is always at the root (head) of the heap.

Internally, the following mechanisms are used:

- Elements are inserted in an array-backed binary heap.
- The heap is not sorted, but is organized so that the smallest element can be retrieved in O(1).
- Insertion and removal maintain the heap property using heapify operations: **siftUp()** and **siftDown()**.

Here is a basic example of the add method in a PriorityQueue:

```
Object[] queue;
int size;

public boolean add(E e) {
    if (e == null)
        throw new NullPointerException();
    int i = size;
    if (i >= queue.length)
        grow();                    // Expand the array if full
    size = i + 1;
    if (i == 0)
        queue[0] = e;              // First element directly added
    else
        siftUp(i, e);              // Maintain heap order
    return true;
}
```

When an element is added at the end, we need to bubble it up if it violates the heap property. The **siftUp** method is used to move the new element into its correct position in the heap, as shown in the following figure:

```
private void siftUp(int k, E x) {
    while (k > 0) {
        int parent = (k - 1) >>> 1;      // parent index
        Object e = queue[parent];
        if (compare(x, e) >= 0)
            break;
        queue[k] = e;                     // move parent down
        k = parent;
    }
    queue[k] = x;                         // place new element
}
```

The **siftUp** method: this maintains the min-heap property. The newly inserted element is bubbled up until it is in the correct spot.

Let us say we add the following elements:

```
PriorityQueue<Integer> pq = new PriorityQueue<>();
pq.add(30);
```

```
pq.add(10);
pq.add(20);
```

This is what happens internally:

- Initially, after adding 30, the heap is as shown in the following:

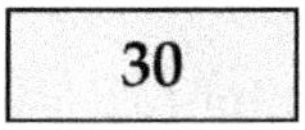

Figure 8.1: Initial heap

- After adding 10, as 10 is smaller than 30, they are swapped. The heap is now as shown in the following:

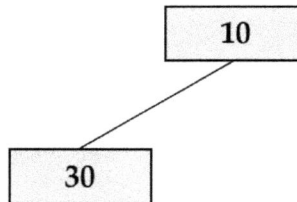

Figure 8.2: Heap after adding 10

- After adding 20, the heap is as shown in the following figure. As 20 is greater than 10, no swapping happens:

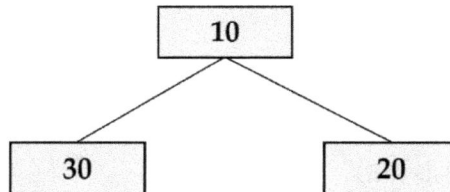

Figure 8.3: Heap after adding 20

When **poll()** is called, **poll()** retrieves and removes the head element (i.e., the smallest element in a min-heap), then reorders the heap.

This is the code snippet for the poll method:

```
public E poll() {
    if (size == 0)
        return null;
    int s = --size;
    E result = (E) queue[0];      // get root (smallest)
    E x = (E) queue[s];           // get last element
```

```
    queue[s] = null;              // clear last slot
    if (s != 0)
        siftDown(0, x);           // restore heap
    return result;
}
```

In the above **poll()** method, the **result = 10** is returned. The index 0 is replaced with the last element, **queue[0] = 20**.

After **poll()**, **siftDown()** is called from index 0 to restore the heap.

The following is the code snippet for the **siftDown()** method:

```
private void siftDown(int k, E x) {
    int half = size >>> 1; // Nodes below this are leaves
    while (k < half) {
        int left = (k << 1) + 1;      // left child
        int right = left + 1;
        int smallest = left;

        Object c = queue[left];
        if (right < size && compare((E) queue[right], (E) c) < 0) {
            smallest = right;
            c = queue[right];
        }
        if (compare(x, (E) c) <= 0)
            break;
        queue[k] = c;                      // move smaller child up
        k = smallest;
    }
    queue[k] = x;
}
```

Now the updated heap looks like the following figure:

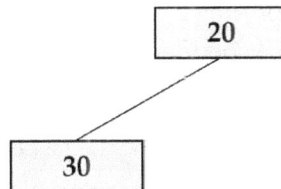

Figure 8.4: After 10 is removed using poll()

So, the array-backed binary heap is the core of the **PriorityQueue**, where insertion and deletion operations ensure that the element with the highest priority (smallest) is always at the top.

Deque interface

The Deque interface, introduced in Java 6, represents a linear collection that supports insertion and removal of elements from both ends. This flexibility allows a Deque to function both as a Queue, FIFO, and a Stack, LIFO.

Unlike a Queue, which restricts insertion and removal to specific ends, a Deque provides a richer set of methods to manipulate elements from the front and rear.

The Deque interface is especially useful when you need constant-time insertions or deletions from both ends of the collection. This is commonly seen in scenarios involving undo/redo stacks, scheduling systems, and palindromic checks.

The Deque interface extends the Queue interface and is part of the **java.util** package.

Common use cases

Let us look at a few real-world scenarios where a Deque proves helpful:

- Implementing stacks (using **push()** and **pop()**).
- Implementing Deque where elements can be added/removed from both ends efficiently.
- Task scheduling where prioritization may require insertion at either end.

Key methods in Deque interface

To enable flexible insertion and removal from both ends, the Deque interface offers a variety of methods. Here are some of the most used:

Method	Description
addFirst(e)	Inserts the specified element at the front of the Deque
addLast(e)	Inserts the specified element at the end of the Deque
offerFirst(e)	Offers the specified element at the front (returns false if not possible)
offerLast(e)	Offers the specified element at the end
removeFirst()	Removes and returns the first element
removeLast()	Removes and returns the last element
pollFirst()	Retrieves and removes the first element, or returns null if empty

`pollLast()`	Retrieves and removes the last element, or returns null if empty
`getFirst()`	Retrieves, but does not remove, the first element
`getLast()`	Retrieves, but does not remove, the last element
`peekFirst()`	Retrieves, but does not remove, the first element, or returns null
`peekLast()`	Retrieves, but does not remove, the last element, or returns null
`push(e)`	Pushes an element onto the stack (same as addFirst)
`pop()`	Pops an element from the stack (same as removeFirst)
`descendingIterator()`	Returns an iterator over the elements in reverse order

Table 8.2: *Key methods in Deque interface*

Using Deque as both Queue and Stack

Let us look at how a Deque can be used to behave like a Queue and a Stack. Consider the following example:

```
Deque<String> deque = new ArrayDeque<>();
// Using deque as a queue (FIFO)
deque.addLast("One");
deque.addLast("Two");
deque.addLast("Three");
System.out.println(deque.removeFirst()); // One
System.out.println(deque.removeFirst()); // Two
// Using deque as a stack (LIFO)
deque.push("A");
deque.push("B");
deque.push("C");

System.out.println(deque.pop()); // C
System.out.println(deque.pop()); // B
```

The following are the output:

One

Two

C

B

The following is the explanation for the above example:

- We are creating a Deque instance using **ArrayDeque**, which is a resizable array-based implementation of the Deque interface. It is efficient and faster than LinkedList for most use cases involving Stacks or Queues.

- We use **addLast()** to add elements to the end of the Deque. This mimics a queue where new elements go to the back.

- **removeFirst()** removes elements from the front of the Deque. So, elements are removed in the order they were added, i.e., FIFO.

- After this, *One* and *Two* are removed and printed. *Three* is still in the Deque.

- **push()** is equivalent to **addFirst()**, it adds elements to the front. So, *C* ends up at the front, followed by *B*, then *A*. This simulates a stack, where the most recently added element is at the top.

- **pop()** removes elements from the front (just like popping from the top of a stack). So, elements are removed in the reverse order of insertion: LIFO.

- At the end, *Three* (from the Queue part) and *A* (from the Stack part) are still present in the deque.

This example shows the versatility of Deque, how it can behave both like a queue and a stack depending on the methods you use.

ArrayDeque implementation

Array Deque (**ArrayDeque**) is a resizable-array implementation of the Deque interface. It supports insertion and removal at both ends with amortized constant time performance.

The following are the key characteristics:

- **Based on a circular array**: Elements are stored in a ring buffer, which is efficient for both ends.

- **No capacity limit**: Grows dynamically when full, usually by doubling its size.

- **Faster than Stack and LinkedList**: Provides better performance for queue and stack operations.

- **Null elements not allowed**: Adding null results in a **NullPointerException**, as null is used internally to indicate empty slots.

- **Not thread-safe**: Should be externally synchronized if used concurrently by multiple threads.

Internal structure

Internally, **ArrayDeque** maintains the following structure:

```
transient Object[] elements;
transient int head;
transient int tail;
```

In the above code:

- The elements array stores the contents.
- The head index points to the first (front) element.
- The tail index is where the next element will be inserted at the end.

When the tail reaches the end of the array, it wraps around to the beginning (hence the circular behaviour).

Let us illustrate a simplified version; refer to the following table:

Operation	Elements	Head	Tail
addLast(10)	[10, null, null, null]	0	1
addFirst(5)	[10, null, null, 5]	3	1
addLast(15)	[10, 15, null, 5]	3	2

Table 8.3: ArrayDeque illustration

When the array becomes full, the internal array is resized (usually doubled), and elements are realigned from head to tail.

Let us understand this with an example. Consider the following code:

```
Deque<String> deque = new ArrayDeque<>();

deque.addFirst("C");
deque.addLast("D");
deque.addFirst("B");
deque.addFirst("A"); // deque = [A, B, C, D]

System.out.println(deque);                  // [A, B, C, D]
System.out.println(deque.removeLast());     // D
System.out.println(deque.removeFirst());    // A
System.out.println(deque);                  // [B, C]
```

The following is the output:

```
[A, B, C, D]
D
A
[B, C]
```

The following is the explanation:

- **addFirst("C")**, the elements would look like the following figure. The head and tail are pointing to the same element.

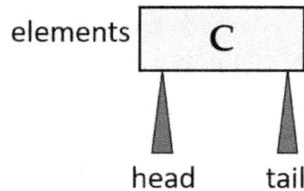

Figure 8.5: ArrayDeque after adding C

- **addLast("D")**, *D* is added to the end of the queue, and tail now points to *D* as shown the following figure:

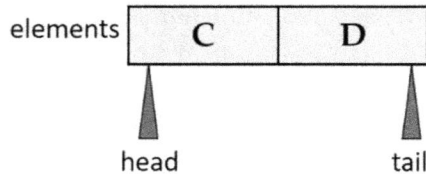

Figure 8.6: ArrayDeque after adding D

- **addFirst("B")**, now when *B* is added to the first, head points to *B*, and the **arraydeque** looks like the following figure:

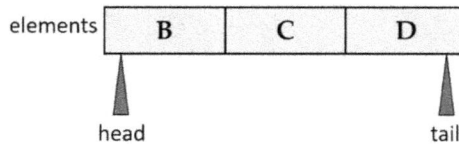

Figure 8.7: ArrayDeque after adding B

- **addFirst("A")**, after adding *A*, the head now points to *A*, and the **arraydeque** looks like the following:

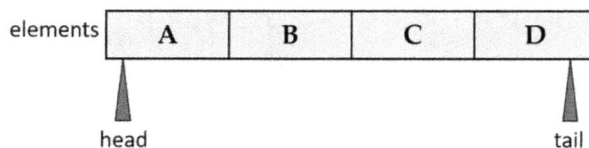

Figure 8.8: ArrayDeque after adding B

- **removeLast()** removes the last element, which is *D*, and the **arraydeque** looks like the following figure:

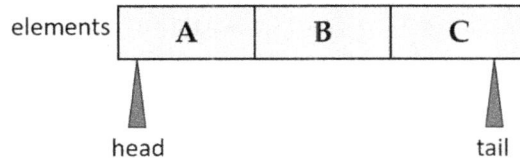

Figure 8.9: ArrayDeque after removing last

- **removeFirst()** removes the first element, which is *A*, and only *B* and *C* are left in the **arraydeque**. The **arraydeque** looks like the following figure:

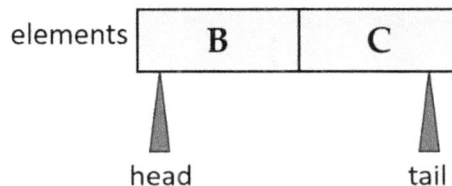

Figure 8.10: ArrayDeque after removing last

The internal resizing logic ensures that even though we are adding/removing at both ends, performance stays efficient.

Constructors

The following are the constructors that can be used to create an **ArrayDeque**:

- **ArrayDeque()**: Default constructor with initial capacity 16. This can be created as shown in the following:

```
ArrayDeque<Integer> deque1 = new ArrayDeque<>();
```

- **ArrayDeque(int initialCapacity)**: Creates a deque with the given capacity, as shown in the following:

```
ArrayDeque<String> deque2 = new ArrayDeque<>(50);
```

- **ArrayDeque(Collection<? extends E> c)**: Constructs a deque containing the elements of the specified collection as shown in the following:

```
ArrayDeque<Character> deque3 = new ArrayDeque<>(List.of('A', 'B', 'C'));
```

Common use cases of ArrayDeque

ArrayDeque is a versatile data structure and can be used to implement both stacks (LIFO) and queues (FIFO) efficiently. Its underlying resizable array and absence of capacity restrictions make it a preferred alternative to legacy classes like Stack and LinkedList in many scenarios. Beyond basic Stack and Queue operations, **ArrayDeque** is also well-suited for advanced use cases such as implementing a sliding window or fixed-size buffer, where elements are added and removed from both ends dynamically. Its constant-time performance for insertions and deletions at both the head and tail makes it ideal for these high-performance, real-time use cases. Let us explore these scenarios with clear examples.

Implementing a Stack

A Stack is a LIFO structure. **ArrayDeque** can be used instead of the Stack class, which is synchronized and slower. Let us consider the following example:

```
Deque<String> stack = new ArrayDeque<>();

stack.push("Page1");
stack.push("Page2");
stack.push("Page3");

System.out.println(stack.pop());
System.out.println(stack.peek());
```

The following is the output:

Page 3

Page 2

The following is the explanation for the above example:

- **push()** adds elements at the front.
- **pop()** removes the last added element
- This mimics undo operations, back navigation in a browser, etc.

Implementing Queue

A queue is a FIFO structure. **ArrayDeque** provides efficient operations for this. Let us understand with the following example:

```
Deque<String> queue = new ArrayDeque<>();

queue.addLast("Alice");
queue.addLast("Bob");
queue.addLast("Charlie");

System.out.println(queue.removeFirst()); // Alice
System.out.println(queue.peekFirst());   // Bob
```

The following is the output:

Alice

Bob

The following is the explanation for the above example:

- **addLast()** inserts elements at the end.
- **removeFirst()** removes from the front.
- This is ideal for print queues, task scheduling, etc.

Sliding window or fixed buffer

You can use **ArrayDeque** to manage a sliding window of fixed size for processing continuous data streams. For example:

```
Deque<Integer> window = new ArrayDeque<>();

for (int i = 1; i <= 6; i++) {
    if (window.size() == 3) {
        window.removeFirst();
    }
    window.addLast(i);
    System.out.println(window);
}
```

The following are the outputs:

```
[1]
[1, 2]
[1, 2, 3]
[2, 3, 4]
[3, 4, 5]
[4, 5, 6]
```

The following is the explanation for the above example:

- We maintain a fixed-size window of size 3.
- This is useful in problems like moving average, windowed search, etc.

LinkedList as a Queue

While LinkedList is commonly known for representing lists, it also implements both the Queue and Deque interfaces, making it a powerful and flexible structure for queue operations.

LinkedList provides an easy way to implement queue-like behavior with dynamic resizing and efficient insertions or removals from both ends.

The following are the key characteristics:

- Implements Deque, so it supports both FIFO and LIFO operations.
- Allows null elements (unlike **ArrayDeque**).
- Insertion and deletion are generally O(1) at the head or tail, but random access is O(n).
- Backed by a doubly linked list, so memory overhead is higher than **ArrayDeque**.

Using LinkedList as a Queue

Let us see how a LinkedList can be used as a simple FIFO queue using the Queue interface.

Consider the following code.

```
Queue<String> queue = new LinkedList<>();
queue.offer("Task1");
queue.offer("Task2");
queue.offer("Task3");
System.out.println(queue.poll());
System.out.println(queue.peek());
```

The following is the explanation for the above example:

- **offer()** adds elements at the end of the queue.
- **poll()** removes the element from the front (FIFO).
- **peek()** returns the front element without removing it.

Using LinkedList as a Deque

The same LinkedList can also be treated as a Deque, allowing insertion and removal from both ends.

Let us understand this with an example. Consider the following code:

```
Deque<String> deque = new LinkedList<>();
deque.addFirst("Start");
deque.addLast("End");
System.out.println(deque.removeFirst());
System.out.println(deque.removeLast());
```

The following is the output:

```
Start
End
```

In the above example:

- **addFirst()** and **addLast()** allow double-ended insertion.
- **removeFirst()** and **removeLast()** remove elements from both ends.
- This usage is ideal when both stack and queue operations are required.

Synchronization in Queues and Deques

In multi-threaded environments, thread safety is crucial when multiple threads access or modify queue-based data structures. Java provides several ways to achieve synchronization for queues and deques.

Choosing the appropriate synchronization mechanism depends on the specific concurrency requirements, such as whether blocking behavior is needed or whether concurrent reads and writes should be supported without locking the entire structure.

One common approach is using concurrent collections such as **ConcurrentLinkedQueue** or **ConcurrentLinkedDeque**, which are non-blocking and allow high-throughput access by multiple threads. For simpler scenarios or legacy codebases, the **Collections. synchronizedQueue()** or **Collections.synchronizedDeque()** methods can be used to wrap existing non-thread-safe implementations and make them synchronized, although these are generally less scalable under high contention.

For use cases that require coordination between producers and consumers, Java provides the **BlockingQueue** and **BlockingDeque** interfaces. Implementations like **ArrayBlockingQueue**, **LinkedBlockingQueue**, and **LinkedBlockingDeque** support thread-safe operations that block when the queue is full (during insertion) or empty (during retrieval). These are particularly well-suited for building task queues, message-passing systems, or bounded buffers.

Let us now explore these alternatives and best practices in detail, along with examples demonstrating their effective use in concurrent applications.

Using concurrent collections

Java provides built-in concurrent implementations as listed in the following:

- **ConcurrentLinkedQueue**: A non-blocking, thread-safe implementation of a FIFO queue.
- **LinkedBlockingQueue, ArrayBlockingQueue**: Blocking queues used in producer-consumer scenarios.
- **ConcurrentLinkedDeque**: A non-blocking deque implementation.

These classes handle synchronization internally and are preferred in concurrent designs.

Wrapping with Synchronized Collections

If you are using a non-thread-safe class like LinkedList as a queue in a multithreaded environment, you must synchronize access to avoid concurrency issues. Java provides a utility method **Collections.synchronizedList()**, which wraps a List (which can be used as a queue) and makes it thread-safe. This can be done as shown in the following:

```
Queue<String> queue = Collections.synchronizedList(new LinkedList<>());
// Synchronize explicitly during iteration
synchronized (queue) {
    for (String item : queue) {
        System.out.println(item);
    }
}
```

The following is the explanation for the above example:

- **Collections.synchronizedList(...)** returns a thread-safe wrapper around the original list.
- However, manual synchronization is still required during iteration to avoid the **ConcurrentModificationException**.
- The synchronized (queue) block ensures that the iteration is atomic and safe from thread interference.

BlockingQueue and BlockingDeque

When you need threads to wait for operations like insertion or removal (e.g., in producer-consumer scenarios), Java provides **BlockingQueue** and **BlockingDeque**. They can be used as shown in the following:

```
BlockingQueue<String> bQueue = new LinkedBlockingQueue<>();

bQueue.put("Data");              // Puts an element; waits if the queue is
full
String val = bQueue.take();      // Retrieves and removes the head; waits if
empty

System.out.println(val); // Outputs: Data
```

The following is the explanation for the above example:

- **LinkedBlockingQueue** is a thread-safe, optionally bounded queue.
- **put()** blocks the thread if the queue is full; this is useful for producers.
- **take()** blocks if the queue is empty; this is useful for consumers.
- This helps manage backpressure and avoid busy-waiting.

When working with queues and deques in concurrent environments, ensuring thread safety is essential. While collections like **ArrayDeque** and LinkedList are not thread-safe by default, Java provides mechanisms such as synchronized wrappers and concurrent implementations like **BlockingQueue** and **BlockingDeque**. Choosing the right approach depends on whether you need basic thread safety or full-fledged coordination between threads (e.g., blocking behaviour).

ArrayDeque vs. LinkedList vs. PriorityQueue

The following table shows a comparison of **ArrayDeque**, LinkedList, and **PriorityQueue**:

Feature	ArrayDeque	LinkedList (as Queue/Deque)	PriorityQueue
Underlying structure	Resizable array	Doubly-linked list	Min-heap (binary heap)
Null elements allowed	Not allowed	Allowed	Not allowed
Ordering	Insertion order	Insertion order	Natural/comparator order
Performance (Add or Remove)	Fast (amortized O(1))	Moderate (O(1) at ends)	O(log n)
Thread safety	Not thread-safe	Not thread-safe	Not thread-safe
Blocking support	No	No	No
Random access	No	No	No
Use case	Stack/queue/deque (non-threaded)	General-purpose queue/deque	Priority-based processing

Table 8.4: *ArrayDeque vs. LinkedList vs. PriorityQueue*

Conclusion

This chapter explored the foundational Queue and Deque interfaces and their primary implementations in the JCF. We examined how Queue supports FIFO operations, while Deque supports insertion and removal from both ends.

Key implementations like ArrayDeque, LinkedList, and PriorityQueue serve different purposes depending on access patterns, performance, and ordering needs. Additionally, we saw how synchronization can be introduced using wrappers or concurrent classes like BlockingQueue for thread-safe operations.

In the next chapter, we will explore Java's utility classes, which provide built-in support for sorting, searching, modifying, and synchronizing collections and arrays.

Exercise

1. **Which method adds an element to the tail of a Queue and throws an exception if it fails?**

    a. offer()

    b. put()

    c. add()

    d. enqueue()

2. **Which interface allows insertion and removal from both ends?**

    a. Queue

    b. Deque

    c. PriorityQueue

    d. Stack

3. **What is the default ordering used by PriorityQueue?**

    a. LIFO

    b. FIFO

    c. Natural ordering

    d. Random ordering

4. **Which method retrieves but does not remove the head of the queue, returning null if empty?**

    a. poll()

    b. remove()

    c. peek()

    d. head()

5. **Which implementation is backed by a resizable array and does not allow null elements?**

    a. ArrayList

    b. ArrayQueue

    c. ArrayDeque

    d. LinkedList

6. **Which of these allows constant-time insertion or removal at both ends and can be used as a stack or queue?**

    a. PriorityQueue

    b. Stack

    c.   LinkedList

    d.   ArrayDeque

7. **What happens if you insert a null element into an ArrayDeque?**

    a.   It's allowed

    b.   It throws a NullPointerException

    c.   It silently fails

    d.   It gets converted to an empty string

8. **Which of the following is not a method defined in the Queue interface?**

    a.   offer()

    b.   add()

    c.   push()

    d.   poll()

9. **Which implementation is most suitable for implementing a priority task scheduler?**

    a.   ArrayDeque

    b.   LinkedList

    c.   PriorityQueue

    d.   Stack

10. **Which interface allows the use of methods like addFirst() and removeLast()?**

    a.   List

    b.   Set

    c.   Queue

    d.   Deque

Answers

1. c

   Explanation: add() adds to the tail and throws an exception if the insertion fails.

2. b

   Explanation: Deque supports element insertion/removal at both ends.

3. c

   Explanation: PriorityQueue uses natural ordering unless a comparator is provided.

4. c

   Explanation: peek() returns the head or null if the queue is empty, without removing it.

5. c

    Explanation: ArrayDeque is a resizable array-based deque that does not permit null elements.

6. d

    Explanation: ArrayDeque supports constant-time insertion/removal at both ends and works as a stack or a queue.

7. b

    Explanation: ArrayDeque does not allow null elements and throws NullPointerException.

8. c

    Explanation: push() is from Deque, not part of the Queue interface.

9. c

    Explanation: PriorityQueue is optimized for priority-based task scheduling.

10. d

    Explanation: Deque provides addFirst(), removeLast(), and other double-ended operations.

Join our Discord space

Join our Discord workspace for latest updates, offers, tech happenings around the world, new releases, and sessions with the authors:

https://discord.bpbonline.com

CHAPTER 9
Utility Classes

Introduction

In real-world Java applications, developers frequently need to sort, search, modify, or synchronize collections. Performing these operations manually can be error-prone and time-consuming. Java's utility classes come to the rescue by providing ready-to-use methods to simplify these common tasks.

This chapter focuses on utility classes like Collections and Arrays that offer static methods to operate on or return collections and arrays. It also covers wrapper classes, synchronization utilities, and how to make collections unmodifiable or type-safe (checked collections). Understanding and effectively using these classes will help you write more efficient, readable, and safe Java code.

Structure

The chapter covers the following topics:

- Collections utility class
- Sorting and searching with Collections
- Modifying collections with Collections
- Arrays utility class

- Working with Arrays and Collections
- Wrapper class
- Synchronization utilities
- Unmodifiable collections
- Checked collections

Objectives

This chapter aims to equip you with practical knowledge of Java's core utility classes that simplify common tasks involving collections and arrays. You will learn how to use the Collections class for sorting, searching, and modifying collections efficiently, and how the Arrays class provides similar capabilities for Arrays. We will also explore the use of wrapper classes that allow primitive types to be used in object-based collections, along with techniques to synchronize collections for thread safety. Finally, you will understand how to create unmodifiable and type-safe (checked) collections using built-in utility methods, enabling you to write safer and more maintainable code in your Java applications.

Collections utility class

The Collections class in Java is a part of the **java.util** package provides a set of static methods that operate on or return collections. These methods are designed to simplify common collection-related tasks such as sorting, searching, reversing, shuffling, filling, copying, and more.

This class cannot be instantiated and serves purely as a utility holder. It is often used alongside the JCF to improve productivity and reduce boilerplate code.

Key methods in the Collections class. The following is a list of commonly used methods provided by the Collections utility class:

Method	Description
`sort(List<T> list)`	Sorts the specified list into ascending order using natural ordering.
`sort(List<T> list, Comparator<? super T> c)`	Sorts the list based on a custom comparator.
`reverse(List<?> list)`	Reverses the order of elements in the list.
`shuffle(List<?> list)`	Randomly permutes the elements in the list.
`swap(List<?> list, int i, int j)`	Swaps the elements at the specified positions.
`fill(List<? super T> list, T obj)`	Replaces all elements of the list with the specified element.

`copy(List<? super T> dest, List<? extends T> src)`	Copies all elements from the source list to the destination list. The destination must be at least the same size as the source.
`binarySearch(List<? extends Comparable<? super T>> list, T key)`	Searches for the key using binary search. The list must be sorted.
`max(Collection<? extends T> coll)`	Returns the maximum element according to natural ordering.
`min(Collection<? extends T> coll)`	Returns the minimum element.
`frequency(Collection<?> c, Object o)`	Returns the number of elements equal to the specified object.
`disjoint(Collection<?> c1, Collection<?> c2)`	Returns true if two collections have no elements in common.

Table 9.1: Key methods in the Collections class

Sorting and reversing a List

Let us look at a simple example of how the Collections class can be used to sort and reverse a list:

```java
import java.util.*;

public class CollectionsExample {
    public static void main(String[] args) {
        List<String> fruits = new ArrayList<>(Arrays.asList("Banana", "Apple",
"Mango", "Cherry"));

        // Sort in ascending order
        Collections.sort(fruits);
        System.out.println("Sorted List: " + fruits); // [Apple, Banana, Cherry, Mango]

        // Reverse the list
        Collections.reverse(fruits);
        System.out.println("Reversed List: " + fruits); // [Mango, Cherry, Banana, Apple]
    }
}
```

The following is the output:
```
Sorted List: [Apple, Banana, Cherry, Mango]
Reversed List: [Mango, Cherry, Banana, Apple]
```

In this example:

- `Collections.sort(fruits)` sorts the list alphabetically.
- `Collections.reverse(fruits)` then reverses the sorted list.

These utility methods abstract away the internal complexity of sorting and reversing, making the code cleaner and easier to maintain.

Sorting and searching with collections

In many real-world applications, you need to present data in a particular order or locate specific elements quickly. Whether you are building a to-do list, a leaderboard, or processing search results, sorting and searching are core operations that help deliver a better user experience.

The Collections class provides ready-to-use static methods for sorting and searching lists. These methods are optimized and widely used in Java applications.

Sorting a List

The most common operation is sorting. Java offers two ways to sort a list:

- **Natural ordering**: When elements implement the comparable interface.
- **Custom ordering**: By using a comparator.

Sorting with natural order

Consider the following example for natural ordering:

```
List<Integer> numbers = Arrays.asList(4, 1, 3, 2);
Collections.sort(numbers);
System.out.println(numbers);
```

The following is the output:

```
[1, 2, 3, 4]
```

The above example explains:

- We create a list of integers with values in random order.
- `Collections.sort(numbers)` sorts the list in-place using natural order, for numbers, that's ascending order.
- The original list is modified, and the elements are rearranged in increasing order.

This works because Integer implements the comparable interface, which defines how two integers should be compared.

Sorting with custom comparator

If you want to sort in descending order, or any other custom order, you need to use a comparator. Let us see an example with a comparator as shown in the following.

```
List<String> fruits = Arrays.asList("Banara", "Apple", "Mango");
Collections.sort(fruits, (a, b) -> b.compareTo(a)); // Reverse alphabetical
System.out.println(fruits);
```

The following is the output:

[Mango, Banana, Apple]

The above example explains:

- The lambda **(a, b) | b.compareTo(a)** flips the comparison, sorting the list in descending (Z to A) order.
- This allows complete control over sorting logic; you can sort based on length, case-insensitive order, or any custom rule.

Note: **You can also use `Comparator.reverseOrder()` or method references for simpler syntax.**

Searching a List

After sorting, you may want to quickly find an element. Linear search is slow for large lists, so Java offers **binarySearch()**, which is much faster but requires the list to be sorted.

This can be done as shown in the following:

```
List<Integer> list = Arrays.asList(10, 20, 30, 40, 50);
int index = Collections.binarySearch(list, 30);
System.out.println("Index of 30: " + index);
```

The following is the output:

Index of 30: 2

The above example explains:

- The list is already sorted in ascending order.
- **binarySearch(scores, 30)** performs a binary search, cutting the list in half each time to find the element.
- It returns the index of the element if found; here, 30 is at index 2.

Note: **The list must be sorted in ascending order before calling binarySearch(). If the element is not found, the method returns a negative value indicating the insertion point.**

Binary search with custom comparator

If your list is sorted using a custom comparator, you must use the same comparator in the **binarySearch()** call:

```
List<String> items = Arrays.asList("X", "M", "A");
Collections.sort(items, Comparator.reverseOrder()); // [X, M, A]
int index = Collections.binarySearch(items, "M", Comparator.reverseOrder());
System.out.println("Index of M: " + index); // 1
```

The following is the output:

Index of M: 1

The above example explains:

- The list is sorted in reverse order.

- Since the order is not natural, we must pass the same comparator to **binarySearch()**.

- If you forget to pass the matching comparator, the search result may be incorrect, or even a negative number.

These utility methods are essential for clean, concise, and efficient collection handling in Java. Whether you are sorting user scores, searching product IDs, or ranking search results, **Collections.sort()** and **Collections.binarySearch()** are the go-to tools.

Modifying collections with Collections

In addition to sorting and searching, the Collections utility class provides several helpful methods to modify the contents of collections in a consistent and efficient manner. These methods allow you to reverse, shuffle, fill, and replace elements, as well as copy data between collections. They are especially useful when you want to manipulate collections without writing your own looping or transformation logic.

Let us go through the commonly used modification methods with examples and explanations.

Reversing a List

Suppose we have a list of student names in the order they registered. We want to reverse the list to show the latest registered students first.

Consider the following example:

```
List<String> students = Arrays.asList("Andrew", "Becky", "Carlos");
Collections.reverse(students);
System.out.println(students);
```

The following is the output:

[Carlos, Becky, Andrew]

The above example explains:

- **reverse()** inverts the order of the list elements.
- This is useful for undoing sort operations or for displaying data in reverse sequence.

Shuffling elements

Consider you are creating a quiz app and want to randomize the order of questions before displaying them to the user. You can do it using the shuffle method as shown in the following:

```
List<Integer> questionIds = Arrays.asList(101, 102, 103, 104, 105);
Collections.shuffle(questionIds);
System.out.println(questionIds);
```

The following is the output:

[103, 102, 105, 104, 101]

The above example explains:

- **shuffle()** reorders the list in a random fashion.
- It is commonly used for gaming, testing, and simulations.

Filling a List with a value

Let us say you are preparing a scoreboard and want to initialize it with default values. You can do this using the **fill()** method as shown in the following:

```
List<String> scoreboard = new ArrayList<>(Arrays.asList("A", "B", "C"));
Collections.fill(scoreboard, "Not Started");
System.out.println(scoreboard);
```

The following is the output:

[Not Started, Not Started, Not Started]

The above example explains:

- **fill()** replaces every element with a specified value.
- It is often used to initialize or reset a list.

Replacing all occurrences of a value

Consider you have a list of cities where a name change occurred. You want to update all old names with the new one. You can do this by using the **replaceAll()** method as shown in the following:

```
List<String> cities = Arrays.asList("Bombay", "Delhi", "Bombay", "Chennai");
Collections.replaceAll(cities, "Bombay", "Mumbai");
System.out.println(cities);
```

The following is the output:

`[Mumbai, Delhi, Mumbai, Chennai]`

The above example explains:

- **replaceAll()** finds all instances of a particular value and replaces them.
- It's helpful for bulk updates or renaming data sets.

Copying one List into another

Suppose you have a master list of team members and want to create a working copy for temporary updates. You can do that by using the **copy()** method as shown in the following:

```
List<String> masterTeam = Arrays.asList("Emily", "John", "Sarah");
List<String> workingCopy = new ArrayList<>(Arrays.asList("X", "Y", "Z"));
Collections.copy(workingCopy, masterTeam);
System.out.println(workingCopy); // [Emily, John, Sarah]
```

The following is the output:

`[Emily, John, Sarah]`

The above example explains:

- **copy(dest, source)** copies data from one list to another.
- The destination list must be at least the same size as the source to avoid an **IndexOut-OfBoundsException**.

These utility methods make collection transformations easy and clean, reducing the need for custom logic and improving code readability.

Arrays utility class

While Collections works with dynamic data structures like List, Java also provides the Arrays utility class to simplify operations on arrays, which are fixed-size data structures. Found in the **java.util** package, the Arrays class offers static methods for sorting, searching, comparing, filling, and converting arrays.

These utilities are helpful when you want to treat arrays like collections, enabling you to manipulate data using a consistent set of tools.

Let us explore some of the most useful features of the Arrays utility class.

Sorting an Array

Let us say you have the marks of students and you want to sort them in ascending order. You can do that by using the **sort()** method as shown in the following:

```
int[] marks = {85, 67, 92, 78, 88};
Arrays.sort(marks);
System.out.println(Arrays.toString(marks));
```

The following is the output:

[67, 78, 85, 88, 92]

The above example explains:

- **sort()** arranges the array in ascending order using a tuned version of quicksort for primitives.
- **Arrays.toString()** is used to print the array content in a readable format.

Searching in an Array

Now, suppose you want to check if a particular mark (say 88) is present in the sorted Array. You can do that by using the **binarySearch()** method as shown in the following:

```
int[] marks = {70, 75, 80, 83, 88, 90, 95};
int index = Arrays.binarySearch(marks, 88);
System.out.println(index);
```

The following is the output:

4

The above example explains:

- **binarySearch()** finds the index of the element in a sorted array.
- If the element is not found, it returns a negative value.

Filling an Array

Suppose you want to initialize an array of size 5 with the default value 10. You can use the **fill()** method as shown in the following:

```
int[] data = new int[5];
Arrays.fill(data, 10);
System.out.println(Arrays.toString(data));
```

The following is the output:

[10, 10, 10, 10, 10]

In the above example, **fill()** assigns the same value to all elements of the Array.

Comparing Arrays

If you are comparing answers submitted by two students to see if they selected the same options, as shown in the following:

```
int[] answers1 = {1, 2, 3};
int[] answers2 = {1, 2, 3};
System.out.println(Arrays.equals(answers1, answers2));
```

The following is the output:

true

You can use the **equals()** method. **equals()** checks whether all elements in two arrays are the same and in the same order.

Copying Arrays

Let us say you want to create a new array that is a copy of an existing one with more room for future data. You can use **copyOf()** method to achieve that, as shown in the following:

```
int[] original = {10, 20, 30};
int[] extended = Arrays.copyOf(original, 5);
System.out.println(Arrays.toString(extended));
```

The following is the output:

[10, 20, 30, 0, 0]

The above example explains:

- **copyOf()** creates a new array of the specified length.
- If the new length is greater, extra elements are filled with default values (0 for int).

The Arrays utility class ensures that working with fixed-size arrays in Java remains powerful, concise, and consistent with the collections paradigm.

Working with Arrays and Collections

In Java, Arrays and Collections are both used to store groups of elements. However, they serve different purposes; Arrays are fixed in size and slightly faster, while Collections are more flexible and provide many utility methods. Sometimes, you may need to convert between the two for convenience or performance.

The Arrays and Collections classes provide methods that help bridge the gap between these two data structures. Let us explore the most common scenarios where Arrays and Collections interact.

Converting an Array to a List

Let us say you collected input from users in a List and now want to store it in an Array for sending over a network. You can do this as shown in the following code:

```
List<String> users = Arrays.asList("Emma", "Michael", "Sophia");
String[] userArray = users.toArray(new String[0]);
System.out.println(Arrays.toString(userArray));
```

The following is the output:

[Emma, Michael, Sophia]

The above example explains:

- **toArray(T[] a)** converts the list to a typed array.
- Passing a zero-length array (**new String[0]**) allows Java to allocate the array with the correct size.

Using collection methods on Arrays

Even though Arrays and Collections are different, you can still perform many collection-like operations on arrays by converting them temporarily.

For example, if you want to reverse an array of names, you can do that as shown in the following:

```
String[] names = {"Alex", "Brian", "Chloe"};
List<String> nameList = Arrays.asList(names);
Collections.reverse(nameList);
System.out.println(Arrays.toString(names));
```

The following is the output:

[Chloe, Brian, Alex]

The above example explains:

- **Arrays.asList()** creates a list view over the array.
- Modifying the list also changes the original array.

Bridging Arrays and Collections allows you to enjoy the best of both worlds: the performance of Arrays and the flexibility of Collections. This is especially useful when working with APIs that expect one format or the other.

Wrapper class

In Java, primitive types like int, char, and Boolean are not objects. This means they cannot be used directly with Collections, generics, or APIs that require objects. To bridge this gap, Java provides wrapper classes: object representations of primitive types such as Integer, Character, and Boolean.

These classes *wrap* primitive types in an object and offer additional functionalities such as parsing from strings, comparing values, converting between types, and accessing predefined constants. All wrapper classes are part of **java.lang** package, making them readily available without needing explicit imports.

Wrapper classes allow primitive values to be stored in collections like List, Set, or Map. They enable the use of primitive values with Java generics, which work only with objects. Additionally, they provide utility methods such as parsing (**Integer.parseInt()**), comparison (**Integer.compare()**), and constant values (**Integer.MAX_VALUE**). Wrapper classes are essential for writing cleaner, safer, and more reusable code in real-world applications.

The following table shows a reference table outlining each primitive type and its associated wrapper class:

Primitive type	Wrapper class	Example of declaration
byte	Byte	`Byte b = Byte.valueOf((byte) 10);`
short	Short	`Short s = Short.valueOf((short) 20);`
int	Integer	`Integer i = Integer.valueOf(100);`
long	Long	`Long l = Long.valueOf(12345L);`
float	Float	`Float f = Float.valueOf(12.34f);`
double	Double	`Double d = Double.valueOf(123.456);`
char	Character	`Character c = Character.valueOf('A');`
boolean	Boolean	`Boolean bool = Boolean.TRUE;`

Table 9.2: Wrapper classes

When working with Java Collections, primitives cannot be added directly. Java handles this automatically using auto-boxing and unboxing.

The following example demonstrates this mechanism:

```
List<Integer> temperatures = new ArrayList<>();
temperatures.add(30);   // Auto-boxing: int → Integer
temperatures.add(35);
temperatures.add(28);

for (Integer temp : temperatures) {
    System.out.println(temp);
}
```

Output:

30

35

28

In the example above, the temperatures list is declared as **List<Integer>**. It cannot store primitive int values directly. When calling **add(30)**, Java automatically converts (auto-boxes) the primitive int into an Integer object. During iteration, auto-unboxing occurs when retrieving the values, converting the Integer back to int if required.

Introduced in Java 5, auto-boxing and unboxing simplify working with wrapper classes. Auto-boxing means automatically converting primitives to wrapper objects. Unboxing means automatically converting wrapper objects back to primitives.

For example:

```
Integer num = 100; // Auto-boxing
int value = num;   // Unboxing
```

Beyond basic storage in collections, wrapper classes provide additional utilities. These include constants such as **Integer.MAX_VALUE** and **Double.MIN_VALUE**, which are useful for boundary checks. They also offer utility methods like **parseInt()**, **parseDouble()**, and **valueOf()** that help convert strings or other data types into primitive values. Methods such as **Integer.compare(10, 20)** allow easy comparison of primitive values while still using the wrapper class methods.

In real-world scenarios, wrapper classes prove essential in multiple areas. In database interaction, frameworks like Hibernate often rely on wrapper classes to handle nullable database columns. While parsing user input, converting string inputs into numeric values through methods like **Integer.parseInt("123")** is common practice. In application configuration and settings, wrapper classes are often used to store application settings in collections such as **Map<String, Integer>**.

Synchronization utilities

In multi-threaded environments, ensuring thread safety is crucial, especially when multiple threads access or modify collections concurrently. Java provides synchronization utilities to help manage this safely without introducing complex locking mechanisms manually.

The Collections class includes several methods to make collections thread-safe by returning synchronized (thread-safe) versions of common collections like List, Set, and Map.

Making a List synchronized

Let us say *Ryan* and *Sophia* are working on different threads, updating a shared list of tasks. To prevent data corruption, the list must be synchronized. A synchronized list can be created as shown in the following:

```
List<String> taskList = new ArrayList<>();
List<String> syncTaskList = Collections.synchronizedList(taskList);
```

The above example explains:

- **Collections.synchronizedList()** wraps the **taskList** with a thread-safe layer.

- All method calls on **syncTaskList** are now synchronized internally.

- However, iteration still needs to be synchronized manually to avoid the **Concurrent-ModificationException**. Iteration can be synchronized as shown in the following:

```
synchronized (syncTaskList) {
    for (String task : syncTaskList) {
        System.out.println(task);
    }
}
```

Synchronized Set and Map

Similar to a List, you can make a Set or Map synchronized as shown in the following:

```
Set<String> names = new HashSet<>();
Set<String> syncNames = Collections.synchronizedSet(names);
Map<Integer, String> employeeMap = new HashMap<>();
Map<Integer, String> syncEmployeeMap = Collections.synchronizedMap(employee-
Map);
```

The above example explains:

- The wrappers ensure that basic operations (like add, remove, get, put) are thread-safe.
- Like with List, iterations must be done within a synchronized block.

When you wrap a collection (like List, Set, or Map) using methods like **Collections.syn-chronizedList()**, Java internally adds synchronization to each method call on that collection. So when two or more threads try to call methods like:

- **add():** To insert an element
- **remove():** To delete an element
- **get():** To access an element by index (for a list)
- **put():** To add a key-value pair (for a map)

The method calls are automatically synchronized using an internal lock. This means only one thread can execute them at a time, avoiding conflicts or data corruption.

However, iteration (like using for-each) is not automatically synchronized, so you still need to do that part manually using a synchronized block.

Unmodifiable collections

In many applications, especially in multi-team projects, it is crucial to prevent accidental changes to certain data structures. For example, a list of default user roles or configuration keys should not be modified once created.

To protect such collections from being altered, Java provides unmodifiable wrappers using the Collections utility class.

When a collection is wrapped as unmodifiable, any attempt to modify it, such as adding, removing, or updating element, will result in an **UnsupportedOperationException**.

Java provides methods like:

- **Collections.unmodifiableList(List<? extends T> list)**
- **Collections.unmodifiableSet(Set<? extends T> set)**
- **Collections.unmodifiableMap(Map<? extends K, ? extends V> map)**

These methods return a read-only view of the original collection. Changes to the underlying collection (if modified directly, outside the wrapper) will still reflect in the unmodifiable view, so it is recommended to avoid modifying the original collection after wrapping it. Creating unmodifiable collections.

Let us say you have a list of departments that should not be changed during runtime. You can create an unmodifiable list as shown in the following:

```
List<String> departments = new ArrayList<>();
departments.add("HR");
departments.add("Finance");
departments.add("IT");

List<String> unmodifiableDepartments = Collections.unmodifiableList(depart-
ments);
```

The above example explains:

- The original department list is wrapped in an unmodifiable layer.

- Now **unmodifiableDepartments** can be read, but any attempt to modify them, like **add()**, **remove()**, or **clear()**, will throw an exception. For example, the following will throw an **UnsupportedOperationException** exception:

  ```
  unmodifiableDepartments.add("Marketing");
  ```

  You can create unmodifiable versions of all major collections like Set or Map, as shown in the following:

  ```
  Set<String> states = Collections.unmodifiableSet(new HashSet<>());

  Map<Integer, String> codes = Collections.unmodifiableMap(new Hash-
  Map<>());
  ```

Note: **The unmodifiable wrapper does not make a deep copy. If the underlying collection is modified, the changes will reflect in the unmodifiable version too.**

This is shown in the following code:

```
departments.add("Legal");
System.out.println(unmodifiableDepartments); // Will include "Legal"
```

Therefore, it is advised to avoid modifying the original Collection after wrapping it in an unmodifiable one.

Java also introduced the **List.of()**, **Set.of()**, and **Map.of()** methods in Java 9, which directly create immutable collections. However, if you are using earlier versions or want to wrap an existing modifiable collection, **Collections.unmodifiableX()** is the standard approach.

Predefined empty collections

In addition to unmodifiable wrappers, the Collections class also provides predefined immutable empty collections, which are especially useful when you need to return an empty result but want to avoid returning null:

- **Collections.emptyList()**
- **Collections.emptySet()**
- **Collections.emptyMap()**

Let us look at examples of how they are used in practical code:

- **Collections.emptyList():** Consider the following example:

```
public class OrderService {
    public List<String> getPendingOrders(String userId) {
        if (userId == null || userId.isEmpty()) {
            return Collections.emptyList();
        }
        // Logic to fetch orders from database
        return Arrays.asList("ORD123", "ORD456");
    }
}
```

Case 1:

```
public static void main(String[] args) {
    OrderService service = new OrderService();
    System.out.println(service.getPendingOrders("user1"));
}
```

Output: [ORD123, ORD456]

Case 2:

```
public static void main(String[] args) {
    OrderService service = new OrderService();
    System.out.println(service.getPendingOrders(""));
}
```

Output: [ ]

The explanation of the above is as follows:

- o If the **userId** is invalid, we return an empty list.
- o **Collections.emptyList()** ensures that no null is returned, eliminating the need for null checks.
- o Since the list is immutable, accidental modification is also prevented.

- **Collections.emptySet()**: Consider the following example:

```
public class Student {
    private final Set<String> enrolledSubjects;

    public Student(boolean isEnrolled) {
        if (isEnrolled) {
            this.enrolledSubjects = new HashSet<>(Arrays.asList("Math",
"Science"));
        } else {
            this.enrolledSubjects = Collections.emptySet();
        }
    }

    public Set<String> getEnrolledSubjects() {
        return enrolledSubjects;
    }
}
```

Case 1:

```
Student s1 = new Student(true);
System.out.println(s1.getEnrolledSubjects());
```

Output: [Math, Science]

Case 2:

```
Student s2 = new Student(false);
System.out.println(s2.getEnrolledSubjects());
```

Output: [ ] (An immutable empty set.)

The explanation of the above is as follows:

- o   When a student is not enrolled, we assign an empty set using **Collections. emptySet()**.

- o   This avoids returning null and also prevents future modification since the returned set is immutable.

- **Collections.emptyMap():** Consider the following example:

```
public class ConfigurationService {
    public Map<String, String> loadConfig(String env) {
        if (env == null || env.isEmpty()) {
            return Collections.emptyMap();
        }
        // Suppose config is loaded from a file or DB
        Map<String, String> config = new HashMap<>();
        config.put("timeout", "30");
        config.put("retry", "5");
        return config;
    }
}
```

The explanation of the above is as follows:

- o   If no environment is provided, an empty map is returned.

- o   **Collections.emptyMap()** helps maintain consistency in return type and avoids returning a null object.

These empty collections are:

- **Unmodifiable**: Any attempt to modify them results in an **UnsupportedOperationException**.

- **Singleton**: The same instance is reused, reducing memory overhead.

- **Safer than null**: Eliminates the need for null checks in calling code.

Each of these methods returns a shared, immutable, and memory-efficient empty instance of the corresponding collection type.

Checked collections

Java is a statically typed language, but due to type erasure, generic type information is removed at runtime. This can sometimes lead to unexpected **ClassCastExceptions** when using raw types or when mixing generic and non-generic code.

To catch such issues early, during runtime but before actual damage, Java provides checked collections through the Collections utility class.

Checked collections wrap a collection and perform runtime type checks whenever elements are added. If someone tries to insert an object of the wrong type, it immediately throws a **ClassCastException**.

Let us consider this situation: *Paul* creates a list of student names, assuming it will only hold String values. Later, *Royston* (working in a different module) accidentally adds an Integer to it.

Without a checked collection, the code would look as shown in the following:

```
List studentNames = new ArrayList(); // raw type
studentNames.add("Alex");
studentNames.add(101); // No compile-time error
String name = (String) studentNames.get(1); // ClassCastException at runtime
```

Now, with a checked collection, it would look as follows:

```
List<String> names = new ArrayList<>();
List<String> checkedNames = Collections.checkedList(names, String.class);
checkedNames.add("Alex");
//checkedNames.add(101); // Compilation fails
```

The above example explains:

- The wrapper **Collections.checkedList()** monitors each addition to the list.
- When a value of the wrong type is added, the error is thrown at the point of insertion, making the error easier to detect and debug.

Similar wrappers exist for other types, as shown in the following:

```
Set<Integer> checkedSet = Collections.checkedSet(new HashSet<>(), Integer.
class);
Map<String, Double> checkedMap = Collections.checkedMap(new HashMap<>(),
String.class, Double.class);
```

Use checked collections in the following scenarios:

- When working with legacy code that does not use generics.
- During testing or debugging to catch incorrect usage early.
- In shared libraries or APIs to enforce type safety for consumers.

Checked collections act as runtime safety nets, not a replacement for generics, but a useful companion when generics cannot guarantee safety alone due to raw type usage.

Conclusion

Utility classes like Collections, Arrays, and the wrapper classes are essential tools in every Java developer's toolkit. They streamline common tasks such as sorting, searching, converting arrays to collections, synchronizing collections, and enforcing immutability or type safety at runtime.

We saw how Collections and Arrays utility methods reduce boilerplate and potential bugs, and how wrapper classes make primitive types work seamlessly with collections. These utilities not only improve productivity but also encourage safer and more readable code.

However, writing effective, high-performance, and bug-free code with collections is not just about using the right data structures; it is also about following best practices in their usage.

In the next chapter, we will shift focus to best practices with generics and collections, where you will learn guidelines, patterns, and common pitfalls to avoid when designing and working with collection-heavy codebases.

Exercise

1. **Which method would you use to make a list unmodifiable?**

    a. Collections.immutableList()

    b. Collections.readOnlyList()

    c. Collections.unmodifiableList()

    d. List.makeReadOnly()

2. **Which utility method would you use to find an element in a sorted list?**

    a. Collections.find()

    b. Collections.binarySearch()

    c. Arrays.lookup()

    d. List.search()

3. **What is the result of converting a primitive array using Arrays.asList()?**

    a. A list of primitive values

    b. Compilation error

    c. A single-element list containing the entire array

    d. A list of boxed values

4. **Which method in the Arrays class would you use to fill an array with a specific value?**

    a. Arrays.assign()

    b. Arrays.fill()

c. Arrays.copy()

d. Arrays.setAll()

5. **What does Collections.checkedList(list, String.class) provide?**

   a. Read-only list

   b. Synchronized list

   c. Type-safe list

   d. Sorted list

6. **Which method converts a list to an array of objects?**

   a. list.convertToArray()

   b. Collections.toArray()

   c. list.toArray()

   d. Arrays.fromList()

7. **Which of these wrappers ensures thread-safe access to a map?**

   a. Collections.lockedMap()

   b. Collections.synchronizedMap()

   c. Collections.concurrentMap()

   d. Map.makeThreadSafe()

8. **What does Collections.reverse(list) do?**

   a. Removes elements from the list

   b. Creates a new reversed list

   c. Sorts the list in descending order

   d. Reverses the order of elements in-place

9. **Which class allows sorting a subrange of an array?**

   a. Collections

   b. SubArray

   c. Arrays

   d. PartialSorter

10. **Which of these Set implementations is most suitable when you frequently need to access elements in sorted order?**

    a. HashSet

    b. LinkedHashSet

    c. TreeSet

    d. None

Answers

1. c

   Explanation: Collections.unmodifiableList() returns a view of the specified list that disallows modification operations and throws UnsupportedOperationException if any are attempted.

2. b

   Explanation: Collections.binarySearch() is used on a sorted list to efficiently locate an element using binary search.

3. c

   Explanation: Arrays.asList() treats primitive arrays as a single object. So passing a primitive array results in a list with one element: the entire array itself.

4. b

   Explanation: Arrays.fill() assigns the given value to each element of the specified array.

5. c

   Explanation: Checked collections provide a dynamically type-safe view of collections to catch type errors at runtime.

6. c

   Explanation: list.toArray() converts the list into an array of Object. A typed array can be obtained using list.toArray(new Type[0]).

7. b

   Explanation: Collections.synchronizedMap() wraps a map to make all its basic operations thread-safe by synchronizing internally.

8. d

   Explanation: Collections.reverse() reverses the order of elements in the given list in-place.

9. c

   Explanation: The Arrays.sort(array, fromIndex, toIndex) method sorts a specific sub-range of the array.

10. c

    Explanation: TreeSet maintains elements in a sorted order (according to their natural ordering or a provided comparator), making it ideal for sorted access.

CHAPTER 10
Best Practices with Generics and Collections

Introduction

As applications grow in complexity, writing clean, safe, and high-performance code becomes critical. Java generics and collections offer powerful tools, but they must be used thoughtfully. From ensuring type safety and preventing runtime errors to designing **application programming interfaces** (**APIs**) that are intuitive and robust, this chapter focuses on the best practices that make Java code maintainable and efficient.

Whether you are building libraries, frameworks, or business logic, knowing how to use generics correctly and leveraging the right collection types can significantly improve your code quality and performance.

Structure

This chapter covers the following topics:

- Writing type-safe code with generics
- Avoiding common pitfalls with generics
- Efficient use of collections
- Designing collections-based APIs
- Performance considerations

- Synchronization best practices
- Using generic algorithms

Objectives

By the end of this chapter, you will be able to apply generic types more safely and effectively, design collection-based APIs that are reusable and clean, select the appropriate data structures based on performance needs, and write thread-safe code using synchronization strategies. You will also learn to avoid subtle pitfalls that may lead to runtime issues or type-safety violations and to harness the power of generic algorithms in real-world Java programs.

Writing type-safe code with generics

Java generics enable developers to enforce compile-time type checks, minimize runtime **ClassCastException**, and write cleaner, more reusable code. In real-world development, however, using generics correctly goes beyond just parameterizing a collection. It is about knowing where to apply them, how to restrict them using bounds, and how to design generic classes or methods that behave consistently across types.

This section explores best practices that help you write robust, type-safe code using generics.

The following are the best practices for type-safe code:

- **Always declare type parameters explicitly**: Avoid using raw types like List or Map. Instead, specify the type to benefit from compile-time checks.

  For example, avoid declaring a list as follows.

  ```
  List list = new ArrayList();
  ```

  This creates a list that can hold *any* object, and mistakes like adding integers into a list of strings will not be caught. Instead, declare it as shown in the following:

  ```
  List<String> names = new ArrayList<>();
  ```

  Now the list can only store String values, and you will get errors if you try to add anything else.

- **Use generic methods for reusability:** Generic methods can work across different types and reduce duplication, as shown in the following:

  ```
  public <T> void printElements(List<T> elements) {
      for (T element : elements) {
          System.out.println(element);
      }
  }
  ```

This method can print a list of strings, integers, or any other type. T stands for *Type*.

- **Leverage bounded type parameters:** You can restrict what types your generic code accepts using bounds:
    - ○ **Upper bound (extends)**: When you want to accept any subtype, as shown in the following:

```
public double sum(List<? extends Number> numbers) {
    double total = 0;
    for (Number num : numbers) {
        total += num.doubleValue();
    }
    return total;
}
```

This method accepts lists of integers, doubles, etc., anything that extends the number.

    - ○ **Lower bound (super)**: When you want to add to the list safely, as shown in the following:

```
public void addIntegers(List<? super Integer> list) {
    list.add(1);
    list.add(2);
}
```

This method can add integers to a list that holds integer or number types.

- **Prefer type parameters over wildcards in your own methods**: If you are writing a method that both reads and writes, define a type parameter.

The following example is not ideal:

```
public void process(List<?> items) {
    // can't safely add items
}
```

Instead, prefer type parameters as shown in the following:

```
public <T> void process(List<T> items) {
    // can read and add items of type T
}
```

Wildcards (**?**) are restrictive, which means you cannot add to them. Use **<T>** if you want more flexibility.

- **Avoid mixing raw and generic types**: Do not mix old non-generic code with generic collections:

```
List rawList = new ArrayList<String>();

rawList.add(10); // No error, but wrong usage
```

The above example defeats the purpose of generics. Use **List<String>** instead.

- **Use @SuppressWarnings("unchecked") carefully:** Only use this when you are sure it is safe, like with legacy code:

```
@SuppressWarnings("unchecked")

List<String> names = (List<String>) getLegacyData();
```

Add a comment explaining why this is safe, and use it only in isolated places.

- **Avoid creating generic Arrays:** Java does not allow new **T[]** due to type erasure. Use **List<T>** instead.

This is invalid, as it would throw a compilation error:

```
T[] array = new T[10]; // Compilation error
```

Instead, use collections like **List<T>** instead of arrays when working with generics, as shown in the following:

```
List<T> list = new ArrayList<>();
```

Avoiding common pitfalls with generics

While generics provide type safety and cleaner code, developers can still fall into subtle traps that reduce their effectiveness or lead to confusing behaviour. In this section, we will explore some practical issues that arise when working with generics and how to avoid them. These examples build on the concepts discussed earlier and highlight less obvious misuses and limitations that developers may face in real-world codebases:

- **Avoid overloading generic methods:** Overloading generic methods with similar signatures can lead to ambiguity or unintended method selection. This is particularly risky when type erasure causes multiple overloads to have indistinguishable bytecode signatures.

Let us understand this with the following code:

```
public class Printer {
    public void print(String data) {
        System.out.println("String: " + data);
    }
    public <T> void print(T data) {
        System.out.println("Generic: " + data);
    }
    public static void main(String[] args) {
```

```
        Printer printer = new Printer();
        printer.print("Hello");
    }
}
```

Explanation: In the above example, although it looks like the generic method **print(T data)** could be chosen, the non-generic **print(String data)** is a better match and will be invoked. This can lead to inconsistent behavior, especially if the method is later overloaded for other types. Developers should avoid creating generic method overloads that can clash with specific ones unless necessary.

- **Avoid using generics with static context:** Generic type parameters are not tied to the class's static context. This means you cannot use the class's type parameter in a static method or static field.

Consider the following example:

```
public class Box<T> {
    private T value;

    // This will cause a compilation error
    // private static T staticValue;

    public static void show(T data) {
        // Compilation error
    }
}
```

Explanation: In the above example, since type parameters are tied to the instance level, static fields and methods do not have access to them. The solution is to make the static method itself generic, as shown in the following:

```
public static <T> void show(T data) {
    System.out.println(data);
}
```

- **Avoid improper use of bounded type parameters:** Incorrect placement or unnecessary complexity in bounded type parameters can make the generic code harder to understand and maintain. Consider the following example:

```
public <T extends Number & Comparable<T>> void process(T value) {}
```

Explanation: While this is valid, complex bounds can often be replaced with simpler alternatives if the use case does not truly require multiple bounds. Overusing bounds without a clear reason adds cognitive load to your code.

- **Avoid redundant use of wildcards in method parameters:** Using wildcards (**?** **extends** T or **?** **super** T) where simple type parameters would suffice will make the API harder to understand. Consider the following example:

```
public <T> void processList(List<? extends T> list) {
    // read-only access
}
```

Explanation: If T is not used elsewhere or if full access to the list is not needed, a simpler signature like void **processList(List<?>** **list)** might be preferable. Wildcards should be used only when needed for flexibility or to follow the **producer extends, consumer super** (**PECS**) rule.

- **Unchecked casts and compiler warnings:** Unchecked warnings are an indication that type safety may be compromised. Ignoring these or suppressing them without care can lead to **ClassCastException** at runtime.

For example:

```
List<String> list = (List<String>) getObject();
```

Explanation: In the above code, if **getObject()** returns a raw type or another generic type like **List<Object>**, the compiler issues a warning. Suppressing it using **@ SuppressWarnings("unchecked")** should be done only after confirming type safety.

- **Generics with varargs**: Using generic types with varargs parameters can cause heap pollution and result in warnings.

Heap pollution happens when a variable of a parameterized type (like **List<String>**) refers to an object that is not actually of that type at runtime.

This usually occurs when you:

- o Mix raw types with generics
- o Use unchecked casts
- o Misuse varargs with generics

Consider the following example:

```
List<String> strings = new ArrayList<>();
List rawList = strings; // raw type
rawList.add(42); // adding Integer into List<String>
String s = strings.get(0); // ClassCastException here
```

Here, the compiler thought strings only held String objects, but due to heap pollution, an Integer slipped in, leading to runtime errors.

With generics and varargs, heap pollution is more likely because varargs arrays are created at runtime, and generics use type erasure; the array might store elements of the wrong type without compile-time safety.

To avoid this, the **@SafeVarargs** annotation can be used as shown below.

```
@SafeVarargs
public static <T> void addAll(List<T> list, T... elements) {
    for (T element : elements) {
        list.add(element);
    }
}
```

The **@SafeVarargs** annotation suppresses warnings and should only be used when the method does not modify or expose the varargs array in a way that could break type safety.

Additionally, **@SafeVarargs** can only be applied to final or static methods or constructors to ensure that the method cannot be overridden and introduce unsafe behavior.

- **Misusing generic exceptions:** Generic classes cannot be directly used to define custom exception types in a way that includes the generic type in the catch clause.

  Consider the following example:

```
public class CustomException<T> extends Exception {
    // This is valid as a declaration
}
// But this is invalid:
// catch (CustomException<String> e) { }
```

Java does not support generic exception catching because the runtime does not retain generic type information. Custom exceptions can still be generic in design, but their type information will not be usable in catch blocks.

Efficient use of collections

Java's Collection Framework provides powerful and flexible tools for managing groups of objects, but using them efficiently requires understanding their performance characteristics and choosing the right data structure for the problem at hand. This section provides actionable guidelines and examples to help you make better choices when working with collections.

Different collection types are optimized for different operations. Using the wrong type can degrade performance or make your code harder to read and maintain.

Let us consider a practical example:

```
List<String> cities = new ArrayList<>();
cities.add("Mumbai");
```

```
cities.add("Delhi");
cities.add("Bengaluru");
System.out.println(cities.get(1)); // Fast access to index 1
```

Just like in the above example, if your use case needs frequent access by index and minimal insertions or removals from the middle, **ArrayList** is the optimal choice.

Consider the following example:

- **Avoid unnecessary resizing:** When using resizable collections like **ArrayList** or HashMap, frequent resizing can be expensive. If you know the expected size, initialize the Collection with an appropriate capacity.

  In the following example, the **ArrayList** and **HashMap** are initialized with a size:

  ```
  List<String> names = new ArrayList<>(100); // Avoids internal resizing
  Map<String, Integer> marks = new HashMap<>(50);
  ```

  Specifying initial capacity minimizes the number of internal array resizings, which can significantly improve performance in large loops or data-heavy operations.

- **Use Streams and enhanced for-loops for readability:** Avoid using traditional for-loops when the index is not needed. This leads to cleaner and safer code. Use enhanced for-loops or Streams as shown in the following:

  ```
  List<String> fruits = Arrays.asList("Mango", "Apple", "Banana");
  //Traditional for-loop
  for (int i=0; i<fruits.size(); i++) {
      System.out.println(fruits.get(i));
  }
  // Enhanced for-loop
  for (String fruit : fruits) {
      System.out.println(fruit);
  }
  // Using Stream API
  fruits.forEach(System.out::println);
  ```

In the above examples, the enhanced for-loop and stream API methods reduce boilerplate code and reduce the chances of errors like **IndexOutOfBoundsException**.

Designing collections-based APIs

When designing applications that expose or consume collections, developers must consider flexibility, usability, maintainability, and safety. A well-designed Collections-based API can make code more intuitive and reduce bugs:

- Always use collection interfaces (List, Set, Map) in method signatures instead of implementation classes (ArrayList, HashSet, etc.). This makes the method flexible and allows callers to pass in any list implementation, such as ArrayList or LinkedList, without breaking compatibility.

- Avoid returning null from a method that returns a collection. Instead, return an empty collection using utility methods as shown in the following:

```
public List<String> getStudents() {
    return Collections.emptyList(); // Safe
}
```

This prevents the calling code from having to perform null checks and reduces the chances of **NullPointerException**

- To avoid accidental or unauthorized modification of internal data, return unmodifiable views or immutable collections. This can be done as shown in the following:

```
private List<String> courses = new ArrayList<>();
public List<String> getCourses() {
    return Collections.unmodifiableList(courses);
}
```

This encapsulates your data and ensures that external code cannot alter internal state unexpectedly.

- If your method expects a small number of fixed elements, use varargs for better readability and convenience, as shown in the following:

```
public void addSubjects(String... subjects) {
    for (String s : subjects) {
        System.out.println("Subject: " + s);
    }
}
```

This allows the caller to pass multiple values in a clean and simple way without explicitly creating a list.

- When returning collections, use more specific interfaces like Set or Queue if the order or uniqueness matters. This can be done as shown in the following:

```
public Set<String> getUniqueCities() {
    return new HashSet<>(Arrays.asList("Delhi", "Mumbai", "Pure"));
}
```

This helps communicate the behavior and expectations clearly to the caller and improves API clarity.

- Accept broader types like collection, iterable, or even stream when you do not need specific operations. Use broader types as shown in the following:

```
public void printAll(Collection<String> items) {
    items.forEach(System.out::println);
}
```

This gives the calling method the flexibility to use any collection without being forced into conversions.

- If you need to enhance or customize a collection, wrap it using composition rather than extending from collection classes, as shown in the following:

```
public class LoggedList<E> {
    private final List<E> list;

    public LoggedList(List<E> list) {
        this.list = list;
    }

    public void add(E element) {
        System.out.println("Adding: " + element);
        list.add(element);
    }
}
```

This avoids the fragility of inheritance and gives more control over behaviour.

Performance considerations

Choosing the right collection implementation is critical for writing efficient code. Each collection has different time and space complexities for basic operations like insertion, deletion, and access. Poor choices can lead to performance bottlenecks, especially in large-scale applications.

Choose the right collection for the task as mentioned in *Table 10.1*. The table is a list of recommended collections based on the use case:

Use case	Recommended collection	Reason
Fast access by index	ArrayList	Backed by array; $O(1)$ access
Frequent insertions or deletions	LinkedList	Efficient add/remove from ends
Unique elements without order	HashSet	Uses a HashMap internally

Unique elements with insertion order	LinkedHashSet	Maintains insertion order
Sorted elements	TreeSet	Elements stored in natural or specified order
Fast key-based lookup	HashMap	O(1) average time for get() and put()
Ordered key-value pairs	LinkedHashMap	Maintains insertion order
Sorted key-value pairs	TreeMap	Maintains natural ordering or custom comparator

Table 10.1: Collection recommendation based on use case

Here are some practical tips to keep in mind:

- Avoid using LinkedList if you need frequent random access. Its get(index) operation is O(n) compared to O(1) in ArrayList.

- Pre-size ArrayList or HashMap if the expected number of elements is known. This reduces costly resizing or rehashing operations.

- Minimize boxing and unboxing of primitive values. Collections like **List<Integer>** store wrapper objects, which use more memory and affect performance. Consider primitive-specific libraries like Trove or fastutil for large datasets.

- Use the enhanced for-each loop for read-only traversal. It is more concise and easier to read.

- Be careful with streams in performance-sensitive code. While they improve readability, they may introduce slight overhead compared to loops:

```
// Use with care in tight loops
students.stream().filter(name -> name.startsWith("A")).toList();
```

- Use maps to cache expensive or repeated computations as shown in the following:

```
Map<String, Integer> factorialCache = new HashMap<>();
int getFactorial(int n) {
    return factorialCache.computeIfAbsent(String.valueOf(n), k ->
computeFactorial(n));
}
```

- Prefer ArrayDeque over Stack and LinkedList for stack or queue operations. It is more efficient and faster for such use cases.

- Remove unused or large temporary collections after use by calling **.clear()** or allowing them to go out of scope for garbage collection.

- Avoid using synchronized collection wrappers (`Collections.synchronizedList`) unless necessary. They add overhead; consider `ConcurrentHashMap` or `CopyOnWriteArrayList` when working with multi-threading.

Synchronization best practices

In multi-threaded applications, using Collections without proper synchronization can lead to data corruption or unpredictable behaviour. The JCF offers multiple ways to safely handle concurrency. However, blindly synchronizing Collections can degrade performance or lead to deadlocks if not done properly. Here are the key best practices to follow when working with synchronized or concurrent collections:

- Prefer concurrent collections over synchronized wrappers. Use classes like `ConcurrentHashMap`, `CopyOnWriteArrayList`, and `ConcurrentLinkedQueue` instead of synchronizing standard collections using `Collections.synchronizedXXX()`.

- Avoid external synchronization on concurrent Collections. Do not use synchronized blocks around operations on concurrent Collections like `ConcurrentHashMap`. These are already designed for thread-safe access, and adding extra synchronization can reduce performance.

- Use synchronized wrappers only for legacy code or single-threaded scenarios needing minimal concurrency. For example, `Collections.synchronizedList()` wraps a list with a thread-safe proxy. However, you must still synchronize during iteration as shown as follows:

```
List<String> syncList = Collections.synchronizedList(new ArrayList<>());
synchronized (syncList) {
    for (String name : syncList) {
        System.out.println(name);
    }
}
```

- Use atomic compound actions carefully. Even with synchronized or concurrent Collections, compound actions like *check-then-act* need additional synchronization. For example, the following code could cause a race condition:

```
// Unsafe even with ConcurrentHashMap
if (!map.containsKey(key)) {
    map.put(key, value); // Race condition possible
}
```

Instead, use atomic methods as shown in the following:

```
map.putIfAbsent(key, value);
```

- Understand the **CopyOnWrite** Collections trade-offs. **CopyOnWriteArrayList** and **CopyOnWriteArraySet** are safe for iteration without locks, but they copy the entire array on every modification, which can be expensive. Use them only when read operations vastly outnumber writes.

- Avoid unnecessary synchronization on unshared data. If a Collection is used by a single thread (or each thread has its own copy), there is no need for synchronization.

- Leverage **ConcurrentSkipListMap** and **ConcurrentSkipListSet** for sorted concurrent access. These provide thread-safe, sorted maps and sets without the overhead of synchronization blocks.

- Do not expose internal Collections directly. Always return an unmodifiable or defensive copy to avoid external threads from modifying internal structures.

- Use thread-safe blocking Collections for producer-consumer scenarios. Classes like **LinkedBlockingQueue**, **ArrayBlockingQueue**, and **PriorityBlockingQueue** are ideal when threads need to wait for data.

- Avoid holding locks for a long time. If synchronizing on a block, keep the critical section as small as possible to reduce contention and the risk of deadlocks.

Using generic algorithms

Java encourages reusability and type safety with Generic algorithms, methods written using Generics that can operate on various data types.

In *Chapter 9, Utility Classes*, we already explored built-in generic algorithms provided by the Collections class, such as **sort()**, **binarySearch()**, and **shuffle()**. These methods demonstrate how generics allow us to write flexible, reusable code without compromising on type safety.

Custom generic algorithms allow you to create reusable logic that works with different types.

Let us walk through an example that is both practical and generic. Imagine you want to count how many times a particular element appears in a collection, be it a list of names, numbers, or even custom objects.

We will define a method called **countOccurrences** that works for any type of data, as shown in the following:

```
public class GenericAlgorithms {
    public static <T> int countOccurrences(Collection<T> collection, T target) {
        int count = 0;
        for (T item : collection) {
            if (item.equals(target)) {
```

```
                count++;
            }
        }
        return count;
    }
}
```

In the above example, the **countOccurrences()** method takes a Collection of any type T (like String, Integer, Employee, etc.). It compares each element with the target and returns how many times the target appears.

The method can be used as shown in the following:

```
List<String> names = Arrays.asList("Liam", "Olivia", "Liam", "Ethan");int
result = GenericAlgorithms.countOccurrences(names, "Liam");  // returns 2
```

This single method works for:

- Counting scores, **countOccurrences(Arrays.asList(85, 90, 85), 85)**

- Counting custom objects (if **equals()** is properly overridden)

- Any other collection type like Set, Queue, etc.

This shows the following:

- You can write the logic once and reuse it across types.

- We do not need type casting or overloading for each type.

- Clear APIs help in building generic utility libraries for teams and projects.

Conclusion

Writing clean, reusable, and efficient code is one of the core goals of Java's generics and Collections Framework. Throughout this chapter, we explored how to write type-safe code using generics, avoid common pitfalls, and make the best use of collection classes by understanding their behaviors, performance characteristics, and synchronization concerns.

We also discussed how to design API methods using generics to improve reusability and readability, and how to approach thread safety using wrappers and concurrent collections. Additionally, we saw how utility methods and custom generic algorithms enable us to write cleaner and more adaptable code across a wide range of applications.

By combining generics with collections wisely, you can build robust and maintainable Java applications. As you move forward, continue to experiment with creating your own generic utility methods and understand the performance trade-offs between different collection types.

In the next chapter, we will bring all this knowledge together in real-world applications.

Exercise

1. **Which of these declarations is type-safe and valid?**

   a. List<Object> list = new ArrayList<Object>();

   b. List<String> list = new ArrayList<String>();

   c. List list = new ArrayList();

   d. List<int> list = new ArrayList<int>();

2. **What will happen if you try to add an Integer to a List<String>?**

   a. Compile-time error

   b. Runtime error

   c. Auto conversion

   d. None

3. **Which Generic wildcard allows read-only access to elements?**

   a. <? super T>

   b. <?>

   c. <? extends T>

   d. <T>

4. **Why should raw types be avoided in Generic code?**

   a. They are faster

   b. They improve performance

   c. They bypass compile-time checks

   d. They support more types

5. **What is the advantage of using Collections.unmodifiableList()?**

   a. Improves performance

   b. Prevents modification

   c. Increases capacity

   d. Supports parallelism

6. **Which method returns a synchronized version of a given Set?**

   a. Collections.unmodifiableSet()

   b. Collections.checkedSet()

   c. Collections.synchronizedSet()

   d. None of the above

7. **How can you enforce type safety at runtime in a Collection?**

   a. Use of raw types

   b. Using checked collections

   c. Casting at runtime

   d. Using reflection

8. **What is the time complexity of accessing an element in an ArrayList?**

   a. O(log n)

   b. O(1)

   c. O(n)

   d. O(n log n)

9. **Which of these Collections allows duplicate elements?**

   a. HashSet

   b. LinkedHashSet

   c. TreeSet

   d. ArrayList

10. **What does <? super T> allow in a Generic method?**

    a. Accepts only T

    b. Accepts any type

    c. Accepts T and its superclasses

    d. Restricts to subclasses only

Answers

1. b

   Explanation: Java generics require the type parameter to be an object type, and b is type-safe.

2. a

   Explanation: You cannot add an Integer to List<String>; it will result in a compile-time error.

3. c

   Explanation: <? extends T> allows read-only access and is used for covariance.

4. c

   Explanation: Raw types skip compile-time checks, making code unsafe and error-prone.

5. b

    Explanation: Unmodifiable lists prevent changes to the Collection after creation.

6. c

    Explanation: Collections.synchronizedSet() provides a thread-safe version of the Set.

7. b

    Explanation: Checked collections throw ClassCastException at runtime if incorrect types are used.

8. b

    Explanation: ArrayList provides constant-time access to elements via index.

9. d

    Explanation: ArrayList allows duplicates, unlike Set implementations.

10. c

    Explanation: <? super T> accepts T and its superclasses, used for contravariant arguments.

Join our Discord space

Join our Discord workspace for latest updates, offers, tech happenings around the world, new releases, and sessions with the authors:

https://discord.bpbonline.com

CHAPTER 11
Real-world Applications

Introduction

Until now, we have explored Java collections and generics from a conceptual and technical standpoint, like how they work, how they are structured, and how they are best used. However, in the real world, you will rarely use these features in isolation. They are often part of larger designs that solve practical, everyday problems in software systems.

This chapter focuses on how generics and collections are applied in real-world Java applications, from handling user sessions to building scalable APIs, from solving concurrency issues to implementing caching and custom data workflows. You will learn how experienced developers use these features to create solutions that are both clean and production-ready.

Structure

This chapter covers the following areas:

- Case studies
- Practical examples
- Common usage patterns
- Solving typical problems
- Best practices in real-world scenarios

Objectives

By the end of this chapter, you will be able to understand how Java collections and generics fit into actual software solutions. You will learn to recognize typical usage patterns, apply collections to common design problems, and follow best practices that improve maintainability, performance, and clarity of your code. Whether it is designing **Representational State Transfer (REST)** APIs, working with large datasets, or managing thread-safe operations, this chapter will equip you with examples and insights that bridge the gap between theory and practice.

Case studies

Case study 1: Managing user sessions in a web application:

- **Problem statement**: Imagine a Java-based web application that allows users to log in and perform tasks based on their roles (admin, editor, viewer). Each user session must be uniquely tracked to ensure:
  - Fast lookup by session ID
  - Prevention of duplicate logins
  - Cleanup of expired sessions based on login time
  - Secure handling of session data with read-only exposure

  The system must scale well as the number of active users grows.

- **Design decision:** Before designing the session manager, it is important to consider why certain data structures and type systems were selected. In large-scale applications, managing state like user sessions requires precision, performance, and clarity. Collections offer fast access and efficient storage, while generics ensure type safety and reusability.

  This combination makes collections and generics ideal for managing session data, where quick lookups, controlled exposure, and maintainable code are crucial.

  Here are the core design factors:
  - **Fast key-based lookup** was essential for retrieving session information quickly using session IDs. A Map implementation was the natural fit.
  - **Insertion order preservation** was needed to track the oldest sessions first for cleanup. Hence, LinkedHashMap was chosen over HashMap.
  - **Type safety** was important to ensure that only valid session data objects were stored and retrieved, which is generics enforced through compile-time checks.
  - **Immutable access to session lists** was required when exposing session data externally. This was achieved using `Collections.unmodifiableList()`.

o   **Maintainability and readability** improved significantly by encapsulating the session logic and using generic collection interfaces.

These choices ensured that the system was both performant and easy to reason about, while also guarding against common runtime errors.

*   **Implementation**: Let us understand the implementation. We first define a class to hold the session-related information, as shown in the following:

```java
public class SessionInfo {
    private final String userId;
    private final String ipAddress;
    private final long loginTime; // epoch time in ms
    private final String role;

    public SessionInfo(String userId, String ipAddress, long loginTime,
String role) {
        this.userId = userId;
        this.ipAddress = ipAddress;
        this.loginTime = loginTime;
        this.role = role;
    }

    // Getters
    public String getUserId() { return userId; }
    public String getIpAddress() { return ipAddress; }
    public long getLoginTime() { return loginTime; }
    public String getRole() { return role; }
}
```

In the above **SessionInfo** class:

o   **userId**: Identifies the user (e.g., *user123*)

o   **ipAddress**: Tracks the user's device or location (e.g., *192.168.1.2*)

o   **loginTime**: Stores when the session started, in epoch milliseconds

o   **role**: Defines what permissions the user has (e.g., *admin*)

We use final to ensure immutability, so that once a session is created, its details cannot be modified.

Now, let us define the **SessionManager** class. This class uses a collection to manage all active sessions, as shown in the following:

```java
import java.util.ArrayList;
import java.util.Collections;
import java.util.Iterator;
import java.util.LinkedHashMap;
```

```java
import java.util.List;
import java.util.Map;

public class SessionManager {

    private final Map<String, SessionInfo> sessionMap = new
LinkedHashMap<>();
    private static final long SESSION_TIMEOUT = 30 * 60 * 1000; // 30 minutes

    // Creates or replaces a session for a user
    public void createSession(String sessionId, SessionInfo info) {
        sessionMap.put(sessionId, info);
    }

    // Retrieve session by session ID
    public SessionInfo getSession(String sessionId) {
        return sessionMap.get(sessionId);
    }

    // Manually remove a session
    public void removeSession(String sessionId) {
        sessionMap.remove(sessionId);
    }

    // Get read-only view of all sessions
    public List<SessionInfo> getAllActiveSessions() {
        return Collections.unmodifiableList(new ArrayList<>(sessionMap.
values()));
    }

    // Cleanup expired sessions
    public void cleanupExpiredSessions() {
        long now = System.currentTimeMillis();
        Iterator<Map.Entry<String, SessionInfo>> iterator = sessionMap.
entrySet().iterator();

        while (iterator.hasNext()) {
            Map.Entry<String, SessionInfo> entry = iterator.next();
            if (now - entry.getValue().getLoginTime() > SESSION_TIMEOUT)
{
                iterator.remove(); // safe way to remove while iterating
            }
```

```
        }
    }
}
```

In the above example:

o   A Map lets us store session IDs (as String) mapped to **SessionInfo** objects.

o   We use **LinkedHashMap** instead of HashMap because it preserves the order in which sessions were added. This helps later when we clean up old sessions.

o   **createSession** adds a new session to the map using a unique session ID. If a session already exists with the same ID, it is replaced (which also allows for re-login logic).

o   **getSession** method looks up the **SessionInfo** object using the session ID key. If no such session exists, it returns null.

o   **removeSession** allows manual removal of a session, such as during logout or security invalidation.

o   The **getAllActiveSessions** method exposes the list of all active sessions, but:

  ▪ We convert the Map values (which are **SessionInfo** objects) into a list.

  ▪ We then wrap it in **Collections.unmodifiableList()** to prevent external code from modifying the internal session data.

o   **cleanUpExpiredSession** is one of the most important features:

  ▪ **SESSION_TIMEOUT** defines the allowed session duration (30 minutes).

  ▪ We iterate through all sessions using an Iterator, so we can safely remove entries without throwing a **ConcurrentModificationException**.

  ▪ We calculate the time since each session started, and if it is more than 30 minutes, we remove it from the map.

The following is an example of using the **SessionManager**:

```
public class TestSessionManager {
    public static void main(String[] args) throws InterruptedException {
        SessionManager manager = new SessionManager();
        manager.
createSession("sess1", new SessionInfo("user123", "192.168.1.1", System.
currentTimeMillis(), "admin"));
        manager.
createSession("sess2", new SessionInfo("user456", "192.168.1.2", System.
currentTimeMillis(), "editor"));
        // Simulate session list
        for (SessionInfo session : manager.getAllActiveSessions()) {
```

```
                System.out.println(session.getUserId() + " - " +
    session.getRole());
        }
        // After 30 minutes, run cleanup (simulate with sleep for
    testing)
        Thread.sleep(1000); // Just for demonstration
        manager.cleanupExpiredSessions();
    }
}
```

Here is what the system does as a whole:

- o Creates a new session when a user logs in
- o Allows lookup, removal, and listing of sessions
- o Cleans up old sessions efficiently based on time
- o Uses generics (**Map<String, SessionInfo>**) to ensure type safety
- o Uses Collections like **LinkedHashMap**, **ArrayList**, and **Collections. unmodifiableList()** to manage state cleanly and securely

This case study demonstrated how Java collections and generics can be used effectively to manage user sessions in a web application. The combination of **LinkedHashMap** for ordered access, generics for type safety, and unmodifiable wrappers for secure exposure resulted in a solution that is clean, maintainable, and performance-aware.

By encapsulating the logic into a dedicated **SessionManager** class and using appropriate data structures, we ensured that the design remains extensible for real-world use cases like session expiration, concurrent access, or role-based filtering. This pattern can be adapted to any Java-based backend system that requires session tracking or similar stateful behavior.

Case study 2: Role-based access control using Sets and Maps:

- **Problem statement:** In an enterprise-grade application, access control must be enforced at multiple levels. Each user is assigned one or more roles, and each role grants access to a set of actions (or permissions). The system must efficiently:
  - o Assign and retrieve roles for users
  - o Define which actions are allowed for each role
  - o Verify whether a user is allowed to perform a specific action
  - o Avoid duplication and ensure fast lookups

- **Design decision**: Access control naturally maps to collections:
  - o A **Set** is used to maintain unique roles per user and unique permissions per role
  - o A **Map** allows quick retrieval of permissions for a given role or roles for a user

o   Generics ensure that mappings like **Map<String, Set<String>>** are strictly type-safe, reducing runtime errors and improving readability

These structures enable scalable, performant, and secure access management logic.

- **Implementation**: Let us build a simple **role-based access control (RBAC)** system where:
    o   Users can have multiple roles
    o   Each role maps to a set of allowed actions
    o   We can check whether a user is allowed to perform a given action

We start with the **RolePermissionRegistry** class, as shown in the following:

```
import java.util.Collections;
import java.util.HashMap;
import java.util.HashSet;
import java.util.Map;
import java.util.Set;
public class RolePermissionRegistry {
  private final Map<String, Set<String>> rolePermissions =
new HashMap<>();
    public void addPermissions(String role, Set<String> permissions) {
        rolePermissions.put(role, new HashSet<>(permissions));
    }
    public Set<String> getPermissions(String role) {
        return Collections.unmodifiableSet(
            rolePermissions.getOrDefault(role, Collections.emptySet())
        );
    }
  }
}
```

The above class holds mappings of roles to their allowed actions.

- o   **rolePermissions** maps each role (e.g., *admin*) to a set of actions (e.g., **{"CREATE", "DELETE"}**).
- o   We return an unmodifiable empty set if the role does not exist, to avoid null checks and modification issues.

To maintain the user-role mapping, we have the **UserAccessManager** class as shown in the following:

```
import java.util.HashMap;
import java.util.Map;
```

```java
import java.util.Set;
public class UserAccessManager {
    private final Map<String, Set<String>> userRoles = new HashMap<>();
    private final RolePermissionRegistry registry;
    public UserAccessManager(RolePermissionRegistry registry) {
        this.registry = registry;
    }
    public void assignRole(String userId, String role) {
        userRoles.computeIfAbsent(userId, k -> new HashSet<>()).add(role);
    }
    public Set<String> getUserRoles(String userId) {
        return Collections.unmodifiableSet(
            userRoles.getOrDefault(userId, Collections.emptySet())
        );
    }
    public boolean isActionAllowed(String userId, String action) {
        Set<String> roles = getUserRoles(userId);
        for (String role : roles) {
            if (registry.getPermissions(role).contains(action)) {
                return true;
            }
        }
        return false;
    }
}
```

In the above example:

o **userRoles** maps each user ID to a set of roles (e.g., **"user123"** | **["editor", "viewer"]**).

o **assignRole()** ensures we initialize the role set if it does not exist.

o **isActionAllowed()** loops through the user's roles and checks if any of them permit the given action.

o **computeIfAbsent** checks if **userId** is present; if not, it creates a new HashSet and associates it with the user before adding the role.

Now, let us test this as shown with the following **AccessManagerTest** class:

```java
import java.util.Set;
```

```
public class AccessControlTest {
    public static void main(String[] args) {
        RolePermissionRegistry registry = new RolePermissionRegistry();
        registry.addPermissions("admin", Set.
of("CREATE", "READ", "UPDATE", "DELETE"));
        registry.addPermissions("editor", Set.of("READ", "UPDATE"));
        registry.addPermissions("viewer", Set.of("READ"));
        UserAccessManager accessManager = new UserAccessManager (registry);
        accessManager.assignRole("Chloe", "viewer");
        accessManager.assignRole("Ray", "editor");
        accessManager.assignRole("Ann", "admin");
        System.out.println("Can Chloe DELETE? " + accessManager.
isActionAllowed("Chloe", "DELETE")); // false
        System.out.println("Can Ray UPDATE? " + accessManager.
isActionAllowed("Ray", "UPDATE"));     // true
        System.out.println("Can Ann CREATE? " + accessManager.
isActionAllowed("Ann", "CREATE")); // true
    }
}
```

In the above example,

- ○ We first populate a **RolePermissionRegistry** with allowed actions for each role.
- ○ Users are then assigned roles using **assignRole()**.
- ○ When **isActionAllowed()** is called, it checks each of the user's roles to see if the requested action is permitted.

This setup is clean, reusable, and scalable. Even in large applications with thousands of users and dozens of roles.

This case study highlighted how Java collections and generics can be effectively used to implement RBAC, a foundational security requirement in many applications. By modeling user-role and role-permission relationships using Map and Set, we were able to enforce access rules cleanly and efficiently.

The use of generics (**Map<String, Set<String>>**) ensured type safety and readability, while avoiding redundant data and enabling fast lookups. This design is both scalable and adaptable for real-world systems where access rights frequently evolve.

Case study 3: Processing product orders in an e-commerce system:

- • **Problem statement:** In an e-commerce platform, orders are received from multiple customers throughout the day. Each order consists of:

o   A unique order ID

o   Customer information

o   A list of items, each with product details and quantity

The system must process incoming orders efficiently by:

o   Storing and grouping them by customer ID

o   Keeping track of all items ordered per customer

o   Calculating total value per customer

o   Providing a read-only summary of orders when needed

The data volume can grow quickly, so the solution must be memory-efficient and safe from accidental modification.

- **Design decision:** To meet the above problem statement, we chose:

  o   A Map to group orders by customer ID

  o   A List to maintain ordered items per customer

  o   A custom class to represent each item in the order

  o   Generics to ensure type-safe handling of orders and avoid casting

  o   Unmodifiable views for reporting order summaries without exposing internal structures

These design choices allow structured storage, easy aggregation, and safe read access for reporting tools.

- **Implementation:** We will model a simplified order-processing module with the following components:

  o   **OrderItem** is a single item in an order

  o   **CustomerOrderManager** stores and groups orders per customer

  o   Utility methods to calculate totals and generate read-only summaries

The following is the **OrderItem** class, which represents a product within a customer's order:

```java
public class OrderItem {
    private final String productId;
    private final String productName;
    private final int quantity;
    private final double pricePerUnit;
    public OrderItem(String productId, String productName, int quantity,
double pricePerUnit) {
        this.productId = productId;
```

```
        this.productName = productName;
        this.quantity = quantity;
        this.pricePerUnit = pricePerUnit;
    }
    public double getTotalPrice() {
        return quantity * pricePerUnit;
    }
    // Getters
    public String getProductId() { return productId; }
    public String getProductName() { return productName; }
    public int getQuantity() { return quantity; }
    public double getPricePerUnit() { return pricePerUnit; }
}
```

In the above example:

  o **getTotalPrice()** calculates the cost for this item
  o The class is immutable, ensuring thread safety and data integrity

Next, we have the **CustomerOrderManager** class that handles the order storage and aggregation:

```
import java.util.ArrayList;
import java.util.Collections;
import java.util.HashMap;
import java.util.List;
import java.util.Map;
import java.util.Set;
public class CustomerOrderManager {
    private final Map<String, List<OrderItem>> customerOrders = new
HashMap<>();
    // Add an item to a customer's order
    public void addOrderItem(String customerId, OrderItem item) {
        customerOrders.computeIfAbsent(customerId, k -> new
ArrayList<>()).add(item);
    }
    // Get all order items for a customer
    public List<OrderItem> getOrderItems(String customerId) {
        return Collections.unmodifiableList(
            customerOrders.getOrDefault(customerId,
```

```
Collections.emptyList())
        );
    }
    // Calculate total order value for a customer
    public double getTotalValue(String customerId) {
        return customerOrders.getOrDefault(customerId,
Collections.emptyList())
                            .stream()
                            .mapToDouble(OrderItem::getTotalPrice)
                            .sum();
    }
    // Get all customers
    public Set<String> getAllCustomerIds() {
        return Collections.unmodifiableSet(customerOrders.keySet());
    }
}
```

In the above example:

o **computeIfAbsent** ensures initialization of a new list when the customer ID is encountered for the first time.

o **unmodifiableList** and **unmodifiableSet** provide safe access to internal data structures.

o The use of streams makes aggregation operations concise and efficient.

The order processing can be tested, as shown in the following:

```
public class OrderProcessingTest {
    public static void main(String[] args) {
        CustomerOrderManager manager = new CustomerOrderManager();
        manager.
addOrderItem("CUST001", new OrderItem("P1001", "Notebook", 2, 120.0));
        manager.
addOrderItem("CUST001", new OrderItem("P1002", "Pen", 5, 10.0));
        manager.
addOrderItem("CUST002", new OrderItem("P1003", "Backpack", 1, 750.0));
        for (String customerId : manager.getAllCustomerIds()) {
            System.out.println("Customer ID: " + customerId);
            System.out.println("Total Value: " + manager.
getTotalValue(customerId));
```

```
        for (OrderItem item : manager.getOrderItems(customerId)) {
            System.out.println("- " + item.
getProductName() + " x" + item.getQuantity());
        }
        System.out.println();
    }
  }
}
```

In the above example:

- o   We add multiple items for each customer using **addOrderItem()**.

- o   All items are grouped by customer ID internally using a Map.

- o   For reporting, we list customer IDs and show their total order value along with each item.

- o   **Collections.unmodifiableList()** ensures consumers cannot alter the order list from outside.

- o   The code can scale to thousands of customers and handle dynamic data reliably.

This case study demonstrated how Java collections and generics can be applied to build a structured, extensible order management system within an e-commerce application. By using a Map to group orders by customer and a List to maintain item sequences, the design naturally aligned with the business logic of processing and reporting customer purchases.

Type-safe constructs such as **Map<String, List<OrderItem>>** ensured that invalid data could not be inserted or retrieved, reducing the potential for bugs. The use of unmodifiable views helped protect internal data while still providing necessary insights for reporting modules or user interfaces.

Overall, the solution illustrates how thoughtfully applying collection types, backed by generic principles, results in code that is clean, scalable, and well-suited for real-world scenarios involving dynamic, structured data.

Practical examples

While case studies help illustrate large-scale applications of collections and generics, most development tasks involve smaller, focused operations. This section presents a set of real-world examples that demonstrate how to use Java collections and generics to solve common problems effectively. These examples are designed to be concise, self-contained, and directly applicable in day-to-day coding, from filtering and sorting to grouping and transforming data structures.

Each example includes a problem statement, Java code, and a short explanation to reinforce both understanding and best practices:

- **Example 11.1:** Filtering items from a list using streams:
  - ○ **Problem**: You have a list of strings representing product names. You want to filter out any product that is out of stock (marked with **(Out of Stock)**) and return a clean list.

    The following is a sample solution for the above problem:

    ```
    List<String> products = List.of(
            "Notebook",
            "Pen",
            "Pencil (Out of Stock)",
            "Marker",
            "Eraser (Out of Stock)"
        );
    List<String> availableProducts = products.stream()
            .filter(p -> !p.contains("(Out of Stock)"))
            .collect(Collectors.toList());
    System.out.println(availableProducts); // [Notebook, Pen, Marker]
    ```

    In the above example:

    - We use a Stream to process the list and apply a **filter** condition.
    - Only products that do not contain **(Out of Stock)** are collected into a new list.
    - The original list remains unchanged due to immutability (**List.of(...)**).

- **Example 11.2**: Grouping elements using **Collectors.groupingBy()**:
  - ○ **Problem:** You want to group employees by their department.

    This can be solved as shown in the following:

    ```
    record Employee(String name, String department) {}
    List<Employee> employees = List.of(
        new Employee("Alex", "HR"),
        new Employee("Rocky", "Engineering"),
        new Employee("Mike", "HR"),
        new Employee("Aron", "Engineering")
    );
    Map<String, List<Employee>> groupedByDept = employees.stream()
        .collect(Collectors.groupingBy(Employee::department));
    System.out.println(groupedByDept);
    ```

In the above example:

- **Collectors.groupingBy()** is used to create a Map where the key is the department name and the value is a list of employees in that department.
- The use of a record (Employee) makes the code more concise and readable.
- This is commonly used in reporting, dashboards, and analytics features.

- **Example 11.3**: Sorting a list of custom objects

  o **Problem:** You have a list of students with names and marks. You want to sort them in descending order of marks.

  This can be solved as shown in the following:

```java
class Student {
    String name;
    int marks;

    public Student(String name, int marks) {
        this.name = name;
        this.marks = marks;
    }

    public String toString() {
        return name + " (" + marks + ")";
    }
}
```

  We define a simple student class as shown, and then we create a list of students and sort them based on their marks:

```java
List<Student> students = new ArrayList<>();
    students.add(new Student("Michael", 88));
    students.add(new Student("Ariel", 95));
    students.add(new Student("Rox", 76));
    students.sort((s1, s2) -> Integer.compare(s2.marks, s1.marks));
    System.out.println(students);
```

  In the example:

  - The list is sorted using a custom comparator that compares marks in descending order.
  - Sorting custom objects using **Collections.sort()** or **List.sort()** is a frequent real-world task.

- **Example 11.4**: Creating a frequency map:
  - o **Problem:** Given a list of product IDs, count how many times each product was sold.

    The following is the code to solve this problem:
    ```
    List<String> productIds = List.
    of("P1", "P2", "P1", "P3", "P2", "P1");
    Map<String, Long> frequencyMap = productIds.stream()
      .collect(Collectors.groupingBy(
      id -> id,
      Collectors.counting()
        ));
    System.out.println(frequencyMap); // {P1=3, P2=2, P3=1}
    ```

    In the above example:

    - **groupingBy** with counting counts occurrences of each element.

    - The result is a Map where keys are product IDs and values are their frequencies.

    - Useful in generating summaries, logs, or dashboards.

- **Example 11.5**: Flattening nested collections with **flatMap()**:
  - o **Problem:** Given a list of students where each student has enrolled in multiple courses, retrieve a flat list of all unique courses taken by all students.

    The following is the code to solve this problem:
    ```
    List<Student> students = List.of(new Student("Aaron", List.
    of("Math", "Physics")),new Student("Rita", List.
    of("Biology", "Chemistry")), new Student("Kaleb", List.
    of("Math", "Biology")));
    List<String> allCourses = students.stream().
    flatMap(student -> student.getCourses().stream()).distinct().
    collect(Collectors.toList());
    System.out.
    println(allCourses); // [Math, Physics, Biology, Chemistry]
    ```

    In the above example:
    - **flatMap** is used to convert multiple course lists into a single stream.
    - **distinct** ensures duplicate course names are removed.
    - The result is a flat list of unique courses across all students.
    - Useful in scenarios like generating curriculum summaries, reports, or analytics dashboards.

Common usage patterns

In enterprise and real-world Java applications, certain patterns of using collections and generics repeatedly emerge. These patterns are not design patterns in the classical sense, but rather recurring idioms or strategies that help solve common problems efficiently and elegantly.

Understanding these usage patterns improves not only your code clarity and performance but also your ability to read and work with other developers' code in a consistent way.

Here are some commonly seen patterns:

- **Factory method for returning unmodifiable lists:**
  - Used when you want to expose a list without allowing modification.
  - For example, `return Collections.unmodifiableList(list);`
  - Prevents callers from altering internal state while safely sharing data.
- **Using Map<K, List<V>> or Map<K, Set<V>> for grouping:**
  - A frequent pattern in organizing entities, like orders by customer or students by class.
  - Promotes organized access and easy aggregation using Java 8 plus streams.
- **Custom comparator via Lambda expressions:**
  - For example, `list.sort((a, b) | Integer.compare(b.getScore(), a.getScore()));`
  - Used for sorting custom objects, such as by age, salary, or date.
  - Keeps sort logic close to usage for one-off or dynamic sorts.
- **Safe defaults using Collections.emptyList() and friends:**
  - Avoids null checks and ensures consistent return types from methods.
  - For example, `return map.getOrDefault(key, Collections.emptyList());`
- **Using computeIfAbsent() to initialize collections in Maps:**
  - Removes boilerplate for checking null before initializing lists or sets.
    For example:
    ```
    map.computeIfAbsent(key, k -> new ArrayList<>()).add(value);
    ```
  - Used in data aggregation, grouping, or building indexes dynamically.
- **Chaining stream operations with collectors:**
  - Combines filtering, mapping, and collecting into one pipeline.
  - For example:
    ```
    List<String> results = list.stream()
        .filter(p -> p.startsWith("A"))
    ```

```
.map(String::toUpperCase)
.collect(Collectors.toList());
```

- o Highly expressive and concise for transforming data.
- **Generics with bounded types:**
  - o Used when writing reusable utility methods.
  - o For example, `<T extends Comparable<T>> T max(List<T> list)`
  - o Ensures that only compatible types are used without sacrificing flexibility.

Solving typical problems

In everyday software development, developers frequently encounter common issues such as data consistency, thread safety, and performance tuning. Java generics and the Collections Framework provide robust solutions to many of these challenges:

- **Ensuring type safety**: Generics allow developers to define the expected type for collections, catching errors during compilation rather than at runtime.

- **Simplifying data transformation**: With the help of Streams and functional interfaces, developers can transform and filter data easily using concise expressions.

- **Providing safe concurrency**: Thread-safe collections like `ConcurrentHashMap` and utilities like `Collections.synchronizedList()` help manage concurrent access to shared data structures.

- **Reducing boilerplate code:** Generics allow the creation of reusable data processing algorithms that work across types, cutting down repetitive logic.

- **Preventing NullPointerExceptions**: Use of empty or unmodifiable collections (like `Collections.emptyList()`) helps avoid returning null and ensures safer API contracts.

- **Handling large datasets**: Using data structures like `ArrayDeque` for queues or `TreeSet` for ordered access allows handling large volumes with optimized memory and access speed.

Best practices in real-world scenarios

When working with collections and generics in large-scale or production-level applications, the difference between average and excellent code often lies in the application of best practices. These practices help you write safer, cleaner, more maintainable, and more performant Java code.

The following are key best practices that are widely recommended and proven effective in real-world software systems:

- **Prefer interfaces over implementations**: Always declare variables and return types using interfaces (List, Set, Map) rather than implementations (ArrayList, HashSet,

HashMap). This improves flexibility and allows switching implementations with minimal impact.

For example:

```
List<String> names = new ArrayList<>();
```

- **Initialize collections with appropriate capacity**: If you know the size in advance, provide initial capacity (e.g., in ArrayList or HashMap) to avoid costly resizing.

    For example:

```
Map<String, String> cache = new HashMap<>(1000); // Reduces rehashing
```

- **Avoid raw types:** Always use generics instead of raw types to maintain type safety and prevent ClassCastException.

    For example:

```
List<String> list = new ArrayList<>();
List rawList = new ArrayList();
```

- **Return empty collections instead of null**: Returning null forces clients to perform null checks. Returning **Collections.emptyList()** or **emptyMap()** avoids errors and simplifies code.

- **Use unmodifiable wrappers when exposing collections:** Prevent callers from accidentally (or intentionally) modifying internal state.

    For example:

```
return Collections.unmodifiableList(orderHistory);
```

- **Use Comparator.comparing() for readable sorting**: Modern Java allows writing expressive sort logic.

    For example:

```
products.sort(Comparator.comparing(Product::getPrice).reversed());
```

- **Minimize mutability:** Use immutable data structures or defensive copies when dealing with shared or sensitive data.

- **Avoid unnecessary boxing in generics:** Use primitive-specialized alternatives (**IntStream, Map<Integer, String>**, etc.) when possible to avoid performance overhead.

- **Use computeIfAbsent() or merge() for aggregations:** These methods eliminate verbose if-else checks when populating or updating maps.

Conclusion

In this chapter, we explored how Java collections and generics go beyond theoretical constructs and become vital tools in building practical, real-world software. Through case studies, common usage patterns, and real-world problem-solving strategies, we saw how to organize, process, and protect data in scalable ways.

Collections provide a structured way to manage groups of data, while generics ensure type safety, reusability, and reduced runtime errors. Whether you are designing an order processing system, implementing RBAC, or analyzing product data, mastering these APIs leads to more robust and maintainable code.

In the next and final chapter, we will explore emerging trends, enhancements in recent Java versions, and the future direction of collections and generics.

Exercise

1. **What collection type should you use to store items in insertion order and avoid duplicates?**

    a. HashSet

    b. TreeSet

    c. LinkedHashSet

    d. ArrayList

2. **Which method returns an unmodifiable version of a list?**

    a. List.unmodifiable()

    b. Collections.freeze()

    c. Collections.unmodifiableList()

    d. List.readOnly()

3. **Which of these is a valid way to count how many times an item appears in a list using streams?**

    a. filter().grouping()

    b. collect(Collectors.counting())

    c. collect(Collectors.groupingBy(..., counting()))

    d. stream().sum()

4. **What does computeIfAbsent() do in a Map?**

    a. Checks if the map contains a value

    b. Inserts a default value if the key is missing

    c. Removes the entry if absent

    d. Merges two maps

5. **Which of the following can be used to create an empty, unmodifiable list?**
    a. new ArrayList<>()
    b. Collections.emptyList()
    c. List.of(null)
    d. Optional.empty()

6. **What is the purpose of generics in Java collections?**
    a. Faster compilation
    b. Memory saving
    c. Type safety and code reusability
    d. Multithreading

7. **Which collection is best suited for fast key-based retrieval?**
    a. List
    b. Set
    c. TreeMap
    d. HashMap

8. **When is Collections.unmodifiableList() most useful?**
    a. When you want thread-safety
    b. When you want synchronization
    c. When you want to prevent modification
    d. When you want immutability during sorting

9. **Which stream method returns the first matching element?**
    a. findAll()
    b. findFirst()
    c. firstMatch()
    d. getFirst()

10. **Which of the following is not a valid benefit of using bounded generics (<T extends SomeType>) in methods?**
    a. Reduces casting
    b. Restricts inputs
    c. Enables more flexible code
    d. Makes code slower

Answers

1. c

   Explanation: LinkedHashSet maintains insertion order and ensures no duplicate entries.

2. c

   Explanation: Collections.unmodifiableList() wraps a list in a read-only view, preventing modifications.

3. c

   Explanation: Collectors.groupingBy(..., counting()) is a standard way to group and count in streams.

4. b

   Explanation: computeIfAbsent() checks if a key is present; if not, inserts a default value returned by the function.

5. b

   Explanation: Collections.emptyList() returns an immutable empty list, ideal as a safe default.

6. c

   Explanation: Generics in collections allow type safety and eliminate the need for explicit casting.

7. d

   Explanation: HashMap is the most efficient for retrieving values using keys in constant time.

8. c

   Explanation: Collections.unmodifiableList() is used to share data safely by preventing modifications.

9. b

   Explanation: findFirst() returns an Optional containing the first matching element from a stream.

10. d

    Explanation: Bounded generics help improve type safety and flexibility, not performance degradation.

CHAPTER 12

Future Trends and Next Steps

Introduction

As Java continues to evolve, developers must stay ahead of the curve to design resilient, efficient, and scalable applications. Java generics and the Collections Framework have long served as the building blocks for type-safe and structured data handling. However, their story does not end with current capabilities.

In this chapter, we explore the future, recent advancements, expected enhancements, shifting development paradigms, and how the language is adapting to the demands of modern software engineering. Whether you are building APIs, backend systems, or libraries, understanding these trends will empower you to make design decisions that are forward-compatible and aligned with industry best practices.

Structure

This chapter covers the following topics:

- Recent advancements in Java generics
- Future updates in collections
- Trends in Java development
- Staying updated with Java innovations
- Future of generics and collections

Objectives

In this chapter, you will gain a thorough understanding of the evolving landscape of Java generics and the Collections Framework. You will explore recent enhancements such as improved type inference, factory methods for creating immutable collections, and the use of sealed classes. The chapter will also guide you through anticipated developments like value types and possible solutions to limitations such as type erasure. In addition, you will examine key trends in modern Java development, including the growing influence of functional and reactive programming. By the end of this chapter, you will be well-equipped to stay current with Java innovations and to design applications that are efficient, maintainable, and aligned with future advancements in the language.

Recent advancements in Java generics

Java generics were introduced in JDK 5 to provide stronger type checks at compile time and to support generic programming. Since then, improvements have focused on syntax simplification, type inference, and integration with newer language features.

The following are the most notable recent advancements:

- **Improved type inference with var (JDK 10+):** The var keyword allows you to declare local variables without explicitly specifying the type, making generic-heavy code cleaner and more concise.

  This can be done as shown in the following:

  ```
  var employeeMap = new HashMap<String, List<String>>();
  employeeMap.put("HR", List.of("Asher", "Satin"));
  System.out.println(employeeMap);
  ```

  Here, var infers the type **HashMap<String, List<String>>** from the right-hand side. This is especially useful when working with deeply nested generic structures.

- **Diamond operator improvements (JDK 7+):** The diamond operator (<>) enables the compiler to infer type parameters, reducing the need to repeat type information. Let us understand this with an example:

  ```
  List<String> cities = new ArrayList<>();
  // Compiler infers type as ArrayList<String>
  cities.add("Delhi");
  ```

  You no longer need to write **new ArrayList<String>();** the compiler infers that from the variable declaration.

- **Intersection types for generic bounds:** Intersection types allow a type parameter to extend multiple interfaces, enabling more flexible and reusable APIs. Consider the following example:

```
public <T extends Runnable & AutoCloseable> void executeAndClose(T
resource) throws Exception {
    resource.run();
    resource.close();
}
```

This method requires any type **T** to implement both **Runnable** and **AutoCloseable**. It ensures compile-time safety while allowing operations that depend on both interfaces.

- **Enhanced support in Lambdas and Streams (JDK 8 Onward):** Generics are now better utilized in functional programming constructs, improving expressiveness and compile-time safety.

Let us look at an example of it:

```
List<String> names = List.of("Asher", "Victor", "Ryan");
List<String> upperNames = names.stream()
    .map(String::toUpperCase)
    .collect(Collectors.toList());
System.out.println(upperNames); // [ASHER, VICTOR, RYAN]
```

In the above example, the **map()** method applies a transformation function to each element in a generic list. Type inference and generics ensure type safety throughout the pipeline.

- **Java specification request (JSR)-335 and improved type inference in complex structures:** In complex chained operations or method references, Java has become better at inferring types without explicit declarations.

Consider the following example:

```
Map<String, List<String>> groupByFirstLetter = List.of("apple",
"banana", "apricot", "blueberry")
    .stream()
    .collect(Collectors.groupingBy(s -> s.substring(0, 1)));
```

In the above example, the compiler correctly infers the type as **Map<String, List<String>>**, even though it is not explicitly declared.

- **Immutable collection factory methods (Introduced in JDK 9):** Java introduced convenient factory methods like **List.of()**, **Set.of()**, and **Map.of()** for creating immutable collections.

They can be defined as shown in the following:

```
List<String> cities = List.of("New York", "Chicago", "San Francisco");
//cities.add("Los Angeles");
```

```
// This line would throw UnsupportedOperationException
System.out.println("Immutable Cities: " + cities);
```

The **List.of()** method creates an immutable list. Any attempt to modify it (like adding "Los Angeles") will throw an **UnsupportedOperationException**. This is useful when you need fixed configurations or want to prevent accidental changes.

- **Sealed classes with Generics (Introduced in JDK 17):** Sealed classes restrict which classes can implement or extend them, improving code readability and safety in domain-driven design. Consider the following example:

```
sealed interface Vehicle permits Car, Bike {}
final class Car implements Vehicle {}
final class Bike implements Vehicle {}

List<Vehicle> vehicles = List.of(new Car(), new Bike());
vehicles.forEach(v -> System.out.println(v.getClass().getSimpleName()));
```

This example uses sealed classes to define a closed type hierarchy. Even when used with generics like **List<Vehicle>**, only the permitted types (Car, Bike) are allowed. This provides better control and safety during code evolution.

These improvements not only improve code readability but also help developers focus on logic rather than boilerplate declarations.

To better appreciate how Java generics and collections have evolved over the years, it is helpful to compare traditional approaches with the more modern features introduced in recent Java versions.

The following table highlights key differences in syntax, capabilities, and programming style, demonstrating how the language has become more expressive, concise, and aligned with current development practices:

Feature	Before (Pre-Java 7)	Now (Java 8 and beyond)
Generic type declaration	`Map<String, List<Integer>> map = new HashMap<String, List<Integer>>();`	`var map = new HashMap<String, List<Integer>>();`
Immutable collections	`Collections.unmodifiableList(new ArrayList<>())`	`List.of("A", "B")`
Functional operations	Manual loops or external libraries	`stream().filter().map().collect()`
Intersection types	Limited support	`public <T extends A & B> void method(T t)`

Exhaustive pattern matching	Manual instance of checks	`Sealed classes and switch pattern matching (preview)`

Table 12.1: Comparison table for old vs. new usage of generics

Understanding the progression of Java generics and related features over various JDK releases helps put recent changes into context.

The following figure shows a timeline that outlines major milestones in the evolution of generics and collections, highlighting how Java has continuously adapted to meet modern programming needs:

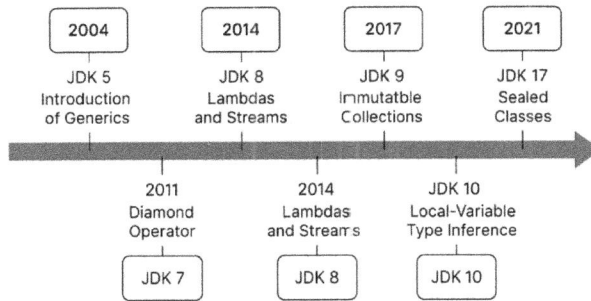

Figure 12.1: Timeline of generics evolution

Future updates in collections

While the foundational structure of Java's Collections Framework has remained robust and reliable for decades, the needs of modern software systems are rapidly changing. Cloud-native development, high-throughput systems, and memory-sensitive environments are all demanding more from language-level abstractions. As a result, the Collections Framework is gradually being extended with new capabilities that align with current and anticipated use cases. These enhancements aim to make collections more performant, safe, and expressive, while still maintaining backward compatibility and the framework's familiar APIs.

Here are some of the most promising directions for future improvements:

- **Value types (Project Valhalla)**: One of the most anticipated changes in the Java ecosystem is the introduction of value types through Project Valhalla. These are lightweight, immutable data carriers that do not incur object header overhead and are stored more compactly in memory.

  Let us understand how value types will change the internal behaviour and performance characteristics of Java collections:

- o In traditional collections, storing thousands of small objects (like points or coordinates) can lead to poor memory locality and performance bottlenecks due to frequent heap allocations.

- o Value types, once fully integrated, will allow collections like **List<Point>** or **Map<Key, Value>** to store data more efficiently, potentially even in-line, reducing GC pressure and improving CPU cache utilization.

This is especially significant for performance-critical applications like real-time analytics, game engines, and financial systems.

- **Pattern matching and structural decomposition**: Java is steadily advancing toward more expressive syntax for common control flow and data access operations.

Let us understand how advancements in pattern matching and structural decomposition are set to impact how we interact with collections:

- o With pattern matching for **instanceof**, and upcoming enhancements to switch, Java is making it easier to de-structure and inspect complex objects.

- o As these features mature, collections may be enhanced to allow structured decomposition of elements during iteration, enabling more concise and readable code patterns.

  Consider the following example:

```
for (Object obj : list) {
    if (obj instanceof Map.Entry(String key, Integer value)) {
        System.out.println("Key: " + key + ", Value: " + value);
    }
}
```

  Future iterations of Java may support patterns like this more broadly in collection traversal, eliminating the need for verbose casting and nested method calls.

- **Immutable collections by default:** Immutability is increasingly seen as a best practice in modern software architecture, especially in concurrent and functional programming models.

Let us examine how Java is evolving toward immutability as a first-class principle in its collections API:

- o The introduction of factory methods, such as **List.of()**, **Set.of()**, and **Map.of()** in Java 9 encourage developers to create immutable collections with ease.

- o Going forward, Java libraries and APIs are expected to embrace immutability by default, reducing the risk of unintended side effects and improving predictability.

In the future, collection creation patterns may prioritize immutability unless the developer explicitly opts into a mutable variant.

- **Concurrent collections enhancements**: Concurrency is a critical concern for today's scalable systems, and Java's concurrent collections like `ConcurrentHashMap` and `CopyOnWriteArrayList` have long supported multi-threaded access.

  Let us explore how concurrent collections in Java are expected to advance to meet the demands of modern, scalable systems:

  o Future improvements aim to reduce contention and improve scalability using lock-free algorithms, fine-grained control over synchronization, and low-overhead atomic operations.

  o Libraries may also integrate structured concurrency to better coordinate collection-related tasks in a thread-safe and organized manner.

  These changes are essential in cloud-native environments, where containers and microservices often face concurrency bottlenecks under heavy load.

- **Memory-efficient implementations**: As Java becomes a preferred language for microservices, edge computing, and serverless platforms, there is a growing need for lightweight and highly optimized data structures.

  Let us analyze how memory-efficient collection implementations are emerging to support Java's role in resource-constrained environments such as microservices, edge computing, and serverless platforms:

  o Libraries are experimenting with compact map implementations, array-backed sets, and compressed storage layouts that offer significant memory savings.

  o These collections may become part of the standard JDK in the future, providing developers with tools that minimize resource usage without compromising functionality.

  Expect to see collections tailored for constrained environments that are ideal for **Internet of Things (IoT)** devices, mobile apps, or backend services running on limited containers.

Together, these enhancements represent the next generation of the Collections Framework that is faster, smarter, and more aligned with the challenges of contemporary software engineering.

Trends in Java development

Modern Java development is evolving rapidly, driven by changes in how software is built, deployed, and maintained. No longer limited to monolithic applications or enterprise backends, Java is now a key player in cloud-native ecosystems, reactive systems, and functional programming paradigms. As the language adapts to meet these demands, the way developers use collections and generics is also undergoing a significant transformation.

The following are the most prominent trends shaping how Java developers think about and apply generics and collections today:

- **Functional programming influence**: Functional programming concepts have found a firm place in modern Java, especially since the introduction of lambdas and the Stream API in JDK 8. Collections are no longer manipulated through traditional loops and if-else logic but are instead transformed using expressive, chainable operations.

  Let us examine how functional programming paradigms have influenced the evolution of collections in modern Java:

  o The use of map, filter, reduce, and collect enables developers to write more concise and intention-revealing code.

  o Collections now support fluent pipelines, where data can be transformed step by step with minimal side effects.

  o This approach encourages immutability and promotes safer concurrent code.

    For example:

    ```
    List<String> names = List.of("Alice", "Bob", "Charlie", "David");
    List<String> shortNames = names.stream()
        .filter(name -> name.length() <= 4)
        .map(String::toUpperCase)
        .collect(Collectors.toList());
    ```

    This kind of usage represents a significant shift in how developers think about processing data collections.

- **Adoption of reactive programming**: Reactive programming is gaining prominence in modern Java development, especially for systems that demand high responsiveness, scalability, and real-time data handling, such as monitoring dashboards, live data feeds, and asynchronous processing pipelines.

  Let us understand how reactive programming is influencing the usage and design of collections in modern Java applications:

  o At its core, reactive programming emphasizes non-blocking operations, event-driven architecture, and the ability to handle streams of data asynchronously.

  o Although the traditional **java.util** collections API is not inherently reactive; its integration with reactive patterns is becoming more common in architectural design.

  o In such scenarios, collections are often used as intermediary structures for gathering, transforming, and delivering batches of data received through reactive streams.

  o Generics play a vital role in ensuring type safety and reusability across these processing flows.

As reactive programming continues to influence Java's direction, it is likely that future iterations of the language and its APIs will introduce more native abstractions to support non-blocking collections and structured asynchronous data handling.

- **Emphasis on readability and simplicity**: Java's reputation for verbosity is gradually fading. Newer language enhancements aim to streamline code without sacrificing readability or type safety:
  - o The introduction of the var keyword in JDK 10, records in JDK 14, and pattern matching in later versions all point toward a more expressive and modern syntax.
  - o Collections benefit directly from these changes. Initializing or transforming them requires fewer lines of code and reduced ceremony.

    For example, the following declaration allows developers to express their logic clearly while still benefiting from compile-time type checking:

    ```
    var employeeMap = new HashMap<String, List<String>>();
    ```

- **Increased use of records and sealed classes**: Java records and sealed classes are reshaping how developers design their data models. These features improve the integration of collections and generics with business logic:
  - o Records provide a compact syntax for immutable data holders, making them ideal for representing DTOs, configuration models, and collection elements.
  - o Sealed classes allow the definition of restricted type hierarchies, helping enforce domain constraints and improving generic type safety.

Collections like **List<RecordType>** or **Map<KeyType, Record>** are becoming standard in APIs that require clear, maintainable, and immutable data structures.

In short, these features support a more declarative, safe, and predictable design philosophy.

- **Modular and cloud-native design:** Java applications are now often deployed as lightweight, containerized microservices that must start quickly, consume minimal memory, and scale effectively. This shift has led to new considerations in how collections and generics are used:
  - o The **Java Platform Module System (JPMS)** encourages modular codebases that load only what is necessary.
  - o Libraries and frameworks prefer using immutable collections or primitive-specialized data structures to reduce memory usage.
  - o Concurrent collections and thread-safe patterns are now the default in many backend services, ensuring better behavior in distributed systems.

Collections must now be lean, responsive, and safe to use in stateless and multi-threaded environments, where even small inefficiencies can have a large impact at scale.

- **Integration with cloud tooling and DevOps:** Collections and generics are also heavily used in areas outside application logic, such as configuration handling, telemetry, logging, and metrics aggregation:
  - ○ Configuration properties (from YAML/JSON files) are often parsed into collections of key-value pairs or object lists.
  - ○ Logs and structured events use maps and generics to ensure flexibility and schema evolution.
  - ○ Generic interfaces make it easier to build reusable services like caching, audit logging, and tracing.

Together, these trends reflect a shift in how Java developers structure their code: from imperative to declarative, from mutable to immutable, and from isolated systems to scalable, cloud-ready services. As Java continues to evolve, so too will its idioms, and the Collections Framework and generics will remain at the core of that evolution.

Staying updated with Java innovations

Java is one of the few programming languages with a consistent, predictable release cadence. Since the introduction of the six-month release cycle in 2017, developers can expect new features, improvements, and bug fixes twice a year. Additionally, **long-term support** (**LTS**) versions are released every three years, such as JDK 11, JDK 17, and the recent JDK 21, making it easier for organizations to plan stable upgrades.

However, staying current with Java's evolution is not just about reading release notes or waiting for an LTS version. The language is actively shaped by its community, and informed developers are better positioned to write modern, efficient, and forward-compatible code. Here is how you can stay ahead in your Java development journey:

- **Follow JEPs (JDK Enhancement Proposals):** JEPs (JDK Enhancement Proposals) are formal documents that define the goals, motivation, and technical details of proposed Java features. They are one of the most transparent and detailed ways to track Java's future direction:
  - ○ JEPs cover everything from language features to JVM improvements and library changes.
  - ○ Monitoring active and draft JEPs helps you anticipate upcoming additions and adapt your codebase or learning plan accordingly.

    For example:
    - ▪ **JEP 401, primitive classes (Preview):** Part of Project Valhalla, aimed at improving performance by introducing value types.
    - ▪ **JEP 430, string templates (Preview):** Designed to simplify dynamic string construction, making code more readable and secure.

You can track all JEPs at the official OpenJDK site: **https://openjdk.org/jeps/0**

- **Read community blogs and watch conferences**: The Java community is one of the most active in the programming world, and community-driven content plays a vital role in knowledge dissemination.

Let us recognize the importance of community-driven learning resources in staying current with the evolving Java ecosystem:

  o Conferences like JavaOne, Devoxx, Oracle CodeOne, and JNation feature hands-on sessions, keynote announcements, and discussions from the engineers behind Java itself.

  o Prominent blogs (like those by Baeldung, InfoQ, JetBrains, and Oracle's official blog) break down complex topics, provide real-world use cases, and cover subtle updates that might not be apparent in documentation alone.

  o Recorded talks and demos often explain *why* a feature exists and *how* it is meant to be used, bridging the gap between theoretical specs and practical usage.

This content is invaluable for staying current and deepening your understanding of how new features integrate with existing tools like collections and generics.

- **Experiment with preview features:** Many features in modern Java are introduced as *preview features*, allowing developers to experiment and provide feedback before they are finalized.

Let us explore how experimenting with preview features enables developers to stay ahead of upcoming changes in the Java language:

  o To enable preview features, compile and run code using the --enable-preview flag in the command line or through IDE configuration.

    Examples of preview features include:

    ▪ Pattern matching for instanceof and switch

    ▪ Sealed classes

    ▪ Record patterns

  o Preview features give you early access to future capabilities, enabling you to test integration strategies and determine where legacy code may need revision.

Experimenting with these features ensures you are not caught off guard when they become stable in future versions.

- **Use early-access builds**: The OpenJDK project offers **early-access (EA)** builds of upcoming Java versions. These builds include the latest proposed features and fixes, giving developers a chance to explore and validate them in controlled environments:

  o These builds are free to download and regularly updated.

- o You can test how your libraries, collections, and APIs perform with new language features, JVM tweaks, or compiler behaviours.

- o Ideal for developers working on frameworks, tooling, or libraries that need to be version-compatible early.

Visit **https://jdk.java.net** to access EA builds of the next Java version.

- **Contribute to OpenJDK**: Java's development is open and community-driven. If you are passionate about influencing the direction of Java, whether in collections, generics, or JVM optimizations, contributing to OpenJDK is the most direct route:

  - o Contributions can include bug reports, test cases, feature suggestions, documentation, or even patches.

  - o Active participation in mailing lists such as `compiler-dev`, `core-libs-dev`, or `valhalla-dev` exposes you to ongoing technical discussions and design decisions.

  - o Developers can also contribute by participating in community voting, joining working groups, or reviewing JEP proposals.

Being part of the OpenJDK community helps you understand Java not just as a language, but as an evolving platform shaped by collective engineering effort.

In the rapidly evolving ecosystem of software development, continuous learning is not optional; it is essential. Java offers all the tools to help you stay current. All you need to do is make the most of them.

Future of generics and collections

As Java continues to modernize while maintaining its core principles of backward compatibility, safety, and platform independence, we can expect substantial improvements in how generics and collections are designed, implemented, and consumed. The increasing demands for performance, concurrency, and developer productivity are likely to shape these enhancements. Based on current trends, ongoing JEPs, and broader ecosystem influences, here are some well-founded predictions for the future evolution of Java generics and the Collections Framework.

Here are a few educated predictions:

- **Support for reified generics**: One of the most commonly discussed limitations in Java generics is type erasure, where generic type information is removed at runtime. This prevents operations such as checking an object's type parameter using instanceof or creating generic arrays.

  Let us consider how reified generics could address long-standing limitations imposed by type erasure in Java:

- Future versions of Java may introduce reified generics, enabling full type retention at runtime. This would:
  - Allow safer and more expressive reflective operations.
  - Eliminate the need for unchecked casts in many common scenarios.
  - Facilitate more robust serialization and deserialization mechanisms.
- This improvement aligns with long-term goals of Project Valhalla, which aims to introduce value types and improved runtime type handling.

Although introducing reified generics poses challenges in terms of backward compatibility, gradual integration (possibly through new syntax or opt-in annotations) could offer a path forward.

- **Specialized collections for primitives**: Current generic collections (like List<Integer>) rely on boxing and unboxing of primitive types, which incurs performance and memory overhead. Although third-party libraries like Trove and FastUtil address this need, core Java lacks built-in support.

Let us evaluate how introducing primitive-specialized collections could significantly enhance performance and efficiency in Java applications:

- The introduction of primitive-specialized collections (such as IntList, DoubleMap) would allow:
  - Improved performance through avoidance of boxing.
  - Reduced memory footprint, especially in large-scale numeric or data-processing applications.
  - Seamless usage in data science, machine learning, or high-frequency trading systems.
- These collections could be built into **java.util**, extending the usability and efficiency of the standard library.

Project Valhalla's value classes would make this enhancement more feasible by treating primitive wrappers as inline types with identity-less semantics.

- **More fluent collection APIs:** Languages like Kotlin, Scala, and JavaScript offer concise and expressive methods for constructing, transforming, and chaining collections. Java is gradually moving in this direction with features like Streams and Collectors.

Future Java releases may enhance collection APIs to support:

- Fluent builders (e.g., **ListBuilder.add("A").add("B").build()**)
- Inline filtering, mapping, and merging of collections outside of stream contexts.
- Direct transformation methods (e.g., **map.replaceAllKeys(...)**, **list.groupBy(...)**) in the core **java.util** package.

Such APIs would make collection handling more declarative, readable, and maintainable, especially in business logic-heavy codebases.

- **Integration with structured concurrency**: Structured concurrency is an emerging paradigm that simplifies multithreaded programming by treating concurrent tasks like structured code blocks. As Java integrates structured concurrency (e.g., via Project Loom), collections will likely evolve to support parallel, concurrent workflows more natively.

Potential enhancements include:

  o Stream-like APIs that work seamlessly with lightweight threads (virtual threads).

  o Thread-safe collectors and partitioners optimized for concurrent streams.

  o Collection utilities that integrate with `ExecutorService`, `ScopedValue`, or structured tasks.

These improvements would allow developers to process large datasets or real-time streams efficiently while ensuring safe resource management and simpler thread lifecycle handling.

- **Enhanced IDE and compiler support for generics**: As generics become more expressive and widely used in modern Java applications, developer tooling must keep pace.

Future improvements in compilers and IDEs (such as IntelliJ IDEA, Eclipse, and NetBeans) will likely include:

  o **Smarter type inference**: Reducing the need to explicitly declare verbose generic types.

  o **Real-time refactoring assistance**: Safely generalize or specialize methods using generics.

  o **Context-aware code generation**: Suggesting generic wrappers, streams, and type constraints during development.

  o **Stronger static analysis**: Detecting potential runtime issues due to unsafe type conversions or misuse of bounded wildcards.

Such tooling support not only improves productivity but also encourages correct and elegant use of generics, especially among newer developers.

- **Greater emphasis on immutability and functional design**: The shift toward **immutability**, already visible with `List.of()` and `Set.of()`, is expected to continue.

Future enhancements might:

  o Offer first-class immutable collection types with no reliance on wrappers.

  o Encourage functional-style usage with lazy evaluation and persistent data structures.

o Provide collection utilities designed specifically for functional pipelines.

These features align with trends seen in other languages and respond to modern needs like concurrency, testability, and ease of reasoning about state.

Java collections and generics are poised to become more powerful, expressive, and performance-oriented without sacrificing the language's core principles. Whether it is through the adoption of reified types, performance gains with primitive collections, or seamless concurrency integrations, the evolution is geared toward making Java more robust and future-ready.

For developers, this means embracing a mindset of continuous learning, experimentation, and readiness to adapt to upcoming changes, ensuring that your code remains modern, efficient, and scalable in the years to come.

Conclusion

The future of Java collections and generics is promising. While the core principles of safety, reusability, and performance remain unchanged, the ecosystem is continuously refined to meet the challenges of modern development. Developers who stay informed, experiment with new features, and adopt evolving patterns will remain productive and relevant in the years ahead.

With this chapter, we conclude our journey through the powerful world of Collections and Generics in Java. Whether you are a student, a backend developer, or a system architect, the knowledge gained here forms a critical foundation for building maintainable, scalable, and forward-compatible Java applications.

Exercise

1. **What feature introduced in JDK 10 reduces verbosity when working with generics?**

   a. Diamond operator

   b. Sealed classes

   c. var keyword

   d. Pattern matching

2. **Which method is used to create an immutable list in modern Java?**

   a. new ArrayList<>()

   b. List.copyOf()

   c. Collections.emptyList()

   d. Arrays.asList()

3. **What is the primary limitation of Java generics that may be addressed in future versions?**

   a. Lack of interfaces

   b. No support for inheritance

   c. Type erasure

   d. No lambda support

4. **What does Project Valhalla focus on?**

   a. Reducing syntax verbosity

   b. Improving Javadoc

   c. Supporting value types

   d. Upgrading HashMap

5. **What will List.of("A", "B") return?**

   a. A mutable list

   b. A list with null elements

   c. An immutable list

   d. A synchronized list

6. **Which feature enables declaring a generic class with specific allowed implementations?**

   a. Streams

   b. Lambdas

   c. Sealed classes

   d. Functional interfaces

7. **What type of collection helps with concurrent writes and reads?**

   a. HashMap

   b. LinkedList

   c. ConcurrentHashMap

   d. TreeMap

8. **What language feature simplifies creating read-only collection views?**

   a. Optional

   b. switch-case

   c. Collections.unmodifiableList()

   d. List.addAll()

9. **What does flatMap() help with?**

    a. Sorting collections

    b. Creating nested structures

    c. Flattening nested streams

    d. Skipping elements

10. **What is a major reason to use records in Java?**

    a. To write mutable data holders

    b. To define behavior-rich classes

    c. To simplify data containers with immutability

    d. To improve runtime performance only

Answers

1. c

    Explanation: The var keyword, introduced in JDK 10, enables local variable type inference. It allows developers to declare variables without repeating generic types, thus reducing verbosity while maintaining type safety.

2. b

    Explanation: List.copyOf() creates an unmodifiable copy of the provided list. This is preferred over Collections.emptyList() or Arrays.asList() when you need an immutable list with actual elements. It throws exceptions if the input list contains null.

3. c

    Explanation: Java Generics use type erasure, which removes generic type information at runtime. This prevents certain operations like checking the actual type parameter using instanceof. Future enhancements may address this limitation with reified generics.

4. c

    Explanation: Project Valhalla aims to introduce value types (also called inline classes) that optimize memory and CPU usage. These types are especially useful in collections by reducing overhead associated with object references and boxing.

5. c

    Explanation: The factory methods like List.of() return immutable collections. Any attempt to add or remove elements will result in an UnsupportedOperationException.

6. c

    Explanation: Sealed classes, introduced in JDK 17, allow you to control which classes or interfaces can extend or implement a type. When combined with generics, this helps enforce strict type hierarchies and controlled polymorphism.

7. c

   Explanation: ConcurrentHashMap is designed for concurrent access and modification. It uses fine-grained locking (or lock-free mechanisms) to ensure thread safety without sacrificing performance, making it ideal for multi-threaded applications.

8. c

   Explanation: Collections.unmodifiableList() creates a view of a given list that is read-only. Attempts to modify it will result in runtime exceptions, making it suitable for defensive programming and API safety.

9. c

   Explanation: The flatMap() function is used to flatten nested structures—especially when working with streams of lists. It transforms each element into a stream and then flattens them into a single stream, making it easier to process complex data.

10. c

   Explanation: Records in Java provide a concise syntax for immutable data holders. They automatically generate constructors, getters, and toString() methods, reducing boilerplate and promoting value-based design.

Join our Discord space

Join our Discord workspace for latest updates, offers, tech happenings around the world, new releases, and sessions with the authors:

https://discord.bpbonline.com

Index

A

application programming interfaces
(APIs) 1
Array Deque (ArrayDeque) 162
characteristics 162
constructors 165
implementation 162
internal structure 162-165
use cases 165, 166
ArrayList implementation 86-89
custom implementation 91, 92
performance considerations 89-91
Arrays and Collections classes 184
array, converting to list 185
collection methods, using on arrays 185
Arrays utility class 182

array, filling 183
arrays, comparing 184
arrays, copying 184
array, searching 183
array, sorting 183

B

BlockingDeque 170
BlockingQueue 170
bounded types 19
examples 27-33
lower bounds 21-23
parameters 27
upper bounds 20, 21

C

case studies 216-227

checked collections 106, 192, 193

  benefits 106

collection interface 61, 62

  key methods 62-65

collections

  future 248-251

  future updates 241-243

  performance considerations 206, 207

collections-based APIs

  designing 204-206

Collections class 176

  key methods 65-69

  List, reversing 177

  List, sorting 177

collections hierarchy 60, 61

collections, modifying with

      Collections utility class 180

  all occurrences of value, replacing 181, 182

  elements, shuffling 181

  list, copying into another 182

  list, filling with value 181

  list, reversing 180, 181

concurrent collections

  using 169

D

Deque interface 160

  methods 160

  real-world scenarios 160

  using, as Queue and Stack 161, 162

E

enhanced for loop 71, 72

F

Follow JEPs (JDK Enhancement Proposals) 246

G

generic algorithms

  using 209, 210

generic classes

  defining 11, 12

generic methods

  using 12, 13

generics 2

  background 2

  basic syntax 6

  benefits 3-6

  best practices 50-52

  common pitfalls 50-52

  common pitfalls, avoiding 200-203

  future 248-251

  recent advancements 238-241

  with constructors 13

generics, applying to List<T> 39-41

  wildcards in generic lists 41-44

generics, applying to Map<K,V> 46, 47

  wildcards in generic maps 47-50

generics, applying to Set<T> 44

  wildcards in generic sets 44-46

H

HashMap 114

  characteristics 114

  constructors 118

  internal structure 114-118

HashSet 137

constructors 138

implementation 137

internal structure 137, 138

Hashtable implementation 125

constructors 125, 126

internal working 125

I

iterable interface 70

Iterator interface 70, 71

iterators 70

J

Java 246

enhanced for loop 71, 72

innovations 246-248

Java 8

enhancements, for Set interface 145

Java Collections Framework (JCF) 60

collection interface 61, 62

collections hierarchy 60, 61

efficient usage 203, 204

nested classes 72

overview 38, 39

Java Development Kit 5 (JDK 5) 2

Java Development Kit (JDK) 59

Java Platform Module System (JPMS) 245

Java Virtual Machine (JVM) 39

just-in-time compiler (JIT compiler) 39

L

Lambdas

using, for iteration 72

LinkedHashMap implementation 118, 119

constructors 120

internal structure 119, 120

LinkedHashSet 138

constructors 140, 141

implementation 138, 139

internal structure 139, 140

LinkedList as Queue 167

characteristics 168

using 168

LinkedList implementation 92, 93

custom LinkedList implementation 97-100

internal structure 93-96

performance considerations 96, 97

list

binary search with custom comparator 180

reversing 177

searching 178, 179

sorting 177, 178

sorting, with custom comparator 179

sorting, with natural order 178

List interface 84

characteristics 84-86

long-term support (LTS) 246

lower bounds 21-23

versus, upper bounds 24

M

Map interface 111-113

comparing 127

generic algorithms 130, 131

performance considerations 128

synchronization 129, 130

use cases 129

N

nested classes, in collections
  checked collections 75
  empty collections 72, 73
  immutable collections 75, 76
  singleton collections 73
  synchronized collections 74

P

parameterized types
  defining 6
practical examples 227-230
predefined empty collections 190-192
PriorityQueue 156
  characteristics 156
  implementation 156
  internal structure 156-159
problem solving 232
producer extends, consumer
      super (PECS) rule 24

Q

queue 166
  implementing 166, 167
  sliding window or fixed buffer 167
Queue interface 154
  characteristics 154-156
  implementations 154
  methods 155

R

real-world scenarios
  best practices 232, 233

S

Set interface 135-137
  generic algorithms 147, 148
  performance considerations 146
  synchronization 146, 147
Stack 166
  implementation 166
synchronization
  best practices 208, 209
  in Queues and Deques 169
synchronization in lists 103
  Collections.synchronizedList() 103, 104
  CopyOnWriteArrayList 104
synchronization utilities 187
  synchronized lists, creating 187, 188
  synchronized Set and Map 188
Synchronized Collections
  wrapping with 170
syntax of generics
  bounded type parameters 9, 10
  generic classes 6-8
  generic methods 8
  overview 6
  wildcard types 10, 11

T

TreeMap implementation 120
  characteristics 121
  common methods 124
  constructors 124
  internal structure 121, 123
TreeSet 141
  characteristics 141

common methods 143, 144

constructors 143

eligibility requirements, for elements 142, 143

implementation 141

internal structure 141, 142

trends 243-246

type erasure 53

impact 54, 55

in generics 53, 54

type-safe code

writing, with generics 198-200

U

unmodifiable collections 105, 189, 190

upper bounds 20

benefits 21

versus, lower bounds 24

usage patterns 231, 232

utility classes 175, 176

V

Vector implementation 100, 101

W

wildcards 24

best practice 26, 27

lower bounded wildcard 25, 26

unbounded wildcard 25

upper bounded wildcard 25

wrapper class 77-80, 185-187

wrapper classes

benefits 77

www.ingramcontent.com/pod-product-compliance
Lightning Source LLC
Chambersburg PA
CBHW061807210326
41599CB00034B/6908